Storytelling and Ima ͜
Beyond Basic Literacy 8–14

Storytelling helps pupils develop a wide range of skills. Do they dream and fantasize? Do they lie, waffle and distract? These are not just bad habits but marvellous starting points for teaching an art that can help them to pass on experience, train and use imagination, develop language skills, promote their own confidence, communication and creativity and much more. Storytelling and story making may indeed be essential catalysts in developing critical and analytical thinking skills too.

Storytelling and Imagination: Beyond Basic Literacy 8–14 is the complete guide to using creative storytelling in the primary school classroom and for transitions to Key Stage 3 at secondary school. Taking a holistic approach incorporating reading, writing, speaking and listening, this book covers the skills of developing stories from conceiving a tale through to performance and the oral tradition. Tried and tested by the author and by teachers in hundreds of workshops, this book provides:

- ideas for sparking children's imaginations and harnessing creativity;
- information on using storytelling in cross-curricular contexts with examples and ideas;
- games and practical activities in each chapter;
- a range of original and traditional stories for use in the classroom;
- different stages of work to suit all abilities;
- joined-up thinking about stories and storytelling.

More than a box of good tricks, this book is an indispensable guide for all literacy co-ordinators, practising and student teachers who are looking to create an inspiring and cross-curricular approach to literacy.

Rob Parkinson is a former teacher who now works as a freelance storyteller, musician, writer and educational speaker. He has visited over 2000 schools in the UK giving workshops on storytelling, stories and music as well as using storytelling in therapy and counselling.

Storytelling and Imagination: Beyond Basic Literacy 8–14

Rob Parkinson

Routledge
Taylor & Francis Group

LONDON AND NEW YORK

First published 2011
by Routledge
2 Park Square, Milton Park, Abingdon, Oxon, OX14 4RN

Simultaneously published in the USA and Canada
by Routledge
270 Madison Avenue, New York, NY 10016

Routledge is an imprint of the Taylor & Francis Group, an informa business

Typeset in Bembo by Swales & Willis Ltd, Exeter, Devon
Printed and bound in Great Britain by TJ International Ltd, Padstow, Cornwall

British Library Cataloguing in Publication Data
A catalogue record for this book is available from the British Library

Library of Congress Cataloging-in-Publication Data
Parkinson, Rob.
Storytelling and imagination: beyond basic literacy 8–14 / by Rob Parkinson.
p. cm.
Includes bibliographical references and index.
1. Storytelling. 2. Literacy—Study and teaching (Primary) I. Title.
LB1042.P28 2011
372.67'7—dc22
2010022697

ISBN13: 978–0–415–57186–9 (hbk)
ISBN13: 978–0–415–57187–6 (pbk)
ISBN13: 978–0–203–83640–8 (ebk)

For Asha,
a talented, much-loved daughter
and a fine storyteller already

Story-telling has a real mission to perform in setting free the natural creative expression of children, and in vitalising the general atmosphere of the school.

(Sara Cone Bryant, 1910)

Contents

Acknowledgements

Grateful acknowledgement is made to Sam Cannarozzi for permission to quote copyright material from his Society for Storytelling publication *When Tigers Smoked Pipes* (Cannarozzi 2008). All tales told in this book are from the author's repertoire. They are either brief outline summaries or original reworkings of traditional plots and motifs, using techniques described in this book, and are not based on single published sources.

Personal acknowledgements

I should like to thank all the many teachers, writers and others with whom I have worked over more than a quarter of a century as a storyteller in education, many of whom have contributed in different ways to the development of ideas described in this book. Thanks are particularly due to June Barlow, Kathy Hinde and Alicia Davies, each of whom made essential contributions in making the most basic of these techniques practically focused for classroom use very many years ago. James Carter, Brian Moses and Mary Medlicott gave invaluable professional advice and so on at the early stage of the creation of this book. Thanks also to Aisha May, Dave Wilson, Mike Dawson, Jayne Simpson, Jenny Williams, Owen Davies, Rachel Evetts and Jason Simms for their helpful comments on the manuscript. Finally my wife Ruth Herbert, a much finer scholar than I am, has provided me with essential insights from her own research as well as much very practical support, whilst my daughter Asha has been a willing and wonderfully imaginative 'tester of the tastes'.

Introduction

Smuggle it across any border with no risk. What is it?

There is currently a new wave of interest in the immense possibilities of oral storytelling amongst literacy specialists. The many ways that listening to stories being told and then being involved in retelling them can plant the seeds from which the capacity to write interestingly and fluently can grow are being more widely trumpeted – and very justly so. But there is always a danger with enthusiasms in the educational field, which is littered with discarded fads – crumpled copies of yesterday's news, as it were. Storytelling is much more than a fad; it's always current news, because it's a central part of being human and humanly intelligent, as I'll explain in Chapter 1. We should expect it to have a tremendous amount to offer, much of it still undiscovered, much of it taking us beyond basic literacy.

The practical ideas in this book focus on ways you can unleash more of the imaginative power of storytelling, for literacy and beyond. They have all come out of very extensive practice, in the many hundreds of workshops I have run with school-age pupils and in the work of teachers who have taken the ideas on in their own way. They can be adapted for use across a very broad age range – with stories and storytelling, it's very often not the ideas and the material that are age specific; rather it's the way you tell and use them and, crucially, the notions you use to organize and integrate that use.

Some of the story game techniques included here are adapted from my four-booklet series Natural Storytellers,[1] though with more guidance on integrating them into a larger scheme than was possible in those short publications. There are many more creative 'one-off' ideas in that series to complement the ideas here. A small number were also included in my *Transforming Tales: How Stories Can Change People*,[2] though with a different emphasis, focused for a different purpose in change work.

1

Thinking about story

It's a powerful treasure that's invisible and weightless. What is it?

The importance of story

The way we think about story is vital to teaching, as it is to many other sides of life and the way we live it. Perhaps you won't mind too much if I spend this first chapter explaining why this is so and exploring the implications and evidence at the start of a practical book about practical ideas you can use to develop a good, ongoing, creative and rewarding storytelling culture within a school context in particular, a culture that links to and feeds literacy and also reaches out beyond, making teaching of many other areas of the curriculum more effective and imaginative in general. There are insights that will make much more sense of those practical ideas than would be the case were I to present them simply as a box of good tricks.

Now by 'story' I mean the whole field of story making, storytelling, story writing, hearing stories, reading stories and all sorts more that will become clearer by the time you are familiar with the contents of this book. Why do we tell stories? Why do we read them? Why do tales fascinate us? It's customary at this early stage of writing on storytelling to point to the very clear evidence you can get, that we do tell and take in tales constantly, by simply listening to people all around you, as they are passing on the news and gossip, telling anecdotes and jokes and all sorts more. Some also point to the way we so easily become absorbed in the 'stories' the media hook us in with, or the politicians spin for us, or the advertisers pitch for us. Others (myself included) have liked to flag up the way that we all, in a sense, make a story of ourselves, a story that we revise and edit from time to time to suit different people and different contexts, different circumstances, a story of how we have been, are and will be. You can add to that the way, according to neuroscientists, the brain constantly constructs a narrative from the clues of our essentially limited senses. Then there are the weird stories we tell ourselves in dreams. And all that is before anyone gets to the more obvious day-to-day story magic – say the way you have only to start a good story, in the right circumstance and with a reasonable degree of competence, to have a room full of recently restless young children staring at you, wide-eyed, wondering and apparently awake in a new way, or indeed the not dissimilar effect you can get (trust me, I've tried it many times and it works) by doing something not altogether different, if suitably disguised and cunningly presented, with adult professionals from therapists and health workers to hardened sales reps and business executives – and even (on a good day) teachers. Stories are a natural medium to us; we take to that medium with the ease with which week-old ducklings take to the water and swim in a line behind their mums. Perhaps the answer to the 'why' questions with which I started this paragraph should simply be 'It is so, so it is.' Perhaps we should leave it at that.

On the other hand, that might just be selling the curiosity that ought to be aroused by giving some attention to the ubiquity of tale telling in one form or another a little short. Because, if stories are natural to us, how and why did this all start? Why is it that our nearest relatives, the apes, appear not to spend much time clustering around bardic bonobos or peering at imaginative scratchings on banana peel? After all they are, by some estimates, as much as 99 per cent genetically the same as us. Language and cultures, thinkers point out here, make a very big difference, not to mention human intelligence. But why and whence language and culture and, indeed, human intelligence?

These are not questions to which glib, quick answers are acceptable – there are contending, considerably elaborated theories amongst experts. None of us was around to witness how it all happened anyway, so we are left with speculation and speculation on speculation – an assortment of just so stories if you want to be cynical. But, beyond cynicism, most would agree that the point at which our ancestors were able to focus and use imagination to some extent must have been pivotal in our development. You can't have language that recalls the past or suggests the future or even accurately registers and records the present without imagination – the ability to represent mentally, to form mental images, to follow where those images lead, backwards and forwards in time. And you can't have much of a culture without language, even if that language is partly non-verbal and is figured more in images in stone and paint and signs and symbols. Language of any degree of sophistication, you could say, is a kind of story – not just a set of labels for this, that and the other, but a framing, a way of thinking about and understanding the world and how we exist and act in it. Culture too is a shared tale we tell ourselves of what we are, how we are, what is important to us. A sense of story, in other words and in brief, underpins both language and culture. It's the capacity that holds imaginings together, makes them coherent and usable.

The language and the words early humans spoke are of course lost to us and, with them, the stories they told. What we do have is archaeological evidence that shows something remarkable. From around 35,000 or 40,000 years ago, there was a sudden acceleration in the complexity, style and type of artefacts created by our ancestors, as evidenced by surviving fragments. Figures that are part human and part beast along with decorative patterns of increasing complexity begin to appear in (for example) carved and shaped materials retrieved and duly dated by experts, indicating the existence of increasingly complex mythologies – stories of one kind and another, stories present at the very birth of what we know as human intelligence. Interestingly, there is speculation that these probably did not come out of an arbitrary process of combination, but out of our capacity to dream awake, to imagine, to tell ourselves stories. Animals, it seems, may well have dreams – they certainly have the rapid eye movements (REMs) sleep research has shown indicate the dreaming phase of sleep. Humans, uniquely so far as we know, can daydream and fantasize. It's a sophisticated faculty, closely allied to our storying capacities – and possibly at the very root of them.

Now that's a very rapid gallop through territory that deserves a fuller explanation – which indeed I have previously given it in an earlier book, in which it was more appropriate to explore the idea at greater length (Parkinson 2009). This book, as I say, is a practical book of practical ideas, though I will come back to some different angles on this theme in the 'Framing ideas' section at the beginning of each chapter. But what is the relevance? Just this. Stories are natural to us, as I said. They are not just accidentally so, however; they're the natural mode in which we think about life, review our relationships, relate to each other, make guesses about the future, plan, design, create, explore, express and pass on experience. It is from stories and associated imagination, from our capacity for metaphor, combined with our ability to be logical and rational (sometimes) and to be social creatures sharing cultures that we get and sustain our intelligence. It is bred in the bone. You can trust it to be there, at least in some degree. Granted it can be damaged, stunted, compromised, underdeveloped, starved and all the rest, just like any other faculty. It is there all the same. You can find it if you look in the right places in the right way.

You cannot live without telling a story. Once we connect with and understand this very simple fact, a lot of pennies start dropping – or, putting it another metaphorical way, a lot of hitherto separate and sometimes puzzling pieces start slotting into the jigsaw with a satisfying click. Being a human being is being a storytelling creature. The other species don't do it, can't do it so far as we know. Hence children are storytellers – naturally. Hence in story work you can draw on what is a basic given of human nature. You really can make teaching of and through stories much more effective once you grasp the implications fully. You really can apply the understanding that comes out of it way beyond the more obvious sphere of story work as a branch of literacy. These are themes I'll be amplifying throughout the book.

The proof of the story

I've known this vital importance of story to come as an epiphany to some who have never considered it fully before – and, if we are honest, few of us do consider it as fully as it deserves. Yet this is not exactly an original notion. Recent decades have seen the beginnings of a confluence amongst thinkers, with people in many different disciplines with many different perspectives converging on the importance of narrative in human intelligence and indeed existence.

Take Antonio Damasio, for example. He has been described as 'a pioneer at the furthest reaches of the human brain and human intelligence' (Charlton 2007). His first two highly influential books, *Descartes' Error* (Damasio 1994) and *The Feeling of What Happens* (Damasio 2000), were thoroughly grounded in a deep understanding of neuroscience, coming out of his role as an internationally famous physician and leading expert on the neurophysiology of emotions. For Damasio, storytelling is a fundamental of human brain functioning: 'Telling stories precedes language, since it is, in fact, a condition for language. . . . The brain naturally weaves wordless stories about what happens to an organism immersed in an environment' (Damasio 2000: 189).

Or take leading evolutionary psychology theorists John Tooby and Leda Cosmides. They have this to say about sources for the power of story:

We evolved not so long ago from organisms whose sole source of (non innate) information was the individual's own experience. Therefore, even now our richest systems for information extraction and learning are designed to operate on our own experience. . . . We process [such information] more deeply when we receive it in a form that resembles individual experience. . . . What form is this? People prefer to receive information in the form of stories.

(Tooby and Cosmides 2001: 24)

Then again there is Jerome Bruner, one of the most influential educational thinkers of the last half-century, with major contributions to cognitive psychology and cognitive learning theory in educational psychology, a major inspiration behind so-called narrative learning theory. Bruner reckons that narrative thinking – telling yourself a story, more or less – is one of the two primary modes of thought, what he called the paradigmatic mode (the logical and analytic, scientific way) being the other. Indeed he feels that our sense of narrative actively 'constructs reality'. The two modes are complementary: 'Efforts to reduce one mode or to ignore one at the expense of the other inevitably fail to capture the rich diversity of thought' (Bruner 1986: 11).

I could go on citing expert after recent expert – and indeed not-so-recent expert. They might not agree on the sense it all makes – the perspectives and priorities of the disciplines from which they come differ anyway. But narrative and story have been very relevant themes for thinkers in different, yet ultimately complementary, ways – which perhaps in the end is nothing new. After all, the founders of most major religions were storytellers – Christ with his parables, the Buddha with his Jataka tales, Mohammed weaving teaching tales into the Qur'an and so on. These days, however, we do like to have evidence that goes beyond both pragmatic practice and tantalizing theory. Fortunately, an abundance of it has been arriving in recent times, proving the effectiveness and usefulness of story and indeed storytelling to an extent that should be much better known. Much of this is applicable to education and could in time redefine it.

In 2007, the American storyteller, writer and trained scientist Kendall Haven published his own meta-study of studies of the practical power and value of story. The worth of this contribution is likely to prove enormous. For the first time, the results of a lot of research into at least some of what stories can do for us have been gathered together in one very accessible, very well-written short volume, suitably grounded in relatively mainstream theory lucidly presented with a richness of references.

So what were Haven's conclusions, based on the studies he looked at? First, one would need to explain that Haven, appreciating the quicksilver nature of story definition (*Yeah, like a story's what you wannit to be, man*), grounded his study of story studies in a particular definition of a story as opposed to a simple factual narrative, focusing his attention on those researchers who, he felt reasonably sure, underpinned their testing of story effects with a similar understanding. This understanding is built up and supported in the book through a broad and impressive review of ideas from very many sources about story, stories and storytelling, including a thorough look at the findings and suggestions of neuroscience, psychology and memory studies as to how the brain uses specific story structures to 'impose order' on experience, how the mind works through a combination of assumption, expectation, inference, pattern matching, prior knowledge, metaphor, blending and various other strategies, how language and memory work, and more. Hence his definition is considerably more sophisticated than it may seem at first sight. 'A story', he says, 'is a detailed, character-based narration of a character's struggles to overcome obstacles and reach an important goal.' This he compares with a standard dictionary story definition ('a narrative account of a real or imagined event or events'), which he considers plot based – 'Plot-based narratives', he insists, 'do not spark your interest or create meaning' (Haven 2007: 79).

Leaving aside for the moment possible objections to this (the study results are fascinating regardless), Haven's conclusions are compelling. He read over 100,000 pages of research from 15 fields touching on 'how the mind receives, processes and responds to stories', including over 350 books and qualitative and quantitative studies plus 70 articles based on 1,500 studies and descriptive articles, also collecting accounts of over 1,300 practitioners, adding his own informal research. Most of the research he quotes in his results section, which references 120 credible studies (representing an analysis of more than 800 other studies and reports), has been published through major universities or in peer-reviewed journals. He describes them as 'powerful, valid and rigorous'.

The first extraordinary thing he draws attention to regarding all of his sources (and, if you have any experience of studies and research results in any other area, you will know that this level of agreement is truly extraordinary) is summarized in a short paragraph early in the book:

> The mind-boggling and extraordinary truth is that each and every one of these thousands of independent sources agrees with the premise that stories work, that they are effective and efficient. I could not find one shred of evidence to suggest that stories aren't effective vehicles to teach, to inspire, to inform, to educate.
>
> (Haven 2007: 7)

Specifically, the studies he quotes show that using stories and/or story structure:

- improves comprehension;
- improves logical thinking and general (cross-curriculum) learning;
- enhances meaning;
- creates motivation and enthusiasm for learning;
- creates involvement and a sense of community;
- improves literacy and language mastery;
- improves writing success;
- enhances memory.

Any one-person study has its limits: we all have our agendas and priorities. Haven's should certainly match with those of many educationalists, and indeed he spells out the implications for the educational context. Fundamentally, he implies, we need to put story nearer the centre of educational effort. It's not something to visit every now and then for a bit of light relief, but something to value and use practically for its very real and, as the studies show, well-established benefits.

Results from subsequent studies go on confirming and indeed extending the list of those benefits. For example, recently published articles indicate the usefulness of storytelling approaches in a wide variety of areas, from problem solving (Hernandez-Serrano and Stefanou 2009) to instructional design (McDonald 2009) to language teaching (Kariuki and Bush 2008) to teaching accounting (Miley 2009). In the UK, a joint initiative between the School Effectiveness Division (Curriculum Innovation) and Birmingham Library Services introduced teachers and children from Reception to Year 6/7 to the Story Spinner series of stories from around the world, told on DVD by the actor/storyteller Phil Dermott. Classroom work was focused around these in different ways, and the project ran during the National Year of Reading in 2008. Eve Bearne and Marilyn Mottram report significant impacts from the project, including raised standards in speaking and listening, noticeable gains in writing and raised reading attainment, as well as important developments in teachers' classroom practice and increases in children's imaginative and emotional engagement (Bearne and Mottram 2009).

But, to return to Haven's study, his definition of story could leave some nagging doubts. Maybe that is a drawback of any brief definition of something as large as story; maybe, too, his is a useful practical definition – it certainly gives a very good formula you can apply if you want to create an effective story for teaching facts in narrative form, for example. There are also lots of stories it fits perfectly. Yet there remain too many exceptions to the rule – good stories whose main dynamic is not details of character and struggles and goal achievement, that work in different ways yet can still engage listeners or readers thoroughly, leaving behind something vital and valuable. You don't have to go far beyond the standard nursery repertoire of tales that engage very young children to see that that is so. Although you can just about make 'Red Riding Hood' or 'The Three Little Pigs' fit the formula, is it really their characters' struggles and goals *alone* that draw children in? Or how about short fables like 'The Boy Who Cried Wolf' or 'The Lion and the Mouse'? Are they character driven *primarily*? If not, are they hence bad stories? And that is before we start on tales of wonder and fantasy, say, or of subtle wisdom and wit, which do not necessarily hinge on the struggles of characters to achieve goals.

Clearly characters and struggles you can identify with are very important ingredients in many (perhaps the majority of) stories. They are generally a central dynamic of the novel, one reason Haven's definition resonates with many people – we are used to fiction that works like that. Some might say it also reflects the dominant values of our individualistic culture. But talking about ingredients is not talking about essence. Focusing attention on another ingredient or two might indicate vital things that may be missing here.

For example, researchers at the University of Pennsylvania Department of Psychology studied what they call 'transportation into narrative worlds' – the means by which people are absorbed in literature to the point where they are, in a sense, 'lost in it' – precisely from the point of view of what it is about character that draws people in. They found that small but vivid details of physical description may be equally (or alternatively) effective in absorbing people in a narrative as descriptions of mental state and motivation. If readers (in this case) were effectively presented with details that encouraged them to imagine the narrative world clearly, they identified with the characters and were drawn in, as if experiencing events with them (Green *et al.* 2004).

This brings up the question not just of what it is that draws people into a story but what it is that they are drawn into – what 'state' they are in when they are, as it were, transported into story country. Hence also by what other means might a person be similarly 'moved'? The first answer seems to be that the 'state' is at least analogous to what in our culture is described as light trance or hypnosis. It's not just hyperbole; stories may literally entrance.

There are, incidentally, many ancient traditions relating to this. In 1912, in the market place at Kordofan in Sudan, a similar tradition was related by one Arakh-ben-Hassul, as part of 'The Legend of the Destruction of Kash', a story by chance recorded by German students of comparative mythology. According to the storyteller, the king asked for a story and Far-li-mas began to tell one: 'The king listened; the guests also listened. The king and his guests forgot to drink, forgot to breathe. The slaves forgot to serve. They forgot, too, to breathe. The art of Far-li-mas was like hashish, and, when he had ended, all were as though enveloped in a delightful swoon' (Campbell 1976: 153–4).

For something perhaps a little closer to home, however, we might turn to Sarah Cone Bryant. She was an early advocate of practical storytelling ideas for teachers. She described a not dissimilar experience of a school storytelling session that didn't start too well but evidently got better and better in her 1910 book *How to Tell Stories to Children*: 'After about five minutes, I was suddenly conscious of a sense of ease and relief, a familiar restful feeling in the atmosphere; and then, at last, I knew my audience was "with me" . . . interacting without obstruction. Absolutely quiet, entirely unconscious of themselves' (Cone Bryant 1910: 11).

It's a feeling quite a few teachers will be familiar with, and it has led some theorists and researchers to speculate on the identity of hypnotic trance and involvement in a story. Research on hypnosis itself and what creates it is a vast field with many controversies, and there is no space to do justice to these here. It shades into separate or sometimes combined research strands in studies of absorption, non-pathological (or normative) dissociation and so-called 'imaginative involvement'. This last was a term more or less coined by Josephine Hilgard in her 1970s studies of 'hypnotizability': Hilgard indeed cites deep absorption in reading of fiction as one characteristic of a general capacity for deeper imaginative involvement (Hilgard 1979: 4–5).

Actual studies of the telling of stories and how it relates to 'hypnotic trance' and so on are less common than studies of reading absorption. Victor Nell reviewed research and theory in what remains, over 20 years on, the most comprehensive published general survey of this field, including various phenomenological approaches to the experience and some of his own laboratory research on physiological effects in absorbed readers, involving both arousal and relaxation. He found the analogy with hypnosis promising enough to christen the effect 'the story reading trance' (Nell 1988). In the same year the American storyteller and writer Fran Stallings quite separately published an influential article in which she drew parallels between the methods employed by Ericksonian therapists and those of traditional storytellers, christening the state of absorption in stories 'the story listening trance' (Stallings 1988). She called attention to the long history of the association of trance-like states with story listening and called for research. In the 1990s, Brian Sturm of the University of North Carolina carried out a study of listeners at American storytelling festivals, finding that they exhibited many of the markers recognized as indicators of trance (Sturm 1999). In a 2008 study, Ruth Herbert of the Open University, in a study of musical absorption, compared the experiences of 20 adult subjects involved in diverse parallel activities including storytelling and story listening, finding a variety of absorbed and sometimes dissociated, trance-like experiences (Herbert 2009, forthcoming a, forthcoming b).

Everyday evidence for this kind of effect in stories can be found in the work of many modern hypnotherapists who make use of stories extensively in their work, following the inspiration of the highly influential twentieth-century American psychiatrist and hypnotist Milton Erickson. Erickson was very much a teller of homely yet powerful anecdotes, often based around his own life and experience. He developed conversational methods of informal 'naturalistic trance' in which stories and other metaphorical communications played a large part – and which were, indeed, often superficially indistinguishable (to clients at least) from ordinary social yarning (Rosen 1982).

Where does all this take us? Well, the second answer to the question I posed about what kinds of things draw a person into the story 'world' (and hence what makes it work as a good story rather than a simple factual narrative) may well include some of the same things (if in different disguises) as trance therapists might use – maybe vividly conveyed sensory details or surprising imagery or intrigue or paradox or (perhaps very centrally) meaningful metaphor in addition to character involvement and indeed plot fascination, but things that essentially fix attention, drawing the listener or reader inwards, into a world of inner imagery. This is crucial if one is to reap all of the advantages of story work in education. There may be some qualities intrinsic to a story and its structure, with other qualities emerging through the way the story is told that are still vital to the deeper engagement it creates – which is where storytelling rather than story reading or script performance retains advantages of flexibility and adjustment. It's the way you tell 'em, as they say.

Finally, it may also be that this 'state' one promotes in telling a tale is not entirely unlike a waking dream – which would accord entirely with the ideas about how our capacity to imagine may have evolved touched on in the last section (and further explored in Chapter 5). If dream is where our capacity for imaginative narrative comes from, one would expect involvement in imaginatively engaging narrative now to have some kindred qualities. What is more, it may indeed be that the kinds of inner focus that seem to be a natural concomitant of that 'dreaming awake', with associated enhanced ability to use and partly control imagination, could be a very useful counterbalance to the more intentional, strained 'left brain'[1] sequential reasoning mode favoured in much recent educational practice. This awaits research findings to confirm it with specific reference to both education and story work, though there seems plenty of evidence that switching into more relaxed and spontaneous imaginative mode in general has all sorts of potential benefits,[2] whilst the kind of creative storytelling advocated in this book fits well with developing approaches seeking to broaden the learning styles and creative capacities of pupils[3] – connections to make whilst perhaps keeping in mind the 'all sorts more' we are likely to find hidden away within that strangely fascinating and magical mirror of life we call story.

The skill of the story

In his best-selling book *Outliers*, author and social commentator Malcolm Gladwell developed a notion that passed almost immediately into popular 'thought lore'. Major concert pianists, rock groups, lawyers, superb sportspeople and many more who have mastered complex and admired skills are not simply natural-born geniuses who don't have to try, but will have somehow or other had the chance to put in about 10,000 hours practising and honing those skills to achieve their success (Gladwell 2008).

Gladwell's point is well made, but there is some good news about telling stories. It might not take pupils that long to become pretty good at it, bearing in mind that they have already put in a lot of hours in the kind of everyday 'storytelling' already mentioned.

Take lying as a first, slightly controversial example. So far as we know, we are the only species with a very extensive capacity for telling fibs. Some other mammals, like those ape cousins I mentioned, certainly seem to have a try at it; the problem for them is that they are already expert in reading non-verbal cues – you have to be a virtuosic actor to convince using actions, squeaks and grunts without the help of words. We do have words, of course, and words can confuse that more primitive signalling system.

Leaving aside moral difficulties for the moment, consider how vital the ability to tell lies is in human life. The person who blurts out the 'truth', regardless of the circumstance and the feelings of others, is clearly not socially skilled for a start. Simply to get on with other people, we need to be able to tell at least the odd white lie here and there. Similarly with excuse making: there can be few people who have never elaborated a necessary excuse that at least bent the truth a little. Then there is bragging – not a thing we (officially and openly at least) are supposed to admire, though a fair number of people have, say, doctored their own CVs a little to suit different job applications or found themselves having to otherwise 'blow their own trumpets' in a world where there aren't too many people to blow them for us. These and other socially necessary types of 'fiction spinning' are not often spoken of in the same breath as the telling and writing of stories, but they clearly use some of the same 'mental muscles'.

There are many other sides to what I'll call the 'natural storyteller', from our ability to daydream, fantasize and imagine to our instinctive ability to embroider and embellish the plain facts or (people vary in this of course) to spice up a banal anecdote. In themselves these are neither positive nor negative skills: a person can use imagination plus elaboration to create a major novel or a stunning film script, or to play cruel and criminal con tricks on others or simply to exaggerate (or sometimes even solve) their own fears and worries and personal problems. In this book I'll be using such natural skills as starting places and reference points for their positive use in more structured story work – to develop the skill of the story, which is, in its full reality, much more than an aspect of literacy.

Stories are not just a bunch of clever and entertaining lies – however much pejorative phrases like 'telling tales' betray what you might call an engrained cultural mistrust of them. The paradox of good fiction is that it has for long been recognized as, potentially, a way of understanding things better – as a stepping-stone to truth. We generally recognize that there is a skill or an art in doing that, in making a story work, in moving from the level of 'telling porky pies' all the way to 'making it true'. That is the essence of story skill: making it true.

There has been no human culture without stories. They may vary immensely on the surface. One culture may not have a word for fiction; another may have hundreds. One culture may have trained storytellers with honed and refined skills; others may have no specialists at all. There are, though, common skills, ways of 'making it true'. Rather than doing a multicultural tour, I'll focus on those here.

The first divide that many will identify, of course, will be between the literate culture of the book and oral cultures. This is a much more artificial split than is often appreciated. You could say that many literacy skills are about being able to notate speech and the many manners and modes of it effectively within established conventions. You could also point out that written modes feed back into and influence everyday talk. But speech came first; oral skills are by the far the more senior. There remains a close relationship between the way we speak and the way we write, even though there are obviously very different 'on-the-page' styles. Fiction writers and poets, for example, often talk about 'finding their own voice'; many actually hear that voice inside their own heads, just about telling them what to write. Similarly, many ordinary people know how an official letter or a job application or an advert for the local paper should 'sound' as they write it.

Literacy skills and conventions of story writing are well enough described elsewhere; it would be irrelevant to list them here. Yet it is not sufficiently appreciated that there are many comparably advanced skills in oral storytelling, some of which coincide with literary skills, but some of which do not. This is important if one is going to release some of the educational potential in oral storytelling. Whilst there is every reason to use storytelling as what you might describe as a 'pre-literacy' (or literacy support) tool and to return to it as a way into writing (for which purposes it is currently being promoted), it is too easy to miss its more subtle and unique qualities and skills, partly through preconception.

Some might be tempted to think of storytelling as literary plus thespian, a misconception that may be fuelled by the stagy, scripted-sounding style of some professional storytellers. Essentially there are skills in storytelling that resemble other skills, even sharing some of the same ground; there are other skills that do not. Many grow out the soil of those natural skills I was talking about, developing them into much finer and more conscious arts. Here is a list of some that will be touched on in this book. You can decide which are familiar and which are less so:

- ways of making up stories and making them work;
- ways of finding one's own story or one's own way into stories;
- ways of learning stories made up by others or passed on in tradition flexibly;
- ways of elaborating and stretching a story;
- ways of choosing a story to suit the circumstance;
- ways of adapting and changing stories 'on the hoof', to suit circumstance, time and different people;
- ways of reshaping the pattern in stories in new and creative ways;
- ways of improvising and adjusting the detail in a story to suit the occasion;

- ways of practically using and disciplining the dreaming, imaginative mind;
- ways of connecting and weaving together stories seamlessly;
- ways of presenting stories, to draw individuals and groups into a tale;
- ways of using the power of the voice;
- ways of using the body and body language;
- ways of using other arts and skills to enhance the telling of a tale;
- ways of developing sensitivity to the dynamics of occasion and rapport with individuals and groups;
- ways of learning practical ideas from stories;
- ways of understanding the metaphorical language of stories in depth and developing wisdom.

Listening to stories is an art too, one we'll touch on further in the next chapter. One of the things that distinguishes storytelling from theatre as usually understood is that the 'pictures' are on the mental stage, in the mind's eye. Seeing them feeds what seems to be a natural appetite too often starved, and develops powers of a concentration and 'inner focus' perhaps too often neglected.

Traditional or not?

Storytelling doesn't have to be traditional. You can usefully separate the two terms. But we should take a closer look at what is meant by tradition in this context anyway, to clear out the clutter from the cupboard so to speak – or to find the gold and discard the dross maybe.

First, though, a remarkable phenomenon without which I would not have written this book and you would not be reading it. A reawakening of interest in oral storytelling and its potential has been gathering momentum across the globe over the last four decades. The revival in the US is usually dated from the mid-1970s, that in the UK (with quite different origins – it was by no means an imitation) from the early 1980s, and there is a range of start dates in all sorts of other countries, even some in which you would have thought storytelling had never ceased to be part of the 'scene'. There is now a burgeoning international storytelling movement, with festivals of storytelling in many countries, societies, clubs for adults, and storytellers appearing on arts centre schedules and at major venues. It may be a minority interest, but it's growing, it's for all ages, not just for children, and it's 'traditional' – that's how it's very often described and marketed.

Now the interest in storytelling goes much further than the storytelling movement, as indicated earlier in the chapter. Indeed a long line of excellent books promoting storytelling in education goes right back, way beyond the current 'movement' through pioneers like Ruth Sawyer and Eileen Colwell to early twentieth-century writers like Sara Cone Bryant and Elizabeth Clark.[4] At one time, Froebel-trained primary teachers automatically learned to tell stories as part of their training; stories and storytelling have long been very much part of less mainstream movements, for example Steiner education. The idea, however, that pupils themselves should tell stories is one that has been gathering pace along with the modern storytelling movement, partly as professional storytellers have run workshops here and there in schools and elsewhere, partly as the result of the work of writers like Betty Rosen, Teresa Grainger, Martha Hamilton, Mitch Weiss and others,[5] including most recently and very influentially in the UK poet, storyteller and former schools inspector Pie Corbett. You could argue, however, that the notion that children might tell stories was there all along. Sara Cone Bryant, indeed, points out that, when a deeply engaging tale is told to young children, they remember it without effort and are eager to tell it back, describing ways you can develop this in the classroom. Cone Bryant, however, was presenting her ideas in an age that was less cynical than our own, less inclined to stereotype.

The notion of 'tradition' exists in a culture and time, and the modern culture of this particular time is fond of images. It's a climate in which 'traditional' easily becomes, effectively, a brand and a label. There is a danger that pairing the words 'storytelling' and 'traditional' suggests something not unlike a verbal barn dance – good old-fashioned fun now and then, something our ancestors used to do we can dig out and try out and marvel at from time to time, all right for weekends and quite an art if you're really into it, but scarcely cutting-edge and contemporary and *cool*.

Something of the 'barn dance slant' seems to have been influencing the way that storytelling has been finding its way back into the curriculum in many schools, where something often called 'traditional storytelling' is 'done' as a separate unit or module or as part of a special focus event and then never referred to again. The idea that there could be any ongoing relevance just doesn't come into it; you give the kids a taster and then move on. I'm not quite sure what the effect would be on some maths skills were one to take a similar approach: 'We've done number, so let's not bring it into any other subjects now.' Hmm . . .

Anyway, enough has been said already to make it clear that the art of storytelling could have a tremendous amount to offer in education. Why root it in tradition? Why not break the link and have a properly modern storytelling, with pupils making up and developing their own contemporary tales to tell aloud? Actually that is precisely one of the things that can and should happen: pupils making up and telling new stories is very much explored in this book. But asserting that we can ditch tradition entirely is simply daft, for several very good reasons:

- Story makers need models. There are many hundreds of excellent models in traditional stories. These can inform makers of new stories in all sorts of ways.

- Traditional stories have been passed on and moulded through oral storytelling. They are hence perfect for retelling.

- Retelling a traditional story and reshaping it teach the craft of fiction and the art of plot in a very practical way.

- There are many language forms associated with traditional oral telling from which one can 'pick up' important things like the importance of rhythm or how imagery works in communication (and much more).

- Traditional stories often reflect the accumulated wisdom of generations. This is why they are passed on: they mean something important. They can mean something important and relevant now. At best, they can focus meaning in an extraordinary way.

The last point needs amplifying. (The others do too, but that will happen in the course of the book anyway.) Meaning is very central to human existence one way or another. Stories are at the heart of the way we create and communicate meaning. You may recall the short passage I quoted earlier from evolutionary theorists Tooby and Cosmides in which they asserted that we receive information best in a form that resembles experience, that such a form is the story. But the information in a traditional story is rarely flat and literal; it's metaphorical. Story is a language of metaphor. We don't tell fables that say 'If you are a hare, don't get cocky and have a nap when you're racing with a tortoise'; or rather we do, but we say it in a way that means something like 'Look, there are lots of situations in life like that and you might be just like that hare one day, so look out!' and we leave it to sit in your imagination as a metaphorical guide. Fables are relatively simple traditional forms; there are much more complex examples, but the principle holds: there has to be meaning in a tale that goes beyond the specifics of a limited time and a circumscribed place for it to survive. People tend to forget stories that make no sense to them.

This does not mean that the words 'traditional' and 'good' are synonymous; neither does it mean that all folk tales are resonant and meaningful for all people at all times. The sterling work folklore collectors have done over the last two centuries has ensured that traditional stories from many parts of the world have 'made it' into print, but at a price. Some of them have lost any sense they may have had in the process of being 'exhibited', becoming instead otherwise useless 'examples of a genre'. Some would have been justly forgotten had they never been collected anyway. Others reflect attitudes and ideas that belong to other times and places; there is no larger symbolic resonance. But there are many more that have exactly that, especially in the case of so-called 'universal' tales – the kinds of stories that crop up in different forms in many cultures in the world.[6] It's that kind of material we should be exposing pupils to: because it can nourish understanding, imagination and independent, creative thought, perhaps even wisdom and spiritual insight, not just because we are genuflecting in front of the shrine of tradition.

There is a profound depth in many of the marvellous materials carried in the traditions of the peoples of the world, whether transmitted purely orally or recorded in literary forms, and we truly need to find ways to connect with the value in that. I suggest that, to do so, we need to assign many approaches involving ultimately limiting generalizations largely to history. That would include some arguments for the traditional tale in education favoured by advocates in the past, including for example Bruno Bettelheim's bizarrely Freudian interpretations (Bettelheim 1976),[7] Jack Zipes's more recent emphasis on what he sees as abuse metaphors in fairy tales (Zipes 1995)[8] or neo-Jungian writers who want to base things around Joseph Campbell's extraordinary exploration of the universal theme of the hero's quest (Campbell 1993). Traditional stories, I've said, are a language. In a language, you should expect to find all sorts of things described, some of them less attractive than others, it is true, and there is no reason to shirk that, but others extraordinary and astonishing. The best way to understand a language, though, is not to theorize but to first listen to and then to speak it.

Atomizing the curriculum

A woman went into a shop and she bought some coffee, some margarine, a loaf of bread, a cauliflower, half a kilo of tomatoes, a carton of milk and two cans of beans. 'Would you like a bag?' the girl at the checkout said helpfully, seeing her struggling. 'No, thanks,' the woman insisted stolidly. 'I've got enough to carry already.'

A bag is not just another something to carry but a thing on quite another level, something that helps you to carry more in a much more efficient way. Probably it was hard for the woman in the joke to appreciate that, in the midst of the desperate juggling game she was playing. Probably it is hard for teachers, in the midst of the daily struggles to balance time and target demands, to appreciate something that works similarly: storytelling, oral and written, is not just another something to fit into a curriculum already bulging at the seams, but actually something that can make it easier to deliver that curriculum effectively, to teach better at the same time as improving pupils' capacities to absorb what they are taught.

Yet there is a factor that is almost bound to work against that research-supported insight, ensuring that story in general risks being underplayed and marginalized. It's something perhaps endemic in curricula in general: the tendency to atomize knowledge and learning, implying discrete units that accumulate to become an education.

Before taking that further, how important do stories look? As important as, say, maths or science? Probably not to the parent at the school gate or the businessperson on the board of governors. Not as important as a whole lot of other more practical things. Do you write or tell stories on an everyday basis, as part of your work – unless you're a writer or some other sort of creative? Do you go around telling tales to folk you meet? I've already argued that we do, without noticing, in all sorts of ways, but that won't carry much weight in this 'common-sense'-style debate. Young children like them, of course; that's what we give them to get them into books and reading. But it's just as well if we gradually phase that sort of thing out in favour of more worldly things like explanation or information texts, which we all need to work with. That's being street-wise, isn't it?

I don't know that anyone ever said it in so many words. It's more an underlying feeling, yet it does reflect what has happened not just in the UK but across the United States and in all sorts of other countries too, as a result of the strict if distorting logic of another process: the creation of curricula and the setting of targets.

Again this all appears very logical. You analyse and argue about what you think children should know and be able to do. The discussion reflects a series of disparate pressures – cultural values, educational thinking (of different kinds), the avowed needs of business, economic competition, fashion, popular opinion and so on, not to mention whatever political drum is beating. In the end it's agreed and it's all spelled out clearly. It's a sort of list. Stories come into that list in several places. Particularly, they are one of quite a few 'atoms' you have to assemble to produce a substance called literacy.

Whilst we think of story in that way, it won't yield anything like its full value – rather like the car some people keep to polish up on a Sunday but almost never drive anywhere. I asked my own daughter not so long ago how often she had to write stories at school (she had just finished Year 5 at the time). Oh, she said ruefully (she, not unnaturally in a storyteller's daughter, loves stories), these days about three times. In a week? That's really good going, I said, surprised that I'd not noticed this renaissance. No, she replied, in a year. It couldn't be so, I insisted, but we checked on the assignment list and she was not wrong. There were plenty of worthy and effective literacy tasks, some of them imaginative and very interesting, but few demanded any developed knowledge of story structures and storytelling skills, on or off the page.

We need, I would suggest, to change the thinking here. The way you use a tool depends on your conception of what it can do – you can use a chisel to make a fine carving or to open a tin of coffee but probably not both for very long. And you won't get round to the carving unless you begin to understand the whole skill and idea set involved and how you use and maintain the sharpness, the cutting power, the shaping power, plus a lot of other inherent powers too. We need not only to abandon the 'barn dance slant' I talked about with respect to oral storytelling but also to abandon the conceptual hierarchy where we see stories as just one relatively minor aspect of literacy, with something called traditional storytelling as a quaint little detour along the way. We also need to go beyond the notion of storytelling as rather a good gimmick for teaching the basics of literacy, to be abandoned once children can write and punctuate. We need to understand story in general, and oral storytelling as a vital expression of it, as something much larger, potentially much more powerful.

To be precise, we should expect to find in story and storytelling:

- a basic way of understanding and expression that is natural to human beings that you can always draw on and develop;
- a superb aid to learning;
- a way of developing and disciplining imagination;
- a creative form of self-expression;
- a way of developing lucid, inspired speaking;
- a way of connecting natural creative abilities;
- a vital way of understanding narrative structure;
- an underlying tool in both creative and critical thinking;

- a tool for multicultural understanding;
- a way of working with pupils according to their current capacity and improving it (storytelling is as appropriate to and adaptable for all abilities);
- a way of developing new perspectives (reframing) and insight;
- a subtle way of changing behaviour positively;
- a way into wisdom.

According to one quick definition I heard recently, knowledge is understanding that a tomato is a fruit, but wisdom is knowing not to put it in the fruit salad. Fun, but not quite enough. We are, in essence, centres of awareness in what seems (whatever your philosophy) a sleeping universe. The storyteller in us is, at its best, a fundamental expression of that 'super' capacity, the part of us that is not only aware but aware of awareness enough to make a good story of it, which is why stories and storytelling can be wiser than we are.

2

Practical protocols

Give it away a hundred times, you'll still have more left. What is it?

How, why, when and where could you run storytelling sessions in schools or any comparable educational circumstance? There is, of course, no one context, no one way to run storytelling sessions, just as there is no one way to tell stories and indeed no one and only way to teach. The more people use storytelling approaches and the more open-mindedly they do so, the more they evolve their own ways to use them and the broader the relevance they find in them. There are, though, some basic questions to answer and some general methods and practical tips to pass on, as well as some important principles, all of which will help in getting the best out of the material in this book and making them relevant to your practice. Those are what I'll deal with in this chapter. Hints about the use of specific ideas will follow throughout the book.

Subject context

Many may assume that the first and perhaps only subject context for the kinds of ideas presented in this book should be literacy or English. I've argued in Chapter 1 that stories and storytelling need to be considered as much more than minor aspects of literacy. Throughout the following chapters, there is a great deal to spice up literacy work and improve its effectiveness: that will obviously be the first context. I'll also make suggestions for uses beyond that field whenever appropriate.

There is at present generally more opportunity for inter-disciplinary links at primary level than in most secondary schedules. Indeed the recent return to topic-based approaches at primary level, combined with new freedom in approaching literacy, should add much contemporary relevance to many of these ideas, which can simultaneously deliver targets in literacy, PSHE, history, geography and even science, as well as overlapping with drama and music and many other areas of the curriculum. However, many secondary teachers with whom I have worked have been grateful for the chance to link with ideas that colleagues are pursuing in other subject areas, if only during special focus events like book weeks, arts fortnights, festivals and so on, whilst speaking and listening development generally comes under the remit of the English departments. Drama and English are often associated; despite caveats about the differences between acting and storytelling, this is always a natural connection for storytelling, especially when also developed as performance. There are natural enough links, too, between English and other arts/humanities subjects, and some secondary schools explore these. Storytelling approaches have the potential to make a lot of connections, dissolving subject boundaries, whilst the relevance of some aspects of stories to pastoral care and individual counselling is increasingly understood.[1] Overall, practical ideas are presented here to be used flexibly and adapted to context, not fitted into the kinds of rigidly modal scheme that have dogged some aspects of education in recent times.

Adapting to age range

Storytelling is not quite a one-size-fits-all art. There are definitely some ways of working that suit young children, some that work best with adults, some that are great for engaging reluctant teenagers and so on. Again I'll flag that up as I go along. Having said that, however, a lot of experience has convinced me that you can very often make the same story or the same tale telling game or technique of elaborating and exploring a narrative work with (say) a 7-year-old one day and a 14-year-old on another. Hence much of the material here is not age-specific and can be revisited in different ways at different stages of development many times over.

Using the story trance

In Chapter 1, I drew attention to connections between the feeling of being, as it were, lost in a story with a 'state' sometimes characterized as light hypnotic trance. The 'story trance' is a useful working conceptualization. Most teachers will recognize that (often very welcome) hush that can miraculously descend on a class when they are truly absorbed in and fascinated by a subject. This is especially true of stories of any kind, whether told or read or indeed delivered in other ways. It's something often described with adjectives like 'magical' or indeed 'entrancing'. Practically, we recognize that something different is happening, a slightly altered state of consciousness has been entered where, if you're lucky, 'you could almost hear a pin drop'.

There are good reasons why it's useful to find ways to encourage this 'hushed trance'. Firstly it appears to be psychologically healthy to go into such dreamy states periodically.[2] Secondly, because such a 'state' is a natural concomitant of absorption in inner imagery, you can be fairly certain that pupils are taking in a story at a deeper level, seeing the 'pictures', responding to the imagery and moods of the story inwardly. Because of this, the story or elements of it will stay with them for further work, whilst the part of the mind that responds more intuitively to metaphor has been at least stirred.[3] Learning in the listening trance state and recall afterwards also tend to be 'whole pattern': pupils may take in the total energy and feel and manner with which the story is presented and may naturally find themselves taking on the 'voice' and mannerisms of the telling, learning to use that voice themselves in improved expression on and off the page. Finally, the change of mode and mood benefits classroom practice: it simply makes it easier to focus in general.

No one should expect all story activity to automatically produce this response and mood. Conditions vary; pupils vary; we all vary. Sometimes you are after a more outwardly active mood anyway. It's helpful, however, to be aware of the possibility, to promote it and to spot the signs, which generally include (amongst other things) these external markers in individual listeners:

- diminished physical activity;
- fixed gaze (looking, as it were, through and beyond);
- enlargement of pupils of eyes;
- slower breathing;
- marked response to emotionally loaded story events and other suggestions.

You can, from time to time, discuss with many groups how they feel when absorbed in a story, whether anyone has felt themselves almost in another world, how they have felt when this happens and so on. Usually this is quite a rich seam. Quite a few claim to see very vividly in imagination, many more to feel, some to taste, touch and smell. (This is a theme we'll follow up in Chapter 5.)

Drawing attention to the possibility of absorption generally amplifies it and makes it hence more possible for more pupils: though it's important to make allowances for those who, for one reason or another, don't get it – yet.

Story listening is a skill too

Many of the activities in the book help to develop and focus the skill of listening and then also responding through focused questioning. It can't be emphasized enough that listening to a tale is as much a skill as telling and shaping a story. A skill needs practice of the right kind in the right circumstance – which of course means minimizing distractions. Working with distractions, bouncing off them, being able to refocus and to hone down one's attention – these are advanced skills, not givens one can depend on. Advanced skills are less likely to flourish if there are simply too many variables. To plan a session in (for example) a hall with a swimming-bath acoustic, where there will be regular interruptions from other classes trooping off to games sessions, not to mention the sound of peripatetic trumpet lessons from an adjoining area, is to doom it to unnecessarily limited success.

Noisy talk sessions

Storytelling and story games in pairs and groups can also be, contrastingly, quite noisy activities. You want pupils to be able to talk to each other in a relatively uninhibited way, telling their stories, asking their questions or doing whatever else is required. Noise levels tend to rise as they relax into activities and have more to say, because they are having to make themselves heard over an increasing hubbub, so it's useful to have a signal agreed in advance to suggest that noise levels need to drop if there is a danger of disturbing other groups and classes excessively.

Many pupils mistake some telling activities for drama work and will begin to act out the story. This is as true of secondary pupils as it is of younger primary children and can sometimes, indeed, suit the circumstance and aims anyway. But story may be most powerful when viewed, as it were, with the inner eye in the mental theatre, so again it may be useful to establish in advance that acting out responses might not (at least yet) be required.

Do teachers need to be storytellers for this to work?

You don't have to be an expert storyteller to make story sessions in which pupils tell tales work. If you are presenting a story that is to be the focus for further work, however, you have to find a way to do that. If storytelling is a skill you have already developed, that's fine. If it's something you're happy to experiment with doing, that's also great. Storytelling is relatively easy to do at a level that gets the tale across well, even if it means referring to a book from time to time, and there's a lot of fun to be had in sharing a tale, not to mention interesting discoveries you can make about pupils through the way they respond to your tale. But you could, alternatively, use an equivalent story told on CD or DVD if available. Or it may be enough to simply read the story aloud, with plenty of expression, allowing the activity to 'take it off the page' later. Or again, if you have quite able pupils, you can get them to read and remember the story themselves, perhaps allowing them to retell it to all the class or group, maybe with different people adding different parts of the tale. The main thing is to find a way, whatever it might be, to pass on stories appropriate to the age range involved.

Fitting it in

Some of the activities in this book require longer sessions specifically focused around them. Some, it should be said, will fit into quite short times, especially when they are familiar and are being revisited. This is hence one good use for those 'spare' five- or ten-minute slots that sometimes crop up unexpectedly in a teaching schedule, when something didn't take quite as long as expected or when one is waiting for this or that to happen and it's not worth starting anything major. A round or more of a familiar story game or a chance for one or two pupils to tell tales they are working on can add up to a lot over time. Equally, stories and story game approaches can often fit into the presentation of other subjects as brief illustrative activities. An example plan for a full lesson around oral storytelling activities is given in Appendix A.

Simulating oral traditions

In oral traditions, stories change in various ways as they pass from person to person. Repetition may make a tale almost unrecognizable when compared to its original, often for better though sometimes for worse. It's possible to simulate some of this in classroom and other workshop situations through procedures such as 'Pass it on', which is described in Appendix B, and the variations on this described in Appendix C. 'Pass it on' is recommended at various points in the book for extending tales, and it will be as well to get to know it as you become familiar with the material in Chapter 3 and beyond.

Connecting storytelling to writing: general principles

Many teachers' use of pupils' oral storytelling activities is accompanied by a certain anxiety: when are they going to write? This is entirely understandable – storytelling doesn't 'show' unless it is recorded in some way. It's easy to feel that pupils have simply been entertaining themselves. This perhaps reflects a general cultural value; it's not a problem unique to the current phase of education. We live in a commercial culture; ephemeral things like stories told can't be weighed and valued, not until they become an artefact like a script or a book or a CD – or even a download. But a told story is only weightless if we measure it on a cash scale. As a psychological and maybe even spiritual 'artefact', it could be enormous. From the telling of story a pupil might learn something so important that it will affect the rest of her or his life. Hence a vital caveat here is: *value the oral for itself, as something worthwhile in itself.*

A second point to keep in mind if you are using storytelling as part of teaching literacy skills: on the page is not the only place those skills will be learned. Literacy (as pointed out in Chapter 1) is, in large part, the art of transposing different modes of talk appropriate to different contexts into appropriate words, sentences, paragraphs and so on organized in conventional ways on the page. It's hard to do that if you don't have the voice of that talk and those modes in your head first; storytelling is a good way to get them there. And what seems at first random, fun talk can gradually be shaped to yield many of the understandings that lead to literacy – for example, how the first, second and third person work in narrative, how description can both help and hinder narratives, how the rhythms of sentences work, how punctuation 'feels', how to really interest people in what you are saying through the language you use and so on.

That said, the transition into writing from oral activities can be made natural and smooth, especially with repetition and practice, so that oral activity is not an occasional curiosity but a constant source to which to return for new inspiration. However, there are some definite challenges to be aware of, and the first is an age-old problem in a new guise.

Once it gets some momentum, talk flows relatively easily. If an oral activity has been successful, most will have warmed up to reach at least some level of that flow and imaginative involvement. Confronting the blank page immediately, however, can have an opposite, somewhat chilling effect. There is a sudden feel that what one does shows and hence has to follow received rules. A creative and imaginatively wild oral tale may limp its way on to the page, rather maimed and tamed. It's hence important not to over-emphasize critical thinking at this transition stage.

So-called 'writers' block' is something many fine professional writers have had problems with from time to time, and it can affect pupils too. For professionals it's usually characterized by excessive self-criticism, so that whatever a person produces seems inadequate and trite. (Something quite similar often affects the form of top sportspeople, especially when they are over-coached and publicly criticized.) For pupils, a comparable state may manifest simply as a feeling of 'I can't do it' or 'This isn't cool', but the sources could be similar. Good writing is produced by a balance between the critical faculty and the imaginative side, a theme we'll explore in the next chapter. Too much of the critical and whatever is done seems wrong; too much of the imaginative and what is produced lacks focus and discipline. A big advantage of engaging pupils in oral activity at a level at which they can achieve is that they speak without being excessively self-critical and respond using natural imaginative capacities. To maintain that feeling, you avoid switching them back into over-critical mode. Hence:

- When moving from oral to writing, avoid insistence on detailed linear planning before writing. This obviously has its place elsewhere and will suit some pupils in this context too, so there's no need to forbid it. For many, it switches them into a potentially blocked mode in which knowledge of what *should* happen gets in the way, so quick scribbled notes as reminders of this or that, quick sketches, key words and so on, use of rough mapping methods like story clouds (see Chapter 3) or any other informal way of holding on to ideas may be far better.

- Similarly, if your school system involves always writing down learning objectives, do that before the creative oral stage, not between the oral and the writing.

- Similarly also, giving too many 'helpful' guide points can be confusing. (A few are very useful of course. More is less.)

- Plunging in without an immediate plan straight from an oral game can work for many. Sometimes you can encourage planning after a paragraph or two, looking at the implications and possibilities of what has been written so far. This is a method some writers certainly do use.

- Equally, sometimes it's as well to allow pupils to ramble on the page in exactly the same way they might do in an improvised oral yarn. Remember that the notion that all writers always work in a very planned and intentional ways is actually a myth based on incomplete information, perhaps combined with the feeling some writers have that they should make what they do seem respectably intentional. All good writers have the ability to plan where necessary; most also know how and when to 'fly by the seat of their pants' too – and probably learned their craft by doing exactly that.

- Where time allows you can maintain the mood of light-hearted experiment with some preliminary bits of brief uncritical writing. For example, get the pupils to quickly jot down something funny or scary or silly or serious that might happen in their story, not necessarily in a complete sentence. Follow this with some colours or sounds or smells or tastes (etc.) that might crop up in the tale. You might get them to progress to something a little nearer to their eventual writing, such as inventing a rough sentence they would like to have at or near the beginning, in the middle and/or at the end of the story or some imaginative words and images they would like to work in somewhere (with no absolute obligation to actually use them). You might equally use something slightly crazy and off-the-wall – perhaps a series of silly word associations related to the story theme you are working with.

- You can encourage pupils to 'hear the voice' of the story as if they had a storyteller inside their own heads. Some able pupils naturally hear the 'voice' of the story as they write; others can begin to notice that as a possibility when attention is drawn to it.

- Also bear in mind that the progression from oral activity to writing can be reversed. You can take a written story back to the oral – as suggested in various places throughout the book. This is one way to subtly encourage that balance between the critical and the creative – oral techniques often suggest ways written tales can be improved.

- The aim of gradually integrating the critical faculty with the creative and vice versa needs to be kept in mind. Groups experienced in working from oral to writing and back again should get better at it and be able to be both creative and sensibly self-critical. But that doesn't happen straight away, even with very talented young writers.

Alternatives to writing: recording stories

Technology is advancing very rapidly. By the time these words are published, there will be new devices on offer with new possibilities for even easier audio and video recording. In recent times, there was a hiatus in the recording of spoken word in education as robust and reliable cassette technology became redundant, whilst recording directly through computer was cumbersome, less flexible and rather off-putting. At the time of writing, widespread availability of good recording facilities on mobile phones with blue tooth connections and the current ease of recording on many laptops plus a new range of digital recording devices make sound recording once more feasible and flexible for classroom situations. Some devices also record short video clips, though digital video cameras with much greater capacity are also now quite common in schools. Voice recognition programs in computers are also increasingly sophisticated, leading to speculation that computer keyboards will become redundant – though this currently seems over-optimistic (or over-pessimistic, depending on how you look at it!).

Recording of pupils' storytelling on suitable media, both as sound only and as video clips, yields some interesting possibilities and advantages:

- A lot of pupils enjoy being recorded, as evidenced by the popularity of YouTube, etc.

- With sound-only recording, one can focus on the sound and rhythm and other qualities of the voice. You can focus in on particular positive qualities as well as points for improvement.

- Sound-only also may make it easier for listeners to go into an imaginary world – as in the old chestnut about the pictures on radio being better than in the films.

- Video clips allow you to study the way the body tells the story (or doesn't).

- In literacy teaching, it also allows you to home in on how punctuation 'looks' as well as sounds: you can freeze-frame particular moments of expression, replay particular speech rhythms and so on, perhaps even juxtapose them with short chunks of text on-screen, so that pupils can pick up how the rhythms of speech turn into marks on the page.

- Popular sites on the internet may give you a forum on which you can post clips of stories told by pupils.

There are a couple of negative possibilities to take into account too:

- Video recording in particular may distance viewers and turn them into observers rather than participants – you are watching the way Jess scratches her nose rather than listening to her story, which wouldn't happen in the live situation.

- Some pupils find recording traumatic, especially if a recording that embarrasses them is played to the rest of the group. You can encourage some past that reaction and increase their confidence in doing so; others it may be best to excuse.

Connecting storytelling beyond literacy: general principles

The fundamental point that subject divisions are something we impose on knowledge rather than being intrinsic to it is easy to forget, especially in an age that tends to emphasize categories. But different subjects are received 'in here' by the same brains, the same neural networks, the same overarching selves. Story is the way we understand many things, the way we put things together, the way we organize things provisionally – especially when we don't know the missing bits and have to make a leap of imagination to make sense of facts or theories or schemes or simply of hints and guesses.

It follows that using the story mode in one way or another will have relevance across the curriculum in all sorts of ways. Some of those ways will be mentioned in this book, but there are inevitably many more possibilities. We should expect stories to be relevant in the following contexts:

- For getting across ideas and information. Ideas presented in story form make better sense.

- For enlivening studies and bringing them to life imaginatively. Telling or writing a story around ideas and information makes it live in a new way and inspires exploration – as for example when you research a historical story or a yarn set in a different country and culture or invent a scientific myth (see Chapter 4).

- Storytelling approaches facilitate a synthesis of knowledge, both overtly studied (as in the last point) and 'intuitive', as when we draw on ideas and information unconsciously absorbed.[4]

- It is also a good arena in which to challenge some assumptions, unconsciously taken on with those ideas and information, in a non-threatening way. If I call into question how your characters are behaving or thinking and how accurate it is as a representation of a person at that time or in that situation or of conditions in this or that time or place, I am not challenging you directly as a person and I am encouraging you to think about ways of behaving or about conditions 'out there' you may not have considered.[5]

- For solving problems creatively and making informed imaginative guesses – as for example happened in ancient myth perhaps as much as in science fiction.
- For showing how subject categories blend.
- For showing something more than information and perhaps in the category of wisdom.

Since each one of those uses would merit a major essay, I'll leave them to be illustrated in the rest of the book.

Random choice and razzmatazz

In various places in the book, the suggestion is made that you use stories or ideas on cards or on prepared sheets or sometimes on slips of paper. This is a chance to introduce a little razzmatazz and theatre to sessions, which helps to maintain interest and enthusiasm, though you need to adapt according to age. Cards might be shuffled publicly before pupils choose, slips could be similarly muddled together randomly to be picked from an attractive hat or star-covered box or attractive sack. If available, you can even find ways to use raffle drums or roulette wheels – anything that builds useful excitement and expectancy.

The kind of random choice these devices generate stretches creativity and makes pupils less ready to rebel against what they have been allocated – it seems more like decrees of fate than arbitrary teacher's whim, though you can allow for some flexibility where the 'choice' somehow doesn't 'take'.

Story sticks, telling thrones and so on

A quieter kind of 'theatre' suitable for younger groups is provided by story sticks or special storytelling 'thrones' or any other device that can be used or occupied or (in the case of costume items, badges, etc.) worn only by the storyteller whilst telling. These are inspired by practices rooted in different traditions around the world but are also very practical devices. You establish and enforce the rule that, when a person is holding the specially decorated stick or wearing the crown or seated on the story throne, others must stay still and listen until she or he has finished. With many older 'street-wise' groups this is less likely to work, but you might use some actual ethnic artefact, claiming that it has a power that it's said to be unlucky to disregard. Respect for such practical 'traditions' works best if it is not overused.

Stories remain a language

A final caveat is expressed in the briefly told tale below. Stories are at best a different kind of language that can go on meaning in new ways. It's worth keeping in mind in any story work than you won't ever have discovered everything there is to know or teach about them. They can go on surprising.

The box

A man wooed and married a maiden from another world. The only dowry she brought with her was a strangely patterned box, which he was never to open. Every day she would tell him stories that amazed him, tales that opened vistas he had never suspected, making him somehow wiser and better able to succeed in his own world. Then one day, when she was out, he couldn't resist peeking inside that box, just quickly. There was nothing at all in it, so far as he could see. When his young wife returned, he told her this, asking why she had kept a mere emptiness such a secret. She shook her head, sorrowfully. 'Now I must leave you,' she insisted. 'In that box were all my stories, but you saw nothing.' With that, she vanished, and whether he ever found her again is another story.

3

Telling tall tales

A lie becoming true. What is it?

Framing ideas: why fib?

In the once and never land of perhaps and maybe, they held an annual festival of fibs. Speakers would vie with each other to produce the tallest and most wildly improbable tale of the day, each wanting to win an enormous rainbow rosette and the coveted title of Fabulous Fibber. One year a pompous preacher silenced them all with a long and passionate sermon on the evils of lying. 'Lying is dreadfully wrong,' he concluded. 'I myself have never told a lie.' Well, it was a unanimous decision. The preacher was presented with the rosette and the title, having told the biggest fib of all.

Most of us not blinded by self-righteousness and over-literal adherence to morality like the preacher accept (as I pointed out in Chapter 1) that all human beings tell lies, sooner or later, that it's essential to be able to do so in order to function in this world. By the time children are seven or eight years old, they are generally consummate liars, with a fair appreciation of how to make something false sound at least a bit true. It's a skill they will go on developing and refining. It's also a skill they will go on getting caught out by; for some it will lead to a downfall or several and for not a few, sadly, to serious difficulties. This is of course why we condemn many forms of malicious lying and encourage pupils to avoid self-deception and learn to tell the truth, even though this is clearly simplistic taken too literally.

Telling lies is like storytelling in that you have to somehow or other make both lie and story 'true' – believable, convincing. Hence it's both a good place to start and an excellent reference point to return to again and again, since you can assume that pupils know how to do it already and, what is more, are practising constantly. Working from what we do more or less instinctively is always likely to be more effective than starting way outside a learner's experience. This need not imply approval of lying per se. One recognizes, firstly and without undue cynicism, that there is indeed no such thing as someone who has never told a lie but then goes a little further. For example, one might notice that, by handling lying as a skill to be drawn on, observed, studied and developed in relation to the larger craft of storytelling and making, one is actually drawing attention to its limitations, training tellers, but also crucially listeners and readers, to spot and question lies, to have a vital feel for the truth – if not to slavishly tell it at all times.

Staying only with the 'natural' or, indeed, treating it as a one-off curiosity for occasional temporary use, however, would be lazy – unless one is going for the impact of a short term 'blast' on telling tall tales, as in the 'festival of fibs' idea at the end of this chapter. One needs a set of graded exercises and bright ideas, building on and focusing the basics. That is what this chapter is about.

School context

Games and other activities around various forms of fibbing, developing into tall tale telling in both oral and written form, can be part of a theme for a term's work in literacy/English. This connects well to myths and legends (as illustrated in the next chapter) and makes a good introduction to or reminder of the fun of storytelling. Equally it can be a recurring point of reference in story work over months and even years, as one explores the other kinds of storytelling skill. The notion is to work from a basic idea: it can be fun to tell extraordinary lies. This is then developed further through a series of fun activities, demanding progressively greater levels of skill and perception, but all growing out of that 'natural' skill. Additional games for use here can be found in my short publication *Tall Tale Telling* (Parkinson 2004), from which three of the ideas included here have been taken, as noted in the text.

The essential story game

I originally invented a version of this game well over 30 years ago; it became a great favourite with the first class I ever taught long before I realized that it embodies essential story making and telling principles.[1] In *Tall Tale Telling*, it appears under the title used here. I'll make no apology for including it again here, since it's the best way I know to introduce those principles.

Fantastic fibs (for use with a whole group or in pairs)

- Choose a storyteller to tell her/his fabulous fib to the group (or, in pairs, take it in turns to be fibber and listener).

- The storyteller tells a fabulous fib (e.g. they visited the moon, flew on their beds, became a celebrity or found a fortune) – just a sentence or two will do to begin with.

- The group or partner asks a set number of questions (say seven) about this. Direct doubt ('That's impossible!', etc.) is forbidden. Questions may work best if they are 'open', designed to make the storyteller give as much detail as possible. (See 'Liar and lawyer tools and tricks' below.)

- The group or partner is aiming to make it more difficult to tell the tale, to make storytellers say 'I don't know.' If they say that, they have lost the game.

- Whatever the storyteller says is true. She or he wins by answering all questions.

- (In a group or solo) The story emerging from the game is retold.

This works with any age, from very young children to adults, suitably adapted. Older groups may respond better to the 'Tall tales' title or simply 'The lying game'. Again themes, for example fibs, can be chosen to suit the likely tastes of participants. Complete fantasy (flying on broomsticks, getting superpowers, capturing a unicorn, etc.) often appeals to younger players, but you may need to go for something different with teenagers – perhaps becoming famous (a common enough fantasy) or developing a love potion (dangerous but maybe). Many pupils will need coaching in asking questions that require a response longer than one or two words ('Yes', 'No', 'Black', 'White', etc.); for some, getting them to offer questions of any sensible kind is a very positive start.

In group situations, once the game has been demonstrated, pupils can play the game in pairs and then change partners, try the same fib again and see what different questions the second partner offers. This will toughen the story up for actual telling without questions, which can be done in a straight story swap (i.e. without the game) following another change of partner. The instruction this time is simply to tell as much of the tall tale as you can, working in as many of the answers to questions as possible. It is also very good to follow this with 'Pass it on' (described in Appendix B; see also the lesson plan in Appendix A), in this instance memorizing someone else's 'fib' and passing it on to yet another partner, as a third person story about that person. ('Claire told me that she flew to the moon last Tuesday. She went on a flying bed . . .') A tale can be passed on several times, with tellers adding whatever comes to them, before being retold to the group by the last to receive it.

These two last storytelling stages will work better as you repeat the game – some get the idea straight away; generally what comes out of the game will sound more like a tall tale, with more of the detail that makes such a story work, on the third or fourth or fifth playing. Hence you can come back to this game repeatedly, perhaps using different set themes (see below), as well as developing it into writing.

Twos, threes and small group fibs

A natural development of the solo game is to have two or more people prepare a joint fib or tall tale. The 'story' is told to the group (or another pair/group) by the pair or group, taking it in turns. They also answer questions in turn. (Something similar will work with other questioning games in the book.) In group telling, the speakers have to listen to each other closely to make sure what they say is consistent, whilst inconsistencies may be more easy for listeners to spot and challenge. Group telling helps to support those who are less confident or find the task otherwise more challenging.

Interesting to notice

'Fantastic fibs' gives you a snapshot of the fiction–spinning mind in action, externalized in the form of the two (or more) players. On one side is 'the liar', coming up with fantastic ideas and improbable nonsense. On the other is the 'lawyer', the part of the mind that questions, raises a doubt or two, presses for more detail and explanation. It's something that goes on 'inside' as well as 'out there', an essential side of effective creative thinking. Too much of 'the liar' and you get a rambling and confusing tale that lurches from one impossible to the next (as in many children's 'default style' telling). Too much of 'the lawyer' and the creative flow stops; nothing seems possible. Ideally the creative side and the critical stay in balance, though this is hard to maintain constantly at any age, let alone when you are young and just learning how to handle words and ideas.

The 'Fantastic fibs' game has several other advantages worth noting as possible learning objectives:

- It builds confidence and competence in speaking.
- It improves verbal fluency.

- It demands thinking and imagining 'on your feet'.
- It can lead smoothly into writing.
- It can, equally, develop told tales that can be valued for themselves.
- Like other story games in this book, it is also very good for breaking the ice and getting a group less familiar with each other working together and trusting each other.

Here is what is almost a picture of the game in story form useful for introducing the game, based on a widespread traditional plot you will find repeated in another form with a framing plot at the end of the chapter.

The liar and the lawyer

'I've been to the moon,' the liar insisted, beaming proudly.

The lawyer coughed doubtfully, furrowing his eager legal brow. 'Indeed. How did you get there?'

'On a flying bike.'

'You went to the moon on a bike that flies? Where did you get that from?'

'I didn't get it. I made it myself from an old pram, a toilet chain and a pillow full of feathers.'

'You made a flying bike from an old pram, a toilet chain and a pillow full of feathers and you flew it to the moon?'

'That's so.'

'But what made it fly?'

'Me. It was the power of personal belief, you see. I'm strong on that.'

'What did you believe in?'

'Getting to the moon. It made the journey go by very fast.'

'So, when you got to the moon, what did you do?'

'I scooped up three armfuls of green cheese and set off to come back by way of Mars. I sold the green cheese there to some of those little red guys – you know, the ones with the seven yellow antennae. They paid me with two magic bags full of Mars bars and I'd have made a good profit on the trip, but I got carried away on a solar wind all the way to Saturn and got the biggest bag stuck on the ring. As for me, I bounced off and was pulled back through a black hole all the way here. I'd be showing the other bag of Mars bars now by way of proof, but when I got back someone stole it and ate every single bar.'

'And who stole the amazing bag?'

'It was you of course. You did it!'

'Now that is a lie!' shouted the lawyer angrily.

Repetitions of the 'Fantastic fibs' game with variations would aim to establish and then develop the pattern of fibbing, questioning effectively, then using answering as a springboard for further fantasy and, finally, recalling those answers in more developed tall tales. One way to vary is to set particular themes and limitations. Another is to study more closely how both 'liars' (storytellers) and 'lawyers' (questioners) can be more effective. As the game and variations progress, you would also expect to be mixing writing and telling tasks. Variations and developments of the game and uses of other kinds of fibbing are also very helpful. Some ideas for all of these are included in the following sections.

17 possible themes for fantastic fibs and tall tales

Any of these themes could be explored through the basic game and also in telling and writing tall tales. They will also work with other games and approaches dealt with later in the chapter. It can be very useful to set a theme for a tall tale telling session or exercise, to give it a different flavour and focus – though of course this should not imply that a tall tale can't combine more than one of these categories and themes. Notes are to give teachers and other workshop leaders a few priming thoughts and/or examples for each theme.

An entertaining way to select different themes for tellers in a group is to print several themes (probably previously discussed) on strips of paper and have group members pick them randomly from a hat.

1. *Strange lands, hidden places and far-away planets:* everything from trips to fantasy countries, bizarre distant planets and weird islands to eccentric, but just about believable, towns, villages, areas of cities, etc. (where people shake feet instead of hands, houses are built on flexible stilts, children are considered wise, etc.). (See Chapter 4, 'The voyage of Mael Dun' for a mythical example.)

2. *Strange structures:* for example, houses made of sugar or chocolate or cheese and other unlikely materials (in a fantasy style that always appeals to younger children); towers built from compacted old newspapers, straw and other recycled materials (in an eco-friendly fantasy that could be made to work with many ages); dream castles filled with wonders, mansions with incredible luxuries, haunted ruins: there are many possibilities.

3. *Sudden transformation:* a good dramatic theme. You are suddenly changed into a monster, large animal, mythical creature, etc.; a small shy person suddenly becomes large and bold; your cat takes some pills by mistake and grows to the size of a tiger; a stupid person becomes clever (or vice versa); ugly becomes beautiful (or vice versa); and so on.

4. *Meetings and/or adventures with remarkable creatures:* a perennial theme in children's fiction, as also in local lore and legend (e.g. finding a dragon

or a unicorn, a yeti, an enormous fish, a wild panther in town, the Loch Ness Monster, aliens, etc.).

5. *Getting a special object of power:* This might be traditionally magical (a cloak of invisibility, ring of knowledge, sword of sharpness, etc.), more contemporary or futuristic sci-fi (special lasers, super-powered phones, a mega-computer, etc.) or perhaps intriguingly on the edge of the possible (a special thought-focusing device, intelligence changer, peace maker, etc.).

6. *Against the laws:* Happenings that seem to defy the normal laws of nature (levitating, walking on water, accurate mind reading, sudden appearances and disappearances, teleportation, etc.).

7. *Finding/getting a treasure, riches or wealth:* from lottery wins to magically made fortunes. Many have fantasized on this very theme, so it's an easy one.

8. *Zany and improbable accidents:* the stuff of clowning and situation comedy, for example you knock over a card, which knocks over an ornament, which knocks over a lamp, which drops on the head of a waiter, who staggers out and bumps hard into someone else, who cannons out of the door, causing a car to swerve and knock down the framework that is supporting the house, which falls down on your head. Such a chain reaction gives an easy-to-handle linear plot structure.

9. *Strange contraptions and odd inventions:* a theme currently most familiar in sequences from *Wallace & Gromit* films, which are in a long tradition including Heath Robinson cartoons and some of the old silent films. It's even more possible with words and imagination – you don't have to make a working model.

10. *Developing special skills:* These could include the magical or apparently supernatural, as in 6 above, 'Against the laws' (making things disappear, becoming invisible, flying, etc.), but also more 'possible' things (a special calculating skill, card and conjuring skills, kicking, catching, juggling, throwing, balancing, fighting/martial arts, embroidery, painting, carpentry, carving, etc.).

11. *Amazing coincidences and impossible circumstances:* The trick here is for one impossibility and absurd coincidence to follow on from another, perhaps each one just about explaining (or at least making you forget) the last – as happens in the liar's story of his flight to the moon or, for more complicated reasons, in Chang's story (below).

12. *Power for a day:* becoming king or queen for a while because you are the monarch's double; taking over, because of some odd quirk of fate, as

head teacher, manager, captain, orchestra conductor, etc.). Power for a day is also, delightfully, power without responsibility.

13. *A secret unusual or magical friend or servant:* another perennial in oral tradition as much as in children's fiction. The secret friend might have unusual powers or just be unusual – perhaps very small or invisible, perhaps summoned by a ring or a lamp, perhaps only turning up in dire circumstances.

14. *Encounter with an unusual, weird or specially skilled person or being:* Heroes and heroines meeting with witches and wizards, etc. has been a stock theme in fantasy for children. Similar themes crop up in stories of kung fu masters, crazy but brilliant scientists and inventors, fabulous painters – or even extraordinary storytellers (which allows for developing stories inside stories: the tales told by the extraordinary storyteller of whom you tell stories).[2]

15. *Exaggerated family stories:* This might include the last two categories, with stories of uncles or aunts or great-grandmothers who had unusual talents, or it might include any of the other categories, such as 8 above.[3] Tales within tales are again very much possible – you tell a story about, say, an unusual aunt, making it as believable as possible, and then tell an incredible story she told you.

16. *Peculiar pets and talented animals:* Dogs and cats that do extraordinary tricks, horses that talk, keeping a crocodile in the bath or an eel in the toilets – these and many more are all fun themes many can make their own. Pets could even include walking, talking plants and rocks.

17. *Gifts:* The present that does more than expected is another theme that automatically suggests an easy structure (e.g. unwrapping present – puzzlement – following the instructions – first strange results – bizarre consequences – attempts at control – increasingly extraordinary events – denouement).

Liar and lawyer tools and tricks

These mental and verbal 'tools' can make themes for parts of (or whole) lessons or workshops or storytelling/writing tasks. I have divided them into 'the liar's tools', which are some of the tricks, short cuts, etc. for the fantasist, and 'the lawyer's tools', which are ways of making the questioning more effective and thorough. Players can note down and share any other tricks that don't fit these categories as 'extra secrets'. The questioning skills of 'the lawyer' will be drawn on in other chapters and are excellent and practical skills to learn to use beyond storytelling too. Tips are given in the second person, as direct advice; they will need adapting to suit different ages.

The liar's toolbox

The themes above are all in themselves part of the liar's kit. However, to help make things more extraordinary, funny, fantastical , strange and so on, you might:

- *Exaggerate* size, length, strength, distance, height, difficulty, etc.
- *Make colours unusual:* pink roads, green skies, purple spotted fur, etc.
- *Use all five senses:* not only strange visions but also weird sounds, peculiar smells, odd taste, surprising touch.
- *Use add-ons:* For pure fantasy tales, give animals, mythical beasts, humans, aliens, etc. extra limbs, more than one head, unlikely horns and spikes and so on. Vary trees, mountains, rocks, roads, cars, trucks, rockets, etc. in similar ways. For just–about–believable tales, use similar ideas in more modest ways (a dog with two tails; a fish with a horn, etc.).
- *Reverse norms:* (a) Extreme reversals (fantasy): people walk backwards up the street; stones fall upwards; frogs or ants rule humans; dogs take people for a walk; everything is upside down, etc. (b) Milder reversals: rocks that are very light; feathers that are heavy; it is polite to be rude, etc.
- *Develop exaggerating crazy-sounding metaphors, similes and conceits* you can slip in and vary ('as bent as a barrel-load of bouncing bananas', 'his eyes popped out of his head and rolled away down the street like two blue and white marbles', 'she was so green with envy she matched the grass', etc.). (See also Chapter 7 – descriptions in three.)
- *Pile it on:* One crazy and confusing thing piled on top of another in a narration may stop listeners asking questions (as seems to happen when the liar in the story explains going to the moon, then Mars and then Saturn).
- *Free-associate:* Especially in the free telling situation, let one idea follow on from and suggest another. If stuck for inspiration, look around and see what is there you could weave into the tale in fantastic form – tables could talk, curtains could whisper secrets, doors could slam in time to music, etc.
- *Invent some stock wonders to throw in when necessary:* a hill made of brass, a chocolate fountain, a drum as big as a lake, etc.

- *Bamboozle 'em with big words and specious explanations:* When challenged, explain with something that simply sounds as if it should be true. If you know enough to do this, it's good if you can make this sound vaguely scientific or otherwise clever, including a few big words. A sophisticated refinement for the liar in the story: 'How did you fly?' 'I discovered a way to reverse the body's natural magnetic field, by using the alpha waves of the brain that are created by strong positive belief, which counteracted the earth's own negative gravitational force.' It doesn't have to be as complicated as this, but any piece of information or jargon (historical, geographical or whatever, as well as scientific) will work, especially if presented with confidence.

- *Use flashy labels:* Similarly, by giving something a special name, you can make it sound as though it must work or must be real. Continuing from the last extra question and answer for lawyer and liar above: 'How did you breathe when you were flying to the moon?' 'I had an automatic solar-powered respirator strapped under my armpit.' Made-up words could also work here: 'I used a groggelizer along with a tweezlebud.'

- *Get your listeners to agree with you early:* 'I'm sure you know what I mean . . .' 'Something like that has probably happened to you . . .' Of course, some people wouldn't understand that, but I'm sure you will . . .' These are all good (sometimes flattering) strategies for getting listeners (or readers) on your side, especially early on in the narrative. (See 'The yes set: PSHE relevance', pages 54–55.)

Last but by no means least:

- *Guess the questions and answer them before they are asked* (a skill that develops through the game and is also essential to all storytelling as also to all unscripted public speaking, teaching, etc.).

Exercises

- Go through the story of 'The liar and the lawyer' and check how many of these ideas the liar might be using.
- Develop the liar's story further using some of the above ideas (probably in combination with the similar exercise at the end of 'The lawyer's toolbox' below).
- Similarly, study Chang's story at the end of the chapter and improve on his fibs and those of the princes, etc.

The lawyer's toolbox

Learning the skill of getting information through asking questions and the likely effect of particular kinds of questions is as important a part of the teaching function of this game as the imaginative side. To make questioning effective and varied, mix the following:

- *Closed questions:* These ask for specifics. Examples are 'What colour was its fur?', 'What time did this happen?' and 'Do you know how old it was?' They may not, however, call for much detail (and therefore story-telling) because the answers could be very brief – 'Blue', '11.15 a.m.' and 'One hundred and three' (or simply 'No'), so try not to use them all the time.

- *Open questions/requests:* These make the liar work harder because they could be answered in various different ways. Open questions might begin with 'How did . . .?' or 'Why was it that . . .?' Open requests (another way of phrasing a question) might be 'Please could you tell me more about . . .?' or 'Would you describe the flying bed in more detail, please?' In the game, you can make it a rule that the liar must not answer by saying 'I don't know', 'No' or 'I won't.' (In the case of detail, you can introduce the idea of describing at least three things, explored at length in Chapter 6.)

- *Recap:* You can repeat or summarize what the liar has said, perhaps to show how unlikely it is. (The lawyer in the story does this more than once.) This could be a prelude to pointing out things that don't 'add up'.

- *Leading questions:* These questions suggest what the liar (or other characters in the story) might have done, thought or seen or what else could have happened or come into the story *before* these have been mentioned (e.g. the lawyer might have asked, in open style, 'Could you describe in detail any of the shooting stars or rockets you could have seen along the way?'). Younger children often ask leading questions in story games, usually in closed form: 'Were there any aliens and flying saucers?'

- *Presuppositions (word traps):* Very similar to leading questions, these imply that something not stated or admitted has been done. 'How often have you stolen things in the past?' is a classic real-life lawyer's trap. The example leading question above could be rephrased as a presupposition thus: 'Please describe in detail the shooting stars and rockets you saw along the way.' The phrasing now suggests not that the liar *might* have seen these things but that he *must* have seen them. This is a bit sophisticated for younger players, but they get the idea if it is called a word trap. For example, you can explain that some parents learn to use word traps cunningly to trick children and get what they want, as in 'Would you like to go to bed now or in 15 minutes' time?' (Alter the example to suit the age, of course.) You can also show them how to reverse this trick in their own favour: 'Can I have a chocolate biscuit/phone credit/extra computer time now or after I've finished this bit of homework?'

- *Check specifics:* The time, place or places, people involved in the story and anything else the liar should know can be checked out through any of the ways of questioning above.

- *Does the story add up?* Ask questions to test the logic and consistency of the story. 'If Tom walked on the water, how exactly did he learn to do it? How did he keep it working?' 'Earlier on, you said that Tom hated water, but now you are saying that he walked on it. Can you explain this change?'

- *Challenge the story* if the answer doesn't address the questions asked.

Hence last but by no means least:

- *Develop the skill of thinking about and imagining the kind of answer you might get* with any question you plan to ask.
- *Listen closely* to what has been said.

Exercises

- Go through the lawyer's questions in the story of 'The liar and the lawyer' and identify what kinds of questions and techniques he or she is using – open, closed, recap, checking specifics, etc.

- Are there some ways the lawyer could have been harder on the liar, supposing the lawyer wanted to trap the liar?

- Reshape the story, putting in some different styles of question (developing the liar's fibs further at the same time, as suggested in the exercise at the end of 'The liar's toolbox'.

- Also try this process with Chang's story in 'The Emperor's truth' (page 56).

Ask yourself (silent 'inward' exercise)

'Fantastic fibs' is played inside the head, allowing it to discipline imagination. This does take some developing with more restless groups, but with repetition pays back in generally increased powers of concentration.

1. Think of a fantastic fib (example: 'I learned how to fly using the power of thinking myself into the air'). Imagine this as possible from inside and from outside the 'experience', i.e. as though it were happening to you (inside) and as though you were watching it happening to someone else (outside) (see also exercises in Chapter 5).
2. Now ask a lawyer's question ('How exactly did I learn to fly?').
3. Think and imagine your answer through, again from inside and outside, before continuing with the next bit.
4. Continue this process through the rest of the story, asking and answering questions and going on to the next. Ideas might be noted down using story clouds.

Story clouds: noting and planning

One of the best ways of noting down details, questions, stages and so on of a fantastic fib or tall tale developed in the basic game (or further games in this chapter and elsewhere) is in story clouds or islands, something familiar to many from other kinds of story plotting, mind-mapping, etc. All you do is draw on a board or sheet if working with the whole group (or possibly print out on A4 sheets for smaller group or individual use) a series of cartoon clouds (or rough circles if you use the island image), as many as you will have questions in the game plus an extra one for the storyteller's opening fib. You can link with a thread or arrows to show the order. Within each cloud/circle you write key words to help recall stages of the game as it progresses (or afterwards), the first statement of the story in cloud 1, and then subsequent questions accepted with key words for answers in the others. This will later make a plan for a written telling or for a more developed oral telling of the fib from the game as it becomes an engaging tall tale.

More oral story games

These games are developments of the basic fibbing and questioning game, which will add variety and new challenge, also refining skills. Each could also lead to independent writing tasks, though general guidelines for writing tall tales follow later in the chapter.

Wild exaggerations and weird imaginings

This is the 'Fantastic fibs' game with more preparation and a restriction to encourage tellers to draw on and exaggerate things, events, people and so on within their own experience, using memory and imagination in partnership to create contemporary wonders and oddities.

- Firstly, get the players or group to recall and imagine through a series of ordinary events (e.g. a journey to school with a detour that made you late; some happenings on a holiday; the arrival of friends or relatives at your house, etc.). They must keep these secret, dividing the happenings into a set number of stages – say five for a first attempt. (Story clouds are useful for notating this.)
- Next imagine through each stage, picking events, people, things actually seen, etc. to exaggerate wildly, making them weird and wonderful. (Sketch these in key words into the story clouds.)
- Choose the tall tale teller(s), who will recount events by stages, taking questions at the end of each stage. Tellers are encouraged to tell more than in the basic game and to exaggerate everything as much as possible. (For example, a detour on the journey to school took a whole day and half the night, people seen were tall as trees and small as flowers, the enormous bus was decorated very flamboyantly with red smiles and winking blue eyes, cars had engines so noisy that the sound smashed windows, etc.)
- Again open doubt is forbidden, though challenges based on inconsistency are allowed. (If the journey took all day and half the night, how could you have been at school for registration?) Omniscience (knowing exactly why the bus was so vividly decorated, how the cars were so loud, etc.) is not expected. Reporting in more detail on observations claimed is. Again what the storyteller says is true for the story ('I turned my watch backwards and everything unwound to make me on time').
- Afterwards, the storyteller can (optionally) explain the ordinary experience on which the fantasy was based.

The story cloud 'map' of the story can be used to retell and develop it in telling and on the page. The idea introduced here of breaking the tall tale into stages for telling and questioning works well with most other kinds of tall tale and teaches the idea of a narrative structure.

Wild cards (group game, at least five players)

- Prepare a series of cards or slips of paper. On each is one of the more plausible themes for a tall tale ('Enormous fish caught', 'Strange bird sighted', 'Exotic wild beast seen locally', etc.). Amongst these will be one or more wild cards which will say simply 'True story exaggerated'.

- Players keep what is on the card secret. Those with tall tale themes think and imagine through a story that matches their theme and then take it in turns to tell a tall tale and answer questions. Those with wild cards work out how to exaggerate a true tale. This may be based on personal experience or on something that happened to someone else, which they can tell as if it were their own experience. Stories (of both kinds) are in the first person.

- Questioners try to determine whether they are hearing a pure fib or a tall tale with exaggeration. They have a set number of questions to ask each teller, as in the basic game. They do not guess who is the fibber until all stories have been told (in a small group) or (in a class or large workshop group) when a batch (usually three to six) of tall tales have been told.

Springboards (adapted from *Tall Tale Telling*)

This refinement of the basic game introduces a restricted way of questioning and answering that can make for a smooth nonsense narrative. It is for two players (though can be adapted as a team game) but needs to be demonstrated first in front of the group. The two players (or teams) are called IS and NOT. The game proceeds by stages:

- IS aims to invent an incredible thing he or she has seen, for example a tree a mile high.
- NOT gives one (and only one) reason why this is impossible. ('If the tree were a mile high, aeroplanes would bump into it.')
- IS must use the objection as a springboard for the next idea. ('The tree is covered in lights like a huge Christmas tree.')
- NOT must raise a single objection to this statement. ('If the tree is so big, how could they get all the lights in place and change the bulbs?')
- IS now uses this as a springboard for another idea, which is again challenged with just one objection, and so on.

The game can be limited by the number of moves (at least three but probably seven or more) or by time allowed (say five minutes). At the end the 'story' is recapped by both players, adding a few extra details to make it sound more 'true'. Again it can be noted down using story clouds before being retold to others. 'Others' might be another pair if the 'Pass it on' idea for transmitting and 'growing' tales is followed, or the whole group when reconvened in a lesson or workshop.

In a little-known province of China, there is a tree one mile high. It is covered over with lights like a huge Christmas tree to stop aeroplanes flying into it by night. A team of 125 people are employed to maintain the lights and change the bulbs, which light up all the land for a mile around so that it is like daylight. The lights work by solar power, stored during the daytime and by electricity generated by a windmill, placed at the top of the tree . . .

Extreme excuses

The idea is to invent an unlikely but entertaining extreme excuse.

- List (and discuss) a series of things for which a person might have to invent an excuse. These could range from old favourites like 'why I can't give my homework in yet' or 'why I was late getting here' or 'how it got damaged' to (not necessarily but maybe, for interest and extra challenge) a few way-out things such as 'why I was wearing an orange gorilla suit and balancing on top of a chimney'.

- Players are allocated a topic for their excuse. A good way to add excitement is to give the listed excuse themes numbers (1 to 6, 1 to 12, etc. depending on the number of excuses listed) and then use one, two or more dice. Whatever the number that comes up for a person is the theme for which he or she must now improvise an excuse. (Slips of paper for different themes picked out of a hat or similar cards dealt out are alternative game ways to allocate themes.)

- The group questions each player chosen on the logic and detail of their excuse, following the rules of 'Fantastic fibs', using any lawyer's tricks learned so far and maybe (for extra motivation) playing the role of suspicious parent or teacher, etc.

- Players can later retell their developed fibs orally or as written pieces.

Which person? teaching points

The oral games included so far begin with the first person idiom. Liars (storytellers) are asked to make up an experience they have had and then develop a story by answering questions from others (or by mentally alternating liar and lawyer) and then to retell it in a more developed form. By going on to the 'Pass it on' procedure (Appendix B), stories can be changed automatically into third person stories – the story is passed on as something that happened to Jade or Imran or whoever. More can be made of this as the playing of the game becomes familiar. So, for example, you might play 'Fantastic fibs' insisting that stories are in the third person – about my friend (not present) or aunt or 'someone down my road'. Questions will then change subtly, to include why the person telling the story 'believes that it is true' (since the teller must adopt this stance).

First and third person stories are the usual idiom for stories, including tall ones. There are further examples to teach this distinction in *Tall Tale Telling*. The second person is, however, possible.

Flattery (second person game)

This is a quite sophisticated game for two experienced tall tale tellers. Player 1 is the Flatterer. Player 2 is Mr/Ms Modesty.

- Flatterer tells a flattering tall tale about the partner, using the second person idiom. 'You climbed up a sheer cliff and rescued a little puppy dog that was stuck on a ledge, fighting off a huge eagle that was trying to get it. How did you manage that?'
- Mr/Ms Modesty must explain, modestly emphasizing reasons why doing whatever has been suggested was quite easy. 'I was trialling some special climbing suction pads so I knew I wouldn't fall. Anyway the owner had offered me a thousand pounds to get it and I didn't even see the eagle . . .'
- Flatterer continues the story with a further flattering incident following on from the first, followed by another modest explanation from Mr/Ms Modesty.
- The alternation continues through an agreed series of moves (say five) or until an agreed time limit (say five minutes) has been reached. If either partner gives up before that, the other wins.

- The resulting story about Mr/Ms Modesty can be retold (or passed on) as a first or third person story.

A reverse version of this is called 'Slander'. It works in the same way, but with partners called Slanderer and Defender. Slanderer describes dreadful (but fantastical rather than real-world) deeds done by his or her partner. Defender describes why this only appears to have been dreadful and why it was really done for the best and for good reasons. This works, but again needs careful handling if it is not to produce actual insults. Both versions of the game are good emotional intelligence/PSHE tools. They can also be used as role-playing games around actual or imagined historical characters or political figures and their good and bad deeds.

A second person tall tale writing task

A short fun writing exercise is the fantasy complaining letter, from which a very tall tale might emerge: 'Dear Dr Strangedeeds, I am writing to complain about the way you have been turning all the houses in our street into purple toadstools and yellow puffballs lately . . .'

Writing tall stories

The telling that develops in oral games like those above might be considered a prelude to writing, but they can also be both a reference point to come back to and a continuing stimulus. For example, basic 'Fantastic fibs' can be played without a lot of build-up and explanation, followed by an 'untutored' writing task (see below). Following this, study the invention and questioning tools for liars and lawyers above, go back to the 'Fantastic fibs' game and tell the story again. This time liars tell the story they have written. They could first read the story and answer questions after each sentence (or paragraph for a longer tale), seeing how much the improved questioning draws out further detail, making notes for a redrafting. (All details asked for in the questioning need not be added; some should be useful. Again this is a learning process.) They would then tell the story they have written without the script (from memory, but not as recitation – see Chapter 6 for memorization methods), perhaps again taking questions initially to move the story along, but developing into simply telling and improvising on the telling.

Winging it: the 'untutored' way

Oral storytelling games encourage tellers to loosen up and improvise. It's an essential skill in telling stories, as will become clearer later in the book. As mentioned in Chapter 2, there is a lot also to be said for simply allowing pupils to do this on the page, both at the initial stage and from time to time anyway. An old saying has it that 'If you've not made a mistake you've not made anything.' Creation is a process of learning through mistakes – and indeed developing through mistakes and adapting around mistakes. So the first approach to writing a tall tale can be to encourage pupils to ramble freely – to 'wing it', allowing invention to lead to question to lead to invention. Note that playing the game through reading back the story to other class or group members allows for some of the critical thinking and editing that will help to shape a rambled story in a second or third draft.

Plans: from 'Ask yourself' to story clouds to linear planning

Doing the 'Ask yourself' exercise described above is, if done properly, a powerful kind of mental planning that can guide both telling and writing. It simulates and also speeds up some of the semi-conscious processes writers go through when they are mulling over a possible story and its development, a theme developed in Chapter 5. In the practical classroom or workshop situation, many students will be unfamiliar with the kind of mental concentration and focus this requires. Some will take to it; others may resist and will hence quite possibly distract others as a result, especially at the initial stage. Without practice in this kind of imaginative discipline, it's also easy for good ideas to slip away. Hence combining this approach with written or visual plans of one kind or another is usually helpful.

Written plans, set out in a logical and linear way perhaps with a sketch or two, can also be useful, though it's worth avoiding having 'too much of a good thing'. I once ran a full-day writing workshop in which an 11-year-old girl produced the best and most detailed plan for a tall story I have ever seen. Unfortunately, she never wrote more than the opening paragraphs of the tale. Too much planning can get in the way by setting up an impossible-looking task. The point of a plan is to guide writing – in the same way as a route map guides. Too many detours and you don't get to the destination; none at all and not only is the journey dull but you miss a lot.

Some ways into writing a tall tale

Here are two good ways of developing a written tall tale (there are many more).

Shock tactics: the provocative opener

'I first saw the pink elephants flying in perfect formation when I was on my way to school on a rainy Tuesday morning . . .'

With this approach, you pitch straight into what is clearly very strange or fantastical, without preparation. A dramatic first line is created, perhaps with no idea of what will follow. The plot develops out of explaining that first line (as in 'Fabulous fibs'). Writers are obviously in imagination country from the start, but they have to make some sense out of it – a series of wonders will not make a tall tale. Maybe the pink elephants are followed by giraffes and even flying fishes, but we need to know (say) why they all appeared, what the reaction of people was, what the consequences were and so on. The opening line is asking for that kind of explanation.

You can set the task of brainstorming some provocative openers as a competitive small group task or in solo writing, feeding these back to the group in discussion before asking pupils to pick one to develop further.

The Slow Sting

The principle here is to build belief and trust in the story.

- Start with an ordinary, believable circumstance. (You find an odd-looking large egg in the park and decide to keep it. It is still warm . . .)
- Build up by believable stages. (You put the egg somewhere warm whilst you look for the nest to put it back. Before you can do that, the chick hatches out, so you have to look after it secretly . . .)
- Add the improbable things bit by bit. (The chick grows into a young bird that rapidly gets bigger. You take it out for walks on a lead. One day it starts to fly on the end of its very long lead. Eventually, when it has grown to the size of an ostrich, you can fly on its back.)

The yes set: PSHE relevance

The slow build brings into the spotlight interesting and relevant features of practical human psychology tellers of stories understand intuitively. For example, there is a way of getting people that salespeople and many other 'influencers' good and bad use. It is called 'the yes set'.[4] At the outset, you work to get agreement to several small things, in this case as you tell a story, though it obviously works in other interactions. Research shows that, if you say yes to something small, you are more likely to say yes to something bigger later, asked for by the same person or organization that asked before. The small yes has committed you; you automatically develop a loyalty. Once you are committed, you may very well eventually say yes to something you'd never have dreamed of agreeing to before you said that first yes. This applies to relatively innocuous things – many people have found themselves volunteering for some small extra duty and later found themselves doing all sorts more they had never bargained for. It also applies to some more dangerous things – gang membership, stealing or drug taking, for example.

The way in which belief in a story and trust in a storyteller can develop through the yes set (simply getting people to say yes or otherwise agree to small 'possibilities' in your tale before moving on to bigger impossibilities) provides a safe context in which to look at and understand this principle of influence, firstly as a useful communication tool but then also to understand why one might find oneself, sooner or later, believing something odd or doing something crazy. It is, in other words, a useful way to move from imaginative fun to effective PSHE.

The lawyer's questioning and thinking tools can be applied to some real-life 'fantastic fibs': from adverts to cults to scams of all kinds. Working with games that require both fibbing and sniffing out the false is a training in reasonable suspicion.

This also leads on to sensitive areas of belief, conceptions of self and framing of experience. Older children and younger teenagers may well be beginning to question some of the beliefs they have previously accepted automatically and are, simultaneously, very vulnerable to new beliefs and ideas. Equipping them with the means both to think imaginatively and to take attractive ideas with a large pinch of salt is at least sowing the seeds for practical wisdom, which can be further developed in other sides of storytelling work.

There are, too, supplementary uses of games in this chapter in, for example, developing the ability to be confident (as happens if a pupil lacking confidence is encouraged and supported in developing and imagining through in detail a tall tale about doing something bold) or opening up to the possibility of achieving something previously inconceivable (as happens if the 'Flattery' game is adapted a little, with an adult counsellor or personal tutor taking the role of Flatterer). When a person imagines doing something new thoroughly, it becomes more practically possible.

Assembling tall tales

It's useful to have a larger goal towards which to work. 'The festival of fibs' at the end of the chapter is one way. Some more are:

- *Tales for the once and never land competition:* For an assembly or presentation to parents or simply within the group or class, create a longer version of the story that begins this chapter to be told by a narrator to frame a series of tall tales. Each teller of a tall tale will be one person performing in the fibbing competition in the story. This format also works as a book presentation.

- *Strange voyages of exploration and discovery:* Create a new framing story about a journey to strange and distant lands, islands, planets or regions in any appropriate setting – historical, fantastical, fairy tale, science fiction, futuristic and so on. A mythical example of this pattern is 'The voyage of Mael Dun' in Chapter 4, where this idea for assembling tall tales is also further explained.

- *Extra tales for 'The Emperor's truth':* Another possible framing story for tall tales includes the pattern of 'The liar and the lawyer' and is given in relatively brief form below. The tall tales told to the Emperor before Chang comes to see him can be elaborated by different tellers for a telling and/or reading-aloud presentation or for a book. Similarly, Chang's story can be improved on and further developed as suggested earlier in the chapter, whilst tips from Chapter 7 can be used to develop this outline much further.

The Emperor's truth

The Emperor of China was enjoying it all hugely. He didn't want his daughter to marry any man at all, not really. So he had decreed that any who wished to win her was welcome to try, as long as the daughter would accept that suitor – and as long as he could tell of some extraordinary thing that would make the Emperor say 'That's not true!'

From the day that the proclamation had gone out, they had flocked to the imperial palace. One by one, they had presented themselves, princes and young lords, merchants' sons and all sorts more. One by one, they had recited preposterous tales of all kinds.

'In my land, there is a mountain of glass you can see right through. It is one thousand miles wide and it stretches all the way from the earth to the highest heavens,' a proud young hopeful would announce.

'Yes, that's true I'm sure,' the Emperor would say in very bored tones, and the young man would turn away, disappointed.

'I have a demon in my pocket smaller than your thumbnail and I keep two fierce dogs in my slippers,' another would venture.

'I'm sure that's so,' the Emperor would yawn. It was such fun to see the young men slinking away, looking so ridiculously downhearted. No matter what they claimed, whether it was weird wonders or impossible feats, he simply agreed that it was all quite true. It was so easy!

Eventually the suitors stopped coming. They had realized what kind of game the Emperor was playing. It was the turn of the princess to be disappointed. She had quite liked the look of a few of the young men and certainly didn't want to stay single for the rest of her life.

The Emperor soon missed the fun, so he sent the proclamation out far and wide again and again, but now there were no takers – until eventually a lad called Chang decided to try his luck. He was no prince, no rich man's son, just a clever peasant lad. He arrived at the court carrying a very large bag. 'Oh great lords and noble ladies, I have come here for justice!' he declared, loudly and angrily. 'This bag I have here has been my only home. I have lived inside it since I was born five thousand years ago.'

The Emperor stifled one of his yawns and was about to send Chang away when the lad went on: 'I jumped out of the bag only this very morning. You see, I'd been fast asleep for a hundred years on a bed made from elephant's ears and fish eyes and the thief must have crept in and taken it whilst I was dreaming. Every last bit.'

'The bed?'

'No, my fortune. My magic flying sandals for a start – and my giant jewelled chariot. Then there were my seven golden dragons, of course. But worst of all was my palace.'

'You had a chariot, seven dragons and a palace, all in that bag?'

'Yes, indeed, a wonderful palace stuffed with treasures and a gilded hall with a jade throne – the same throne you are sitting on now. That is my throne and this is my palace. You know very well that you stole it away from me whilst I slept! I demand justice!'

'That's not true!' the Emperor fumed. 'How dare you?' But a moment later, there was a tinkling, excited laugh and the princess appeared in the hall, smiling the biggest smile she had smiled in many long months. She and Chang were soon married, and a good life they had and a long one.

A festival of fibs

Celebrations of lying like the one in the story that begins this chapter have been a tradition in diverse cultures. Tobagan star Lord Nelson tells of King Liar de Lion and a lying contest for participants across the West Indies in a famous funny calypso. In Cumbria in the north-west of England, the World's Biggest Liar Competition is held every November at the Bridge Inn at Santon Bridge and traces its roots back to one Will Ritson, a notorious nineteenth-century local fibber. There's an affinity with the old Yuletide reign of the Lord of Misrule or the Saturnalian feasts, where conventions were abandoned and mischief was obligatory – most societies condemn lying, but paradoxically human beings are natural fiction spinners.

A feast of fibs is a marvellous way to boost a culture of creative tale telling in school. Making it a special event gets over those moral qualms some may still have. It's all made perfectly clear that 'the rules' have been put on one side in the name of pure fun – or indeed for charity or school funds. I've known it to happen once a year in the run-up to Christmas, as part of a book week or during the summer silly season. It can equally work on a more regular basis – one marvellous teacher of Year 3/4 children, now sadly retired, did it once a week with her class and produced some of the best young tellers and writers of stories I've ever seen. You can generate a carnival atmosphere around the larger event, with families invited in to hear top tales – or to help with judging if you decide on a contest. You could get some good publicity in local papers and elsewhere: 'Children learning to lie' is the kind of headline sub-editors love.

4 Likely legends and marvellous myths

However true it gets, it's still a fib. What is it?

Framing ideas: myths, legends and relevance

Many a legend is a tall tale that has somehow become true. At some stage it became accepted in a culture, in a sub-culture, in a locality, in a whole country or just within the family, not as 'just a story' but as something that happened long or not so long ago or is now or used to be. We don't know who made such tales up nor how. They have (generally) been told and then retold over and again, in such a way that they have acquired the feel of a truth, like the patina and glow that much-handled coins get. In fact they can seem so true that some people actually claim to have seen and witnessed parts of them.

For an example from tradition, there was a belief common across many European countries that witches could turn themselves into hares and quite a few stories great and small that supported it – you'll find some in folk and fairy tale books for children and plenty in actual folklore collections. Here's a bit of convincing personal testimony from an 80-year-old English countryman who had never travelled far from his own village and knew nothing of books. It was written down by a listener and published in 1933: 'I tell you, as true as I'm sitting here, she vanished, and instead of her I saw a hare running through a gap in the hedge. I saw it – and you could have knocked me down with a feather. I shall never forget it, not to my dying day.'[1]

Stories like that might seem quaint and full of rustic charm, but the superstitions about witches they somehow amplified and verified could, of course, be dangerous, unpleasant and possibly lethal if you happened to be an old woman in a village where folk took such things as gospel. This shows some of the power of storytelling because, whilst that particular belief is now safely contained in the realms of fantasy archetype for use by the likes of J.K. Rowling *et al.*, strange and peculiar beliefs are still all around us all the time. Legends are not just things in books. There is plenty of contemporary relevance to find in studying how legends come to be, comparing them with rumours, looking at ancient legends, spotting a few modern ones too, learning to question them intelligently as tall tales were questioned in the last chapter, even learning to develop a spoof legend or two for the fun of it.

Legends are not just another kind of tarradiddle, however. They happen. They grow without anyone necessarily intending them to. A story, as the saying goes, 'gets legs'; to extend the metaphor, it starts to gather speed and before you know what has happened it could have run a wrecking riot. Equally it can be or become a valuable thing. It can grow into a useful and illuminating metaphor, something that carries a message about bravery or hope or how a person might struggle against adversity and many things more. It can go on growing and become an epic, full of wonder and adventure and ideals and imaginings. It could become, in fact, a myth in the best sense of the word – not just a tale in some ancient codex but a story that both informs and inspires.

Mythology is often studied as long ago and far away – the beliefs of the Greeks or the Romans, say, or the stories of the ancient Egyptian or Indian or Babylonian or Chinese gods and heroes and chimeras and heroines. All of those should be studied and understood for all sorts of good reasons, cultural and social, as well as for their deeper metaphorical qualities. But there is also every good educational reason to give the idea of a myth and a legend contemporary and immediate relevance, by studying in parallel how legends and myths go on being created all around us. We all have heard legends and absorbed mythologies, without necessarily realizing it. Being more aware of the process is a protection and a creative resource in story making and telling.

Definitions

Since there's a certain amount of confusion in the way the words 'myth' and 'legend' are used, these practical working definitions may be helpful as starting points for discussion with pupils (suitably adapted for age group).

Legends

- *Legend 1 (popular use):* the extraordinary reputation (and stories that support it) of a person or place or activity, etc., as in 'living legend' or 'legendary skills/talent/tricks', etc. or 'contributing to his/her own legend'. Legends in this familiar sense are constantly being created (and these days inflated by media hype, PR and so on).

- *Legend 2 (traditional):* a story passed on in tradition about a person (usually dead) or place (often, though not necessarily, ancient) or landscape feature or mythical monster, etc. The story may be part of a larger epic or cycle of stories, which may in turn be part of a larger mythology. Or it might be a one-off curiosity or sensation, like the modern urban legend/myth or like the local legends (of which one finds a fair number of examples in schools).

Myths

- *Myth 1 (popular use):* a false idea or a story that is probably false. (Legend is used in this way too.)

- *Myth 2 (traditional):* a great story that may have been part of a religion or philosophy.

- *Myth 3 (modern – cultural studies, etc.):* hidden 'stories' that underpin a world view or outlook.

Legends and lies

You can progress directly from 'Fantastic fibs' in the previous chapter to creating legends on different themes. A list of possible themes is given below. Use the same questioning procedures to make it grow, but this time the theme has to be making up (say) a legend about the something that happened in the neighbourhood once or an extra 'little known' tale of a particular hero or heroine from history or myth, etc.

Legend types (not an exhaustive list!)

1. Landscape legends.
2. Mythical hero/heroine legends.
3. Legends about historical characters (ancient or modern).
4. Legends about living people (celebrities, etc.).

5. Legends about localities: towns, cities, villages, estates, etc.
6. Warning legends.
7. Legends about natural things (trees, wind, stars, etc.), including 'just so' type stories explaining how things come to be as they are.
8. Legends about strange powers.
9. Legends about mysterious and unusual beings.
10. Funny or bizarre events.
11. Wonderful tricks that caught people out.
12. Modern urban legends (many kinds).

Lie or legend?

With fairly able and/or experienced groups, you can add an extra dimension to this by using some actual legends alongside the fiction. One way to do this, which resembles some TV and radio bluffing games, is to prepare a series of cards or slips. On the larger percentage of these are the words 'Make it up', possibly combined with some guide points (e.g. 'Near here – buried treasure'). However, on some (say around 25 per cent) is a short description of a legend – perhaps a local legend from a local history book, perhaps a less well-known legend of a mythical hero or heroine summarized very briefly, depending on the theme you are following. Participants prepare their stories for telling (or write them). They must keep these secret. When they are told (or read out or displayed), the group guesses which one is the legend.

From dodgy yarns to creative PSHE

This is also useful (perhaps simultaneously) as a PSHE exercise, especially if you can collect some examples of unusual reports from newspapers and other media. We are often presented with doubtful 'stories'. Spotting those without becoming too cynical about ones that are different but true or are merely exaggerated is an essential (if neglected) life skill. You can take a legend or a tale culled from the news. Here are three from a radio show.[2] They range from the apparently commonplace to the fairly bizarre. After sharing these, you can ask questions about whether the story is newsworthy, whether or not it seems literally true, but also whether or not it *should* be true even if it isn't: whether it might say something worthwhile – does it offer a useful metaphor or moral, for example? Also could it be expanded to make a more interesting tale? (Each story could be used with some of the elaboration ideas for stretching stories in Chapter 7.)

Stuck head

A man got his head stuck between the floorboards in a loft when trying to find a rat he believed to have entered his house. He evidently struggled for some time to free himself, eventually managing to summon a neighbour, who called the fire brigade, who released him after he had spent five hours in what he described as 'a very uncomfortable position'. A crowd of neighbours and curious passers-by watched the man being escorted from the house by medical orderlies. The man described the incident as 'most embarrassing' but said that there was at least now no sign of the rat.

Girl saves grandfather's life

In the Appalachian mountains in the USA, a 12-year-old girl took over the wheel of a pick-up truck when her grandfather, who had been driving, was suddenly taken ill. She drove more than ten miles down dangerous mountain roads to a filling station, where she found adult assistance. Her grandfather was rushed to hospital and made a full recovery.

Seven-mile sleepwalk

In China, a habitual sleepwalker had a surprise when he was awakened seven miles away from home. He was even more surprised when it was established that he had sleepwalked most of the way through the city sewers.

Urban legends

Dubious stories in the news are sometimes recycled urban legends that have been around for quite a long time – some have been traced back hundreds of years. The three stories above may be urban legends. Such stories are usually retailed as true and often passed on as something that happened to a friend of a friend. You can buy whole books of them.[3] As they grow up, children often hear urban legends (especially scary ones) passed on by family members or at weekend camps or on holiday. Discussing stories pupils know and may believe to be true, getting them to tell and/or write them, labelling some as probably urban legends, and comparing them to their models in urban legend collections are also valid, engaging and useful as both a literacy/English and a PSHE project.

Here is a 'true' story told to me some years ago by a lady.

Withering and sinister

A friend of a friend bought a rare and expensive indoor tropical plant from a very reputable supplier, complete with detailed care instructions and just the right plant food. She had looked after it very carefully, giving it the perfect conditions and exactly the correct amount of feed at exactly the correct times, no more and no less. Despite all that, it wasn't doing at all well. In fact it was definitely wither-ing away by the time she decided to take it back to the shop. They agreed with her that it should not be failing in this way, but sent it away for tests. Imagine her shocked surprise when, within a few hours, a large white van arrived at her house and men emerged wearing protective clothing and donning protective masks and gloves. They explained that she must get out immediately and take shelter in the van whilst they searched the house, and she did just that. Fortu-nately they found what they were looking for sooner rather than later, under the mattress on her own bed. Apparently when the plant had been tested, they had found a recently dead male spider from the same tropical regions as the plant amongst its roots. They knew at once that it was highly likely that its mate had recently left it and the lair in the roots – it was one of the species where the female killed the male when it was about to lay eggs. This was precisely what it had done, all along the bottom of her mattress. Fortunately the men found that female and all of the hundred or so eggs, each of which would have hatched out to become a deadly poisonous spider whose bite has no known antidote.

My informant didn't know that this is a classic urban legend, often recorded; she insisted it had happened to a friend and that the store was Marks & Spencer. See whether pupils believe it – they generally will unless primed to disbelieve and until you point out some of the improbabilities.

Scientific myth making

Storytelling, legend and myth making may not seem to have much to do with science. Not so at all. Science merely means 'knowledge' – effectively practical and established knowledge of how the world works. But, since we don't have a God-like eye for the whole picture, that knowledge is partial, provisional, and subject to revision with new discoveries. It's as though we were given bits of the jigsaw puzzle, one at a time, and kept making guesses about what the whole picture would be when all the bits were in place, in the absence of a guiding picture and indeed a lot of the pieces. The guesses are the stories, the myths and sometimes the legends, often very necessary as theoretical working models. Some of them turn out to truly work in prac-tice, whilst others don't. The history of science is littered with discarded science stories; some redundant ones get in the way of scientific progress.

Connecting work on myths and legends in other areas with 'myths' in science is a good way to engage students in the story of science itself and to encourage the spirit of healthy scepticism that is part of scientific enquiry, whilst retaining creative flexibility. Some 'respectable' scientific stories need to be questioned; some might equally be worthy of imaginative elaboration, as in the fabulous fibbing practised in the previous chapter.

This scientific story could start the ball rolling.

Phlogiston

Phlogiston, as most people know, is a fire-like element, first discovered in 1667 by Johann Joachim Becher, a German physicist, alchemist, scholar and adventurer. The word comes from ancient Greek and means 'burning up'. Phlogiston has no taste, smell, colour or mass. You find it in any substance that will burn. When such a substance ignites, phlogiston is released and the substance is 'dephlogisticated'. The substance is then in its true form, the 'caix'. This explains what is happening when you see a flame and also helps us to understand the rusting of metals – as evidenced by the fact that both flame and rust are usually seen as reddish orange.

Present this as literally true and discuss whether pupils have observed the effects of phlogiston before revealing the facts, which are that it is indeed a myth in the popular sense of something proved not true. It could sound true, especially to those not familiar with much current science – the description is based on what was commonly said about this 'element' in the many years during which it was believed to exist and before better explanations replaced it. Though not quite all in formal language, it has some 'sciency' words that help the effect – you might get pupils to pick these out. The concept, though false, is sometimes said to have been a stepping–stone to those better explanations.

Two more historical curiosities follow. They can be introduced simply for interest or as starting points for creative story work – what would happen if we (or other people) still believed these things? How would it change the way people act and think?

Aristotle's radiator brain

The Greek philosopher Aristotle (384–322 BC) is a very influential figure in the history of thought. However, not all of his ideas turned out to be correct. For example, he believed that the brain was a kind of radiator designed to regulate the body's heat, whilst the heart was the seat of thought, reason and feeling as well as the soul itself.

Not a good excuse

Late-nineteenth-century doctors treated a widespread condition called neurasthenia, 'discovered' by American psychiatrist George Beard. The symptoms were tiredness, mental sluggishness and generalized aches and pains. Expensive rest cures and travel to sunny climes were often prescribed for rich sufferers. You won't get far if you put it on your sick note these day. More than a hundred years after Beard named it, the medical establishment decided it was a myth.

For further work around scientific legends, these are some of the current top scientific myths.[4] One or two of them have some truth.

- There is no gravity in space.
- Water drains backwards in the southern hemisphere owing to the Earth's rotation.
- Chickens can live without a head.
- Yawning is contagious.
- A penny dropped from a tall building could kill a pedestrian.
- Chicken soup can cure the common cold.
- Adults don't grow new brain cells.

Pupils can investigate each of these, make up stories that 'prove' them and present these alongside the facts as currently understood. They can also make up new scientific myths and legends.

Geographical and historical fibs: legend and myth to practical fact

Ancient maps once actually used by sailors are a wonderful source of imaginative invention, apparently literally believed, practically illustrating the merging of mythical belief with fact. There were the known trade routes and the areas unknown where legends like 'Here bee monsters' and ' Here Endethe ye Earthe' might be accompanied by graphic illustrations of mermaids, dragons and other chimerical creatures. Similarly, supposed historical accounts by early scholars sound like tall tales and pure fantasy centuries later.

Using actual medieval maps or short passages from ancient historical texts gives good examples. Here is one summarized from the fifth-century BC Greek historian Herodotus, sometimes called the Father of History for his nine-volume mixture of known fact and reported fantasy:

In the far eastern provinces of Indian, there is a furry ant the size of a fox. The region is one of sandy deserts. In those sands, there is much gold dust, which these curious ants unearth in digging their mounds and burrows. The local people collect this gold and have built much wealth from it.

(*Histories of Herodotus*, Book 3, 102–5)

Compare this legend with the legend at the end of the chapter, with reference to some of the islands Mael Dun visited. Scholars have found a certain amount of garbled truth in this legend – evidently the Himalayan marmot (a burrowing squirrel, not an ant of course) does sometimes unearth gold, and the Minaro tribal peoples in Kashmir have evidently been collecting it for generations (Peissel 1984).

Making up historical and geographical tall tales and legends has many fun possibilities, and you can play the 'Lies and legends' bluffing game on this theme. A useful point is that, to make such a legend credible, you have to do at least some research. Stories about Bedouin tribes skiing across snow drifts in the Sahara might not be believed unless you can add some convincing extra facts.

Family legends

This needs a bit of informal research from pupils and is also a good way to practise interviewing techniques that are less combative than the 'lawyer's tricks' in the last chapter. The task of pupils will be to find ways to ask parents, carers, relatives or any suitable and significant others about people in their families (or circle of friends and acquaintances) who are or were interesting or different in some way. The idea is not to get tales of superheroes and saints, but to get the adult (or older relative) to tell something that can be passed on as a fragment (or more than a fragment) of a story. Persuasion is part of the study – choosing the moment to ask, not nagging at the person, showing interest, thinking of encouraging questions: all these are very useful life (as well as word/language) skills, as is knowing how questions can be phrased to get useful answers. So one can discuss a list of question types and approaches, getting pupils to notice how direct commands like 'Tell me now!' or 'Please answer the question' are for more occasional use in this context and are less likely to be effective than 'What would you say was special about (my gran)?' or an implied query-cum-challenge like 'I bet you never knew anyone who was a bit different/special/clever.'

Pourquoi stories and creation myths

Academic folklorists label stories of the 'just so' variety as 'pourquoi tales': the kinds of stories that explain why the pig is fat or the giraffe has a long neck or why there are mountains in Scotland. They blend quite easily into larger creation myths: stories about how the world and indeed the universe came to be, how human beings started out and so on. Both have been fertile fields for creative story making for teachers and children for a long time and should go on being so: any project on legends and myths that doesn't tackle this area is incomplete. Using storytelling questioning games of the kinds already explored works really well with any 'how the (whatever) came to be' themes. Equally, creating pourquoi and/or creation tales by writing and drawing and then simply telling them to the group works very well, as do combinations of both these approaches. These are some obvious and not-so-obvious example themes:

- how the cat/dog/tiger/elephant/peacock got its tail;
- how the leopard/hyena/trout/teenager got its spots;
- why trees are made of wood;
- why Australians (or Americans or Brummies or Scots) talk with special accents;
- why human beings can be both kind and cruel;
- how the moon started out as a piece of green cheese;
- why there are sunspots;
- why kangaroos are not found in the North Sea.

Myth challenges

This is quite an easy story game for making up mythical or pourquoi tales. It is for two players or teams.

- Player/team 1 challenges player/team 2 to invent a myth or just so tale on a particular theme. ('Tell me where ants came from/why rain falls out of the sky.')
- Player/team 2 makes up the myth or just so tale. It should be fanciful, not a scientific explanation. If they are not able to complete this within a limit (say 90 seconds or perhaps seven sentences), player/team 1 must do so. (Hence they can't win the game by setting an impossible theme.) The listening player/team can ask lawyer questions about how the tale works, as in 'Fantastic fibs'.
- Whichever player/team finished the story sets the next theme. Players can keep a tally of rounds won.

Not only but also

However fantastical and unlikely explanations may be, there is often a shred (and sometimes more than a shred) of metaphorical and/or moral truth in such tales as they develop. As an explanation of how this or that happened, they may be entirely unlikely; as a comment about other things (people and the way they behave, how life works, etc.) they can sometimes be very resonant. Looking out for that is a good guard against encouraging the know-it-all cynicism that comes of thinking that such explanation tales are somehow only primitive or babyish. It is, after all, the process by which myths make meanings.

Not only but also (thinking exercise)

Participants are encouraged to offer their ideas about a story using the formula 'Not only . . . but also . . .' to comment on the sense a story makes, which can be a traditional or a new one. So, for the briefly told legend below, 'Not only does this give you a story about the sky, but it also tells you how people are sometimes greedy and foolish . . .' Others can add more ('and also that we shouldn't think that nature's gifts last for ever', etc.). You can do this orally or as a written exercise.

Why the sky is far away

When the world was young, the sky was close. You could stretch up and touch it and even break off pieces. They were good to eat and so people did not have to work to get their food. However, some took too much – there seemed to be plenty, so why not? What they didn't eat they just threw away until pieces of old sky were littered all around.

Now all this made the Sky God angry. He appeared before them. 'You are misusing my sky. You are misusing me! If you are not more careful, I shall leave you!'

People were very careful after that. They only took as much as they needed and no more. It couldn't last. One family was feeling particularly hungry one day, so they carved off a huge chunk of sky. But their eyes, as they say, had been bigger than their bellies: they couldn't finish it so they asked the neighbours to join them. But the neighbours were not very hungry so they asked the neighbours of the neighbours and then the neighbours of the neighbours of the neighbours. Still there was some left, so they hid it under the rubbish pile when it was dark.

But the Sky God sees all. 'Now I am going!' he thundered. And he took the sky so far away that no one could reach it. Since that day, people have had to work for their food.[5]

Mythical fantasy: the voyage of Mael Dun

This mythical story suggests plenty of connection with tall tale work. It was written down, evidently from earlier bardic recitations, in a tenth-century manuscript, *The Book of the Dun Cow*. Alfred, Lord Tennyson wrote his own fanciful version. There is only space for a few of the marvellously fantastical islands visited by Mael Dun – there are more than 30 in the original.[6]

Mael Dun and the quest

The hero Mael Dun never knew his own father, who had died in battle. Mael Dun also never knew his mother, who had died young in the nunnery to which she had retreated. He was brought up by the King and Queen of Erin, with three princes as his foster-brothers. It was not until he had proved himself the mightiest of heroes of Erin that he heard from a druid of how his father had been killed by a coward, who had stabbed him in the back, meanwhile claiming the glory of defeating him. This same druid informed him that his mother's death had been through grief for his father and not as a result of natural illness. Mael Dun vowed vengeance on his father's slayer, who, the druid informed him, lived even now on an island to the north. To seek this murderer, he was told, he should select a band of 17 heroes to accompany him, making 18 in all, no more and no less. He should sail in a large coracle seven hides thick on a certain day from a certain spot. If he followed these instructions, his journey would be blessed.

Mael Dun gathered together the greatest heroes of the day and, following the druid's instructions closely, set sail. However, as they rowed the ship out across the bay and prepared to hoist the sails, the king's three sons came down to the shore begging Mael Dun to take them too. 'Go back!' commanded Mael Dun, but the three princes dived into the waves and swam out towards the ship. A treacherous current was about to sweep them away, so Mael Dun turned his ship around and hauled them into the boat. He then tried to return to the land, but a great wind came up and forced them away to sea. Try and try as they might, Mael Dun and his men could not return to land. So there were 21 men in the boat instead of the proper 18. From that moment, the quest was cursed and bad luck attended them.

The island of the slayer

Mael Dun and his men sailed on until they reached two islands with a fortress built on each of them. From within one of the fortresses, they heard the sounds of revelry and then a man's voice boomed out loudly, boasting of how he had killed Mael Dun's father fairly. They tried over and again to beach that boat so that Mael Dun could kill the slayer of his father, but even as they did so another great wind hurled their boat way out across the waves and over the sea for day after day.

The island of the giant ants

As the storm died away, they glimpsed an island and set a course for it. However, as they approached they saw that this island was infested with huge ants the size of foals, black, white and scarlet and each one of them enormous. They decided not to land on that island.

The island of the great birds

Not long afterwards, however, the heroes reached a third island, where there were birds as big as men and bigger. Yet these birds were not fierce and clearly not used to human beings, so that they did not run away and were easily caught, cooked and eaten. Mael Dun and his men left that island with enough meat to last them the next 40 days of their journey.

The island of the fiery swine

After they had passed more strange islands, seen more strange sights and had more strange adventures, they reached an island where they saw golden apples hanging from the tall trees. But living in caves nearby were pig-like creatures made from fire. They would hurl themselves against the trees, which would shower down golden apples. These they would gobble up. Once a day, however, birds flew across the island and, at this time, the fiery swine went down to the sea and swam out across the waves to cool themselves. When they discovered that this was so, Mael Dun and his men chose that very time to go to the trees and pick the apples, though the ground was still very hot under their feet from the hooves of the red-hot swine. These golden apples restored their strength and fed them for many days.

The island of the pillars and the small but dangerous cat

They came next to an island on a tall white chalky pillar. On it there was a great hall with four pillars. A little black cat leapt from pillar to pillar. Food was laid out in the hall, whilst on the walls there were gold and silver brooches, gold and silver torques and gold and silver swords, all set out in rows. Mael Dun politely asked the cat if they might eat the food, but the cat only glanced at the heroes and went on with its game, so they set to and ate their fill. In the morning, Mael Dun's foster-brother, the first of the king's sons, went to take gold and silver jewellery from the walls, against the command of Mael Dun. As soon as he did so, the cat leapt at him, passing through him like an arrow. He fell to the ground as a pile of ashes, which afterwards Mael Dun and the remaining two princes scattered sadly on the shore. All mourned the loss as they set sail again.

The island of the black and white sheep

Now they reached an island that was divided in half, with a black and white fence in the middle. Black sheep were on the one side and white sheep on the other. Sometimes one of the sheep would leap over the fence from the one side to the other and at once it would change from white to black or from black to white, depending on which side it was jumping towards. Mael Dun threw a white stick among the black sheep and it changed to black. He and the heroes sailed away without landing, realizing that to tread the strange soil of this place would confuse them all completely.

The island of the black-robed mourners

Sobbing and wailing sounds filled the air as Mael Dun's ship sailed into view, though there was no sign of a reason for grief. All of the people on the island were dressed in black as if for a funeral, and all of them wept. Mael Dun's second foster-brother, the second son of the king, jumped ashore and immediately started to lament and cry with the island folk, since he was deeply saddened by the loss of his brother. After a time, two of Mael Dun's men jumped ashore to rescue him, but both instantly began to sob and wail. Mael Dun blindfolded four more men and stopped their ears. These four managed to bring back the two, but not the prince. He refused to come back to the boat, so in the end they were obliged to leave him to his tears and sorrows and sail on. Sometimes you can hear his cries and sobs from across the water, though you might mistake it for the cry of a seagull.

The island of the miracle fountain

The soil of the next island they reached was pale and soft, like down. There was a marvellous fountain in the centre of it. On Wednesdays and Fridays, it ran water and whey, whilst on Sundays and feast days it ran wine and beer.

The sea of clear glass

They crossed a sea that was as clear as glass with neither a ripple nor a wave to cloud it. They could see the bottom of the ocean far below them, with never a fish in sight – no seaweed, nor rocks, nor coral. It was as if they crossed a desert, floating in the air.

The underwater island

Now the heroes found themselves sailing on a sea that seemed thin, like mist, so that they were afraid they would fall through it and perish. Far below, they could see a great monster in a tree, stealing and gobbling up hundreds of sheep and cattle, despite the many warriors who were attacking it without any success.

The island of the water arch and the jumping salmon

A gigantic arch of water spanned this island like a rainbow. The water flowed in a great rush both up and down it, though it was impossible to see where this water came from, nor to where it went. Salmon swam up and down the arch, and a person could put in a hand and pull one out at will.

The island of laughter

There was an island filled with rosy-faced people who laughed and giggled and chortled and wheezed and ho-ho-hoed all day long. The third foster-brother of Mael Dun, the third son of the king, knew at once that this was the place to cheer him up after the loss of his brothers and jumped down from the boat. After a time, two men went to fetch him back, but they were soon chuckling and roaring, so four men were sent blindfolded, with their ears stopped up. They brought back the two companions but not the prince, who stubbornly refused to leave and so was left to his laughter – which floats across the waves sometimes even now, though people again think it only the shrieking of distant gulls.

The island of the monk of Torach

Not long afterwards, they came upon an island where there was a hermit wearing only his pure white hair and pure white beard. This man told his story – the story of how he had stolen the treasure of a monastery, but had at length thrown it away in exchange for God's forgiveness and this simple island on which he offered his prayers fervently each day. He counselled Mael Dun to forgive and then forget the killer of his father. Mael Dun did so at once. The following day they spotted a falcon of the familiar kind they knew in their own land, flying across the sea. They followed, and it led them back to Erin's shores, where they found their own people and told of their adventures, so that the bards could relate them and the scribes could, at last, write them down in The Book of the Dun Cow.

Working with the story

- 'The voyage' makes a marvellous memory and imagination exercise. Young storytellers can be invited to develop their own imaginative/associative ways of training the memory to recall each island in turn. (Memory training is explored further in Chapter 6.)

- Pupils are often intrigued by particular islands. Ask them to pick a particular island to tell or write a tall tale/fantastic fib about – for example, how they visited it, what further things they found out about it, etc. You can also use visits to Mael Dun's islands as a theme for a 'Fantastic fibs' game.

- As part of this, you can also extend the list of islands visited by Mael Dun, asking pupils to invent new islands Mael Dun visited.

- The islands are also great for the kind of multi-sensory picturing described in the next chapter, in which you would imagine particular islands as vividly as possible using sight, sound, smell, taste, touch and overall feel.

- A completely new quest tale can be developed using the pattern of Mael Dun, as in some of the stealing stories ideas described in Chapter 8. It might use (for example) visits to distant planets or strange continents or different fantasy worlds as alternatives.

- Finally, the simple structure of a visit makes an easy presentation structure for a public event or assembly. You have a narrator and then individual pupils or groups of pupils tell the story of each island, whether from the Mael Dun epic or from an entirely new and invented yarn.

(See also 'Magic islands and strange planets' story game in *Tall Tale Telling*.)

New school legends

Why not invent a school or classroom legend? Perhaps it is about the school building – maybe it was built over an ancient treasure vault or an underground lake; maybe people claim to have seen the treasure of the lake. Perhaps there is a ghost that lurks in a certain part of the school at certain times. Perhaps, on the other hand, there is something strange about some of the staff. Maybe they have to undergo a strange initiation and belong to a secret organization to work there. Or maybe there is something weird about some of the pupils or parents. Perhaps there is quite a story behind it all.

A school legend has to be just about believable to 'get legs', so there could be some competition to see which legend could be chosen for further development by the group. Any existing school legends could be shared and discussed in advance. (Interestingly, pupils often describe legends they have actually heard about the school or locality as 'true'.) You can then play a version of 'Fantastic fibs' around the theme of new school legends, either in pairs or with competing groups. Alternatively it can be a writing task, but stories can later be subject to soft criticism and oral redrafting and development through the same game or simply by sharing suggestions.

Pick one or more school legends to work up at length, choosing legends that are harmless. (Discussing why some legends could be harmful can be part of the learning.) All contribute to the chosen legend(s), either in discussion or in further writing. Group members can be sworn to secrecy until the legend is worked out. When it is, it can be passed on to people in other classes and years as a 'true' legend – either formally in an assembly or informally and 'on the side'. This can be a very interesting practical study of the power of belief and rumour.

5
Dreaming awake

A dream without slumber. What is it?

Framing ideas: imagination and dreaming

Where does imagination come from? No one knows exactly, but one quite logical explanation is that it's originally precisely what I called it in Chapter 1: dreaming awake. When we imagine intensively, we go into a dreamlike state; brain activity gets closer to the way it is in dreams. Imagination itself may start to take over, showing us things we didn't expect to see or hear or sense, almost like being asleep and dreaming. The dream state evolved in much earlier life forms, but Homo sapiens (so the theory goes) at some stage began to be able to go into something akin to that state more consciously, for quick, relatively controlled visits as it were.[1] Hence we were able to use that mental image-making faculty more intentionally, to imagine and picture possible future actions and schemes as well as to summon up images of the past. Hence we were able to develop languages with complex past and future tenses, with words for things you could neither see nor touch nor taste.

In dreams, of course, things become confused and combined in unusual ways, which may not be entirely random. Psychologist Joe Griffin has suggested that dreams metaphorically enact and defuse recent unfulfilled expectations, which had put 'the system' on alert so to speak (Griffin 1997). Without that enactment, reactions would gradually lose their sensitivity – as the villagers did to the boy who cried wolf in the famous Aesop fable. So dreams are naturally metaphorical; so too imagination (dreaming awake) works through and with metaphor. And so metaphor is not just something 'out there' but an essential part of the way our minds work – yours and mine and of course children's too.

If we assume that imagining is a kind of dreaming awake, we can and should expect imagining to be both meaningful and metaphorical – and perhaps surprising. What and how we imagine says a lot about us. Anyway, it's a great natural place to start from and indeed to return to in making engaging stories.

From mega-screens to crystal balls: imagining skills and how to develop them

Telling and writing and working with stories as well as listening to them are already a training of imagination. Working directly with imagination, letting your imagination show you a story in guided imaginings, is one highly effective way into storytelling and story making.

Rediscovering guided imagination for story work

Visualization or guided imagining has been a staple of adult creative writing classes for years. It has tended to fall out of favour with teachers in recent years. Partly there are the perceived practical difficulties of getting a class of mentally and physically restless pupils to concentrate for long enough to do it effectively: one giggling, distracted or cynical student could spoil it for all. Partly there was the problem of fitting it into a literacy hour structure at the primary stage; it might take too much time, without any clear external markers of achievement. Partly too there is that underlying distrust of the dreamy states for anything more than recreation that has infused the larger culture: the belief that, to do something well, we must be very alert and intentional. Then, of course, guiding imagination is a skill that's easy to underestimate: it may not often have been done as well as it can be anyway.

There are many good reasons to reinstate guided imagining and learn the skills – and also to debunk myths enshrined in the above 'why-nots'. These are some of them:

- It is not actually particularly difficult if one uses effective methods.
- It really does develop and train imagination when used intelligently and regularly.
- It doesn't need to take long – in a classroom situation, five minutes is enough to do a short picturing for story work.

- It doesn't need the New Age rituals sometimes associated with it (relaxing music, gongs, bells, soft 'meaningful' voices, etc.).

- It need not invariably involve eyes-closed total stillness (though these could develop in time).

- It is, however, a training in being more still – developing 'the story trance' (see Chapter 2) and an inward focus.

- Focus and balance of this kind have many knock-on benefits in other kinds of learning. People of all ages simply function better when they get chances to relax and go inwards for a time during the day (Rossi 1991).

- It balances the use of intentional structures with use of images unconsciously generated.

- It boosts a feeling of creative 'flow' because it can feel effortless.[2]

- Because imaginings are inclined to be or become meaningful, guided imagination can yield personal insights useful in one-to-one tutoring, counselling, PSHE, etc.

- It is also a good way of establishing rapport and empathy with others, getting insight into their different ways of imagining in the safer 'language' of images.

- It can initiate insights crucial to later developments of critical thinking.

- It connects well to practical questioning and story making games.

- It also connects well with subject areas beyond literacy/English.

Practical tips

Imagination may be a given of human nature, but not everyone has equal access to it. Not everyone uses it in the same way either, whilst not everyone gets to it in the same way. To give guided imagination the best possible chance of working:

- *Name it appropriately:* Pick the label according to the group's age and experience. 'Guided imagining' may work well enough for older pupils, as it does for many adults. You can point out that it's a version of something used by sports stars and other top performers in honing their skills.[3] You could also call it (as I do sometimes) multi-sensory picturing. This is a bit of a mouthful but conveys the notion that you don't just have to use the visual sense to imagine, as implied in the term 'visualization'. Younger pupils may respond and understand better if you call it (say) 'letting your mind show you a story' or maybe something a bit more technical like 'exploring mind's eye places'.

- *Make it multi-sensory:* The first mistake made by many teachers and work-shop leaders in guiding imagination is in assuming that it has to be visual. Making mental pictures, as if one were actually looking at something like a film with an inner eye, is the most common form of imagination. The larger percentage of people claim to be able to do this to some degree, but by no means all. Some do so very readily, others only in flashes, others apparently not at all or only rarely. Yet people who don't have the 'inner eye' experience may be imagining strongly in different ways – using bodily or kinaesthetic sensations, for example, or sounds or scents or tastes or just the strong feeling of it happening. It's important to allow for this in the language you use, rather than always talking about seeing. So:

- *Use and overlap all of the senses:* By using words and constructions that suggest the use of more than one sense, you hedge your bets, making sure that individual 'taste' is catered for. ('Maybe you can *hear* that more *clearly*, getting the *sense* out of it and being more *in touch* with it, *grasping* the chance to *see* your way onwards . . .')

- *Assume it's a skill as well as a talent:* Imagination, like many other capaci-ties, can be framed either as a skill or as a talent. A talent (in popular 'thought-myth') is something you either have or you don't; a skill is something you develop with practice. If people imagine solely by see-ing images, they are missing the chance to hear, taste, smell and so on in imagination. People who get no visual images but feel their way through an imagining may need to value that ability and then develop the confi-dence to get flashes of seeing, hearing, etc. Skilled imaginers may work with all the senses, though may still have favourites.

- *Make it appropriate:* Consider whether the subjects are likely to go with this theme. Different themes work with different people and different age groups. Don't assume that, because you like beaches or mountains and find them relaxing, everyone else does too! Fantasy palaces, enchanted castles, unicorns, dragons *et al.* are marvellous up to a certain age, but may be risky unless handled with a certain irony beyond that.

- *Don't be too bossy:* Sometimes it might be appropriate to say 'Imagine now that you are walking along your own path' and to use other more direct instructions. If you do this all the time, it doesn't give imagination much permission to go off on its own tracks. A vaguer-sounding, less bossy way of asking for the same kind of imagining might be: 'I wonder if you can imagine walking along some kind of path, a path you can choose for yourself, anywhere, any time, a very interesting path . . .'

- *Issue challenges:* This works particularly well with younger groups. It goes on working with teenagers and even adults, but you have to adapt. 'I bet you could never imagine what it is like to be on a magic carpet' is good for many primary children. With older groups, you might use clever phrases like 'Not many people can imagine what it is like to be on a magic carpet' or 'Some people find that they can imagine easily what it is like to . . .' The cleverness here is subtle. A person hearing these phrases can pick up the suggestion and do the imagining, feeling a little bit exceptional if they can do it, but can equally feel justified in not being able to do it well (or at all): because 'not many' or only 'some' people can do it.

- *Hint and suggest and leave interpretation open:* The general policy is to hint and suggest in what you say as far as possible, leaving listeners to interpret the instruction in their own way.

- *Take your time:* Leave long intervals between sentences and parts of sentences and linger on words, especially those with an interesting or unusual sound. Listen for silences between phrases. A silence in giving a picturing can seem far too long to the speaker, but much too short to the listening imaginer. Pausing in almost any sentence makes it more likely that listeners begin to guess and imagine what has been said and what might be said next.

- *Use useful nominalizations (reifications):* Nouns like 'peace', 'freedom' and 'power' (and associated adjectives − 'peaceful', 'powerful', etc.) don't have a set, universal meaning; they mean different things to different people. They are nominalizations, a word derived from the idea of creating an abstract noun from a practical action word (verb or adverb). For example, I can free you from some trap or prison but I can't give you something labelled 'freedom' as such. The advantage of using these vague words in guiding imagination is that listeners have to go on an inner search for their own meaning, so that they are automatically going inwards and imagining.

- *Be sensitively aware of the power:* Imagination can be very powerful, so needs a degree of sensitivity in the handling. Some of the themes listed below could be awkward if used gratuitously with more vulnerable pupils − though the same themes, used with sensitivity, could be potentially liberating for precisely those students.

- *Maintain authority, confidence and trust:* If you give images with authority and the confident feeling that listeners can do the imagining you ask them to do in their own way, repeating instructions as necessary in different ways calmly and evenly, they are much more likely to go with the imagining than if you dither and change course often.

- *Pick your time:* It's not usually possible to get perfect circumstances for imagining, and in fact it can work very well in many less-than-perfect situations. But there will always be times in any schedule when it would be more obviously difficult than others.

- *Pick up on it straight away:* Imaginings, like dreams, are too easily forgotten. For story work, it's usually best to pick up on what has been imagined immediately through the various means suggested later in the chapter.

All of the above are suggestions, not rules. You can give an effective guided imagining without following any of them slavishly.

Imagination station

This is a key multi-sensory picturing. Wordings here may suggest younger groups, but it can be adapted to suit any age. The idea is to create a private imaginary mental space where it's easy and safe to relax and imagine vividly. The advantage is that you can then ask pupils to revisit and develop 'your imagination station' whenever necessary, as a prelude to further 'picturings' or to imagining a pre-existing story in more detail, a short cut to getting into the right frame of mind, usefully compared (because the image currently resonates for IT-literate pupils) with clicking an icon on the desktop to bring the 'imagining program' up. It hence saves future time spent on preparation rituals and so on, whilst also allowing for more nervous imaginers. Ideally it's best to improvise the wording on the day to suit the conditions and the listeners, but here is one way of phrasing it that could work if read out slowly with plenty of pregnant gaps (though adjust the imagery for older listeners). For just this one picturing, I have indicated how you might do this, with conventional dots for gaps and with italics for words one might want to emphasize subtly. (I stress that these are suggestions only – there are other ways to deliver the same words, and one has to adapt to conditions.) As a prelude, something about the fact that people imagine in different ways, discussing how different pupils do their own imagining (pictures? sounds? scents? tastes? smells? touch? feeling?), will create the right kind of expectancy and adjustment of mood. Also a bit of further explanation of why you'll be pausing every now and then to allow them space to find out how they imagine will be helpful too.

Creating your own imagination station *inside your own mind* is a very useful thing to do. . . . It can be like . . . a place you . . . can always carry around with you anywhere, somewhere you can *relax* . . . and . . . *feel calm* . . . and *safe* . . . and *distant* . . . as you *imagine incredible and amazing things*. Some people like to *stare off into nowhere in particular* and . . . *imagine it all happening away beyond*. . . . Others like to *close their eyes and sense it all* going on inside. . . . People do their imagining in their own way, of course. . . . Again some like to *imagine a quiet place* where *everything goes still . . . and silent*. Others like it *more active*, like a laboratory with all kinds of potions bubbling away . . . or mega-monitor screens and music and computer terminals. . . . Then there are people who like . . . crystal balls . . . and magic wands . . . as well as lots of others who like much more ordinary things. . . . Some like to *keep changing* their imagination stations; others prefer to *keep it the same*. . . . Whatever works for you is fine. Maybe you can . . . *explore* now *your own* . . . *imagination station*. . . . Maybe you can *see* three things . . . or *touch* three things . . . or *taste* . . . or *hear* . . . or *feel*. . . . I wonder how many things you can *notice for yourself* in the next few seconds . . . (Go silent for a while before ending there, for a short picturing, or adding Part 2 below, for a longer imagining.)

Part 2 (If not continued from Part 1, remind imaginers of that first. Spend a while 'regaining' it – some will think they have forgotten completely; it may take a while to get the mood back):

I wonder if you can start to develop some imagining tools in your imagination station . . . like for example . . . something for *looking at things* in more detail, *close up*: like . . . a magnifying glass . . . or a zoom lens maybe. . . . Then something for looking at things from a *long way off*, making them very tiny – like the wrong end of a telescope. . . . What can you see with these two ways of looking?

Now you can use other ways of imagining. Not everyone can *hear in imagination* but maybe you can find a way to *make sounds louder and sharper* . . . or to *fade away*. . . . Maybe you can make feelings stronger or more faint . . .

Continue with touch, taste and smell on the same formula, as part of the same picturing or in repeat 'visits' to the imagination station. Conclude with a statement such as:

> There are lots of things you might like to . . . *tell other people* about in your imagination station, but it's fine if there are some things you want to *keep private*. It's up to you. You can decide right now which things you will tell people about and how you can make them imagine what you have imagined . . .

Show me what you heard (debriefing pair game)

- Take it in turns to describe what has been seen, heard, smelt, felt, touched or tasted in the imagination station. Speakers give as clear an idea of what they have imagined as possible.

- Listeners ask encouraging questions. They can draw on some of the 'lawyer' questioning patterns studied in Chapter 3, though they are not aiming to catch the speaker out, but rather to explore and discover as much as they can about the other person's imagination.

- If speakers are asked about something they didn't get around to imagining (e.g. the view from a window or door or entrance in their imagination station), they do some more imagining to 'discover' the answer.

- When both partners have spoken and answered questions about their imagination stations, they can together answer these three questions: 1) What was similar about your two imagination stations? 2) What was different about your two imagination stations? 3) What do you notice about your partner's style of imagining?

Teaching notes

You may want to demonstrate with the group how this will work, using a bolder, more forthcoming student who won't mind exposing his or her imaginings. Some lawyer's tricks from Chapter 3 can be used, but the style of questioning needed here (and for further imaginings below) is a little different – the questions are designed to draw the speakers out and help them to imagine more. Speakers can be encouraged to consult imagination again in answering questions, perhaps staring off into the distance or closing their eyes, perhaps using other ways of going into imagining mode. The questions at the end are designed to make players think about imagination: how it works for them and what it can tell them about others.

Optional writing tasks

1. The questions at the end can also be handled as a writing task. Prior to answering the questions, the 'players' can also write down as much as they have been able to recall about their partner's imagining space. (They could use story clouds for this.)
2. Under a title such as 'My imagination station', pupils simply write about what they have imagined, giving as many details as possible of each sense they were able to use in representing the 'place' to themselves.

Another way to start: two preliminary challenges

The following two picturing games are a good way into this kind of imagining, because they show something about how imagination can work unconsciously, without intention, whilst also suggesting ways of training the ability to handle and train imagination. Older students, who could feel that a traditionally presented imagining like the one above is not cool and resist with silliness and 'snark', are usually seduced by these kinds of picturing, especially if you tantalize a little and arouse curiosity in advance with the suggestion that they 'show you something about your mind' or 'tell you a lot about how other people think'. Younger listeners will also go with them, though you would adjust expectations for discussion and 'interpretation'.

The room, the table and the window

Skills developed in this picturing challenge include understanding imagery and symbolism, insight into how literature 'means' and improved understanding of self and others. It has a modern setting, but there are traditional picturings or games with the same flavour from various cultures (Spanish, Indian, Arab, etc.) with quite different imagery.[4] It's about mental images. If you restrict suggestions about how listeners should see (hear, taste, feel, etc.) and just give the (approximately memorized) instructions slowly, very roughly as given here, the images may be triggered fairly unconsciously. This game can be approached without any relaxation ritual. You tell the group that they are going to visit an unusual room in imagination, maybe introducing it as an imagining challenge that can show you a thing or two. Then you go through these stages:

1. You don't know this room and you have never been in it before. When the door opens, you can notice what it is that tells you that this room is for you – things you can see or hear or smell or touch or feel.

2. There is a table in the room. What kind of table is it? Are there any chairs?
3. On the table is something unexpected and very interesting.
4. Underneath it, there is something else, quite different.
5. There is one window. What is it like? What can you see when you look out of the window.
6. How easy is it to get out of the room?
7. What is outside?

Next, you go back over the picturing, simply asking pupils to volunteer a little about what they imagined – which illustrates how differently people can imagine something as simple as a room, a table and a window and helps those who found it hard to imagine. Were you doing one of the 'folkloric/ pop psychology' versions, you would then give each of the stages a precise meaning – the room is you, the table is your respectable interests, what is under the table is less respectable, etc. This is dubious: the way we imagine things rarely tells us precise and limited things like that. What is more interesting and gets pupils animated when handled in an age-appropriate way and with some probing, is to tease out and discuss in an open way what the images *might* mean, *might* show and *could* illustrate. Here are some possible priming questions, one for each stage:

1. What could the room tell you about a person and the ways the person thinks about him - or herself?
2. Why do people choose different kinds of table?
3. Things on the table are on show. Does that give you any idea about the person and what he or she wants to show you?
4. Things that are under the table are more hidden. What could that mean?
5. If people can choose to see whatever they like when they look out of an imaginary window, what does their choice of what to see tell you?
6. Getting out of the room is easy for some and difficult for others. Why?
7. Some people say that what is outside the room shows things about how people think about what they don't know. What do you think about that?

A red ball and a white floor

This intrigues (as well as annoys and frustrates) many, particularly those who have a strong visual imagination, suggesting that imagination might be stronger than will. You first ask a person or group to imagine a circular pure white floor as clearly as they can. To allow for people who don't get clear visual mental images, you can play with other senses (what a white floor might feel like – cold or hot? clean? etc. Does it have a silence around it or some particular noise? Is there a crisp white smell?). Then you ask them to imagine a red ball rolling on to that floor, also very clearly. Imagine it coming to rest exactly in the centre of that floor. (Again, to make it multi-sensory, you can add the sound of the ball, rolling or perhaps bouncing, plus a little accompanying music, etc.) You then challenge them to go back to thinking about just the white floor without the ball. Tell them that they must not think of the red ball now. For most (if they are honest), this is difficult – floor and ball have been linked by the imagining. Also the act of denying the ball makes it more likely that a person will imagine it first and then try to delete it, so that an impossible bind is set up – rather like the famous 'Don't think of pink elephants' instruction.

The game is a very good illustration for pupils of the (sometimes worrying) power of imagination and generally leads to interesting discussion. Here are two good practical solutions to this picturing that have come out of my own work with it and which prove that there are ways to work with imagination rather than be ruled by it. (There are several more.)

- Leave the red ball safely on that first white floor and say that it can stay there. Set about imagining a second, slightly different pure white floor. Following this, you can also imagine the red ball rolling somewhere separate, perhaps to a yellow floor.
- Imagine in great detail slowly painting out the red ball with thick, cold white paint, adding a second and a third coat as necessary, concentrating on the power and strength of the paint, its density, etc.

Creative written task

Create another similar picturing that does not involve a floor or a ball. Set it out as a series of instructions. Try this on someone else. Find a way to solve the 'imagining bind'.

Letting your imagination show you a story (nine more adaptable multi-sensory picturings)

Each of these 'picturings' is presented quite briefly. Simply reading this wording out with plenty of pauses and spaces to allow some imagining may be sufficient for some groups. However, each could be adapted to suit different ages and/or extended simply through improvising around it as you go, using the clues given above. So it's best simply to memorize the idea and adapt as you go. Each picturing could lead to the kind of sharing and discussion (speaking and listening) already illustrated, to oral work through games (as illustrated later in the chapter) or to writing tasks around what has been pictured. Some suggestions for joining some of them together in a more complex plot are also given below. 'Imagination station' can be used as a prelude to each picturing to get into imagining mode. Alternatively, you can issue another challenge, such as 'I don't suppose you will be able to imagine this one because it's hard!' Single picturings can be used for one-off experiments. All nine picturings might be used sooner or later; several (at least six if dice are used) are needed for a linked imaginary journey, as explained below. As you use more of them, you can ask for increasingly detailed imagining, combining senses more systematically.

1. *The house of possibility.* In the house of possibility, there are endless doors. You can choose to open any of them, though it is wise to linger for a while before making that choice. It's good to get an idea in your mind about how you approach the house, how you will get there, where it is, what its surrounding are, what it looks like, how it makes you feel, whether there any sounds that catch your attention. It may change when you go there on different occasions, which could be interesting; people change in the way they feel. Today could be different from tomorrow or this time next week. But, right now, how does it look and feel? What is it like to go into that house and peer at the doors, notice any colours or decorations or patterns or whatever, sense the atmosphere and touch base with a decision on one of them. What is special about that door? What would it be like to slowly turn that handle, allow the door to open? Is it silent or is there that familiar storybook creak or maybe the sudden scent of something surprising?

2. *The art of flying.* Getting the hang of flying may take a while or could be easy, the way it is in some people's dreams. It's up to you. You can design your own way into it. Will you want to do it by just thinking yourself up into the air or by putting your mind on one side and going by feel and instinct? Maybe you prefer a set of wings, in which case maybe you can have a long and careful look at them. Maybe you prefer technology of some kind. Or perhaps you like the idea and the sensation of stepping into the air and being able to walk up it effortlessly. Maybe you want to be just floating there almost without knowing it, way up and away above the clouds or just a metre or several up. Maybe you can imagine being above your brother or your sister or your friends or your teachers, just looking down, feeling powerful.

3. *Darkness and dangers.* Not many people are fond of darkness and dangers. After all, if it is both dark and dangerous, that's a good reason to keep away, is it not? All the same, just supposing you have to go through some dark and dangerous place. It's dark in a way that means you can see nothing, so you just have to grope your way through. It's dangerous – or could be. Knowing that, your imagination might suggest all sorts of possibilities, many more than make sense. You know what imagination can be like; it does that to you sometimes. It's the difficult side of having an imagination. How will you control it and discover the right kind of bravery – not just shutting your eyes and hoping for the best? Given that you can't take a light, what protection will you have? What is it like as you get to the other side, safely, back to the light?

4. *Something very valuable.* People have different ideas of what is valuable. For some it is just lots of money, for others it is jewellery or golden crowns or pictures by famous painters, for some it is something mysterious or strange, whilst some go for very personal and private things that wouldn't seem worth a lot to anyone else. There are even grown-up people for whom one of their most valuable possessions is a toy they had when they were five or six. The thing is that, if you really think about it, everyone has an idea somewhere in their mind about something that would be valuable as far as they are concerned. It might not be like anything mentioned so far; it might be something completely unexpected. So what is it? Can you make a mental picture of it – the way it would feel to have that valuable thing with you right now? How could you describe it to someone else?

5. *Meetings with monsters.* Not everyone is scared of monsters – until they meet one. Of course, a monster to one person might not be a monster to another. Those warty, scaly, weird, peculiar, fantastical, very large and very dangerous creatures you might have once imagined were hiding just outside your house or under the bed might now seem impossible, even silly – at least until you are left alone in a dark place. But everyone has a monster of some kind they just would not want to meet; everyone has had a nightmare sometime, somewhere. So what would it be like to be protected enough, using your imagination station, to take a long cool look at a nightmare monster? What would it be like to sit back at a distance and get a feel for what that monster is? Could you just note three or maybe more things about how it looks, so that you can describe it to someone else? What kind of noise does it make? Imagine several ways to tame it or control it or lock it up securely. Imagine that monster getting smaller, slowly shrinking, until you can fit it on the palm of your hand and make it dance to some crazy music. Make it even smaller. Then clap your hands together and notice that it is gone.

6. *The strange forest.* I don't know what kind of forest this will be because it's your forest, not mine. You can let your own imagination choose it. Maybe it will be the traditional kind of deep dark forest, with tall trees and long

shadows and owl hoots. Maybe it will be a much lighter place with all sorts of many-coloured leaves and flower scents and twisting pathways with the songs of rainbow birds chanting away happily. Maybe it will be a mixture of those two or maybe it will be a very unusual kind of forest that doesn't even have trees. After all, there might be forests on other planets or in weird realms beneath the ground with quite different plants and different tracks. In fantasy kingdoms, there are fruits on branches that are jewels or keys or living heads. In real-life jungles there are plants that are almost stranger. There are all kinds of forest, so you can linger a while a make a choice and then start to make your way or grope your way or follow the scent through it and across it to wherever you want to go.

7. *The ring of knowledge.* The ring of knowledge is something heroes and heroines in ancient tales or modern fantasy films sometimes go on quests to find and sometimes are just given, just as you can be given one in imagination right now. It gives you the power of knowledge, without books or the internet, just knowing things you need to know when you need to know them. First of all, though, you have to get a clear image of it. You could start with the feel of it – on your hand as you take it, slipping it on to a finger. Where does it come from? Who gives you this ring? How heavy or light is it? Some rings sparkle and gleam; some have strange designs. Some you control by the power of thinking, some by pressing some special part of the ring, some by reciting spells, some in other ways. How does your ring work? What kinds of things can it tell you?

8. *The healing potion.* This healing potion can cure all ills – wounds from battles or sickness or anything else. If you have an ache here or a cut there, just a little of the potion will banish it. If you were dying, one sniff of it would bring you back to life. Some people find the potion in out-of-the-way places after long journeys; some get it just down the road, somewhere they had seen often enough and never expected to find such a thing. Some store it in one of those ancient stone flasks decorated with magical patterns, some in a modern glass bottle and some in other kinds of container. The important thing is to be able to put it in something that keeps it safe, something you can open whenever you need to. The important thing is to begin to know the feeling of opening it, the sound of taking out the stopper or unscrewing the top or whatever, the excitement you might notice, the smell of the potion, the colour and the look of it. The important thing is to just get a bit of the feeling of healing right now, just a little taste or a flash – so that you can always come back to it when you need to, so that you can tell someone else how it works.

9. *Perfect place.* There are not so many perfect places in the world, or perhaps there are lots of them, all around. Perhaps it depends how you look at places. Perhaps anywhere is perfect in its own way; perhaps nowhere is ever perfect. In imagination, though, it's possible to create a perfect place – the kind of

place you would find perfect, not someone else, just you. Think, for example, of a long journey you might have taken as the hero or heroine of your own story – a long, dangerous or wearying journey, but now it's over. You are arriving at this perfect place. I don't know what it will look like or feel like or sound like, because it's not my imagination we're talking about. It might be warm; it might be cool; it might be light; it might be dark; it might be all sorts of things that you can decide for yourself it should be. But getting there, to the safety, will be a big relief: getting there and meeting whoever you want to be there and finding expected and unexpected things; noticing what there is to see and do there, the feeling it gives you inside yourself of having reached this point of perfection; just being there.

Making more picturings

These are example imaginings with a common thread of fantasy for reasons that will become clear at the end of the chapter. It is easy enough to make more picturings with similar or quite different themes. Once pupils are familiar with the idea of guiding imagination, it is a good challenge to set them the task of creating their own multi-sensory picturing instruction texts, which they will be able to read out to the group (or partners or small groups), who will feed back how well they were able to imagine through those instructions. Guidance can be given about combining different senses, not being too directive, etc., as described earlier. Popular themes include traditional fantasy, the modern world, fabulous shops and riches, science fiction, faraway places, adventures and dangers, but there are very many more.

I-witness (group game, also pairs and small groups)

This is a storytelling/questioning game from my booklet *Imagine On: 24 Fun Ways to Picture and Tell Marvellous Stories* (Parkinson 2005). (There are other debriefing/story-developing games in this book, plus a series of 18 guided imaginings different from those presented here but possibly complementary.) It works rather like 'Fantastic fibs' in Chapter 3.

- The storyteller is chosen. She or he has 'seen' imaginary or fantastical things through one of the picturings and tells as much as possible about them.

- Questions are asked by the rest of the group, encouraged to be curious, not sceptical – to ask about the kind of natural detail a person who has, say, learned to fly or claims to have met a monster would be likely to know.

- The storyteller is given time to check answers by reimagining (or further developing) the 'picturing', rather than saying the first thing that comes to mind.

- As the idea of the game is established, questioners are encouraged to ask questions about different senses involved in the imagining – how (and if) the teller saw or felt or heard, etc. They might also ask questions about particular parts of the imagining they themselves experienced vividly, sharing their own experience as they ask the question. ('I saw a very bright scarlet and there was a whiff of something like petrol . . .')

Curriculum connections and beyond

Guided imagining and PSHE, counselling, etc.

Many of the themes for guided imagining above were chosen partly for their potential for literal or metaphorical relevance in this area, as well as for their imaginative possibilities. For example, 'Darkness and dangers' is a theme everyone has to deal with in life – working with one's own fears and insecurities. Similarly, healing from illness or injury or psychological wounds ('The healing potion') is an essential that can actually be speeded up through positive imagining. Note too that something like 'Meetings with monsters' can be useful in dealing intelligently with bullying – one can explore imaginatively and metaphorically how to deal with the 'monster' without directly talking about potentially embarrassing bullying. Because work with imaginative themes like these can connect easily to a personal sense of meaning, it often has this kind of power and relevance beyond literacy work,[5] an intrinsic power that story work should not shirk – though of course one retains sensitivity to individuals at the same time. And, as often with storytelling ideas, it is possible to meet more than one educational target as part of the same activity.

History and other subjects

Using guided imagining combined with storytelling can make many other subjects come to life for pupils. For example, if a group have been studying Egyptians and have seen pictures, internet images, perhaps even films, they should be well primed to imagine for themselves how it would be to visit ancient Egypt for a moment or two, particularly if one guides them through a particular scenario – going into a Nile settlement perhaps, seeing an Egyptian priest or two or the Great Sphinx, or perhaps sitting in a temple or by a pyramid. What is imagined need not be accurate but would be imaginatively 'true'. Pupils can then tell each other the story of their 'Time travel to ancient Egypt' in an 'I-witness' game and go on to write the same story in more detail. Similar approaches can be taken to the study of a contemporary country or culture – or indeed of other planets.

Joined-up imagining

Imagine that

Take a story that contains vivid images. ('The voyage of Mael Dun' at the end of the last chapter is a good example; 'Mohammed and the magician' and 'The taming of Fenris' in the next chapter are also recommended.) Ask pupils to imagine parts of it as vividly as possible, working your way through the five senses but not forgetting the holistic 'feel' that comes out of a combination of sense and emotional 'framing'. In the case of Mael Dun, you can take an island or two at a time and encourage imaginers to notice as much detail as possible and then feed back to each other (or the whole group) through the 'I-witness' game. (See also exercises in the next chapter and beyond.)

An imaginary journey

Stories about journeys have been told for centuries. The classic quest plot features a journey – the journey, say, of Jason and the Argonauts in search of the Golden Fleece or of Mael Dun through the many fantastic islands. Journey story plots generally move along a line from setting-out point to final destination, with stop-offs along the way for adventures, trials and tribulations, phantasmagoria and all sorts more here or there. You can make great literature of it, but it's still an easy plot type for novice fiction makers to handle – they can draw out the plot line on paper, with circles (or story clouds) for separate incidents as a plan.

Why not link some of the imaginings from the set of nine above (or any other group of guided imaginings, such as those in *Imagine On*) to make a quest story? Tellers or writers will choose for themselves some that particularly appeal (perhaps three and probably no more than six for a simpler tale) to put together in a story. You might introduce a chance game element. For example, they get number 1, 'The house of possibility', to start, but then pick numbers from a hat or roll dice to get other numbered picturings that have to be included (use 6 of them to one dice). Number 9 in the set ('Perfect place') is included as a possible happy ending point. The order in which the themes come up can be enforced as the order in the story, or it can be left to individual story makers.

The story based on the imaginings could be a told or a written story (or both). The teller/writer must decide who is going on the journey/quest. Is it a first or third person story? How and why does the person (or people) come to be going on this journey? What is the object of the journey? Is it a fantasy story (as the images here suggest) or is something 'real world' – so that you learn to fly not by magic but in a helicopter or hang glider? What will they achieve at the end and at what price? These and many more questions can guide the development of the tale and could emerge from a guided discussion or a questioning game before making a developed telling.

A group telling and/or story reading presentation of a journey tale is good for an assembly, etc., as noted at the end of Chapter 4.

6

Learning stories

A cure for amnesia, long forgotten. What is it?

Framing ideas: memory and stories

If you want to remember something, turn it into a story. Our ancestors probably did just this – anthropologists have found that not only sacred ritual and 'god lore' are passed on in the myth and legends and fireside tales of surviving hunter-gatherer tribes, but also everyday wisdom, practical plant and medicinal knowledge, mapping of the landscape and all sorts more. If you talk to memory champions today, people who perform prodigious feats of instant learning, you will find that they use techniques that are essentially of the same order. They learn to see, taste, hear and feel a mentally 'pictured' story that brings all of the facts, people, places and so on together, making them memorable, making them stick. Stories are supposed to be sticky.

In a sense, memory itself is a story. We need the sense of narrative to string together the pictures and scents and words and numbers and all the other nuggets that come to us when we switch into the chaos of associations that swim into view as attention turns to part of the past or to a topic of passing interest or even a formally studied subject. We need to give it all relevance, context, coherence – in our lives, in our experience, in our wider knowledge. Narrative memory does that for us. It is one of those natural, unconscious abilities we have to have in order to live fully human lives.

All the same, there is no doubt that memory benefits a lot from coaching. There are awe-inspiring examples of prodigious memory, both ancient and modern. Those with a Muslim background will know the term *hafiz*, applied to people who have completely memorized the Qur'an – a daunting enough feat to most of us, though actually the term was originally applied to people who had memorized in addition 100,000 *hadith* (traditions of the prophet) with their narrators and transmission chains. Many cultures of the past have preserved their histories, genealogies and poetry by memory, including the ancient Celts, whose bards evidently had highly trained memory skills. (According to one legend, Celtic bards spent long hours with boulders laid on their bellies, so that they were unable to move whilst focusing their minds on epics they had to relate to royalty and other dignitaries.) The professional bards and minstrels of many cultures have had their memory methods and tricks, some studied and learned only through long and arduous discipline; many have kept extraordinary numbers of stories in their memories, sometimes several thousand.

Like guided imagination, dealt with in the last chapter, memorization in general is currently stressed much less in education than was once the case. You could argue that the increasing availability of more and more sophisticated 'knowledge technologies' makes many traditional memorization skills redundant anyway. Yet the training of memory, in one way or another, has to be an important ingredient of a genuine education we neglect at our peril. A person whose memory is undeveloped is lacking in a vital life skill. And memory is, quite apart from its practical value in day-to-day work, life and play, the place where we store our sense of self.

Direct benefits of memorizing stories for telling aloud include the following:

- The memory 'style' honed in this work is practical for all sorts of other 'performances' involving memory. From exams to interviews, presentation to selling to teaching, there are many situations where a person needs not only to memorize but to do so flexibly.

- In story memorization for telling, you don't learn a script; you take in a template you can adjust to suit. Putting it another way, you first absorb the concept of the story.

- Conceptualization means that you take in the pattern of the tale, its whole structure and an intuitive understanding of how it works.

- That develops a flexible sense of plot and means that 'templates' are available for guiding further story work.

- This in turn leads on to the kind of creative work with stories explored in the following chapters.

- Memorizing is an excellent study in control and use of attention and focus, combining the kind of work with the imaginative mind explored in the last chapter with analytical skill.

- This has knock-on benefits in other work requiring similar combinations of skills.
- It's stimulating fun in itself and feeds into performance work, explored in Chapter 10.

Making it stick: using attention

Actually stories do stick quite naturally. Young children often recall long narratives for some time when they have been truly engaged by them. Many can remember scary or disgusting stories they would prefer to forget. On the other hand most people have been told good jokes or anecdotes they instantly forget. Why can't we remember? The story was a good one; we *should* be able to get it back! The secret of remembering stories well seems to divide into three parts, each embodying good psychological principles, each relating to the way we control and use attention:

1. seeing the pattern in the story;
2. living in the story;
3. practice, practice, practice.

We'll take those first two aspects of story memory in more detail, unpack them a little and introduce some ideas for teaching the skills involved – which will provide the third essential of practice.

Practice seems such an obvious point that it's easy to underestimate its value. In 1949, the Canadian psychologist Donald Hebb outlined a principle since called Hebbian learning. It's frequently simplified in the phrase 'Cells that fire together wire together' and refers to the ways in which neurons in the brain become associated with each other in neural networks by repeatedly 'firing together'. In other words you need repetition to make it stick – evidently around 13 exposures to a piece of information or an idea before it becomes part of your more permanent learning. (This is a good way of understanding why pupils sometimes can't remember what they learned last term – or even yesterday.) A lot of people know the story about the violinist who is wandering around New York with his cased fiddle, looking for a certain venue. He stops an old man. 'Can you tell me how to get to Carnegie Hall?' he asks, and the old man reiterates my final point above, 'Practice, practice, practice!'

Seeing the pattern

To remember a story well, you analyse it – practically, usually on the hoof and probably rather approximately. It's this or that kind of story. This bit at the beginning is an optional extra; this other part is absolutely essential. Maybe a person could skate over that bit of the tale quickly; maybe one could take a little more time over this other part, introduce a little more detail . . . That might all happen almost unconsciously for a person with quite a lot of experience and some sensitivity; one has only to listen to a child ploughing through every irrelevant detail of films they like, or to have one's ear bent by an elderly adult telling you about what the doctor said, to realize that it is something that happens neither automatically nor naturally.

To encourage the skill of seeing the pattern in a story in a lesson or workshop:

- *First* ask for the rough and approximate 'bits' of the story in oral discussion.
- *Next* map and landmark the story (see below) with the group or class and eventually produce a frame.
- *Then* ask if there are any other stories this one reminds anyone of that are like it in some way. Make some comparisons, listing similarities and differences.
- *Lastly* go on to imagining exercises with the story pattern (see below) before having individuals (or pairs or groups) retell the story in outline from memory.

Mapping, landmarking and framing

Mapping a story is a straightforward enough idea. You go back through the story heard or watched or read, noting the key events in approximate order. This can be done in writing, or you can 'draw' the story as a series of linked islands (circles or clouds) of events joined by arrows.

Landmarks are less obviously logical. Memory doesn't necessarily work sequentially and logically. Some things grab your attention and imprint themselves automatically – like the passing landscape features you see on a walk: the rock that looks like a cat's head, the tree that reminds everyone of a fairy tale hag. Landmarks of that kind might not show on the Ordnance Survey map; story landmarks might be missed out if you are just analysing the plot pattern. When you think back on the story (or the walk), it's these that come back first. They're hence very practical for story learning – you can use them as 'centres' through which to grope your way to other parts of the story. To landmark a story, simply ask the group to say or to write down which 'pictures' in the story they recall in any order, starting with whatever comes into their minds first. Landmarks can next be sorted into the order in which they appear in the story.

Frame is the sequence of events you found in the map, reduced to a series of numbered or bulleted points, summarizing as briefly as possible the main points of a story. To make the frame more sticky, you can add the landmarks at the appropriate stages of the frame.

Living in the story

Stories are often taken in only at a superficial level, especially when read through fairly rapidly or listened to with incomplete attention. This is one reason they may afterwards be forgotten. Engaging the imaginative, 'dreaming awake' mind with the story more thoroughly makes it more likely it will stick. Sometimes this happens because the story is particularly well told or read in circumstances that are particularly favourable, so that listeners/readers have gone thoroughly into the story listening trance. These exercises are ways of achieving and indeed practising that kind of engagement, encouraging pupils to live imaginatively in a story in a deeper way than they might otherwise.

Seeing it through (storytellers' exercise)

- Take any story you want to learn well (perhaps one of the stories presented at the end of this chapter).

- Map, landmark and frame the story, as described above.

- Now relax into imagining mode using routines developed in the last chapter, such as 'Imagination station'.

- Take each stage of the story in order, picturing them in the fullest sense (i.e. using as many different sensory modes as possible).

- Hear some of the words you will use to tell parts of the story – hear yourself using some of the words with which you will tell the tale.

- Allow for surprises, when you discover unexpected things in the way you 'see' the story.

- Give it enough time, repeating the sequence more than once.

- Tell the story to someone.

Listening through (tellers' and listeners' exercise)

- Map, landmark and frame a story, as described above.

- Choose a series of storytellers to tell one stage each in the frame of the story (or, with more experienced storytellers in smaller groups, one storyteller to tell all of the story).

- Challenge storytellers to invoke different senses in the way they describe their stage in the story, talking about things listeners might see, hear, touch, taste, etc.

- Before the telling begins, encourage the class or group to go into a quiet imagining state, perhaps by invoking 'Imagination station', perhaps in other ways.

- Challenge listeners to see how much they can see, feel or touch in their imaginations at each stage of the story.

- Discuss the picturing afterwards and get the group to feed back to storytellers on what worked best.

Zooming in and out

To look at detail in the story whilst retaining the ability to look at the whole pattern:

- Ask pupils to invent an imaginary focusing device – anything from traditional things like crystal balls and magic mirrors to telescopes, TV and computer screens and clever mobile phones. (Give them choice with a few suggestions.)

- Get them to practise imagining using this device to imagine something simple – say a fountain or a river or a road or a tree.

- Suggest that this imagining device is very advanced and can do 3D multi-sensory images, though you have to practise to get the hang of the controls. Hence they might try using the controls for different senses – starting with visual, aural and 'feel'.

- Ask them to imagine part of a story previously mapped, landmarked and framed. (Probably start with a particularly vivid story landmark.)

- Ask them to zoom in on the part/landmark, so that they can imagine it in more details, perhaps turning on and off different sensory modes.

- Ask them to zoom out to see the overall pattern of the story, as if from a bird's eye perspective.

- Switch between zooming in to different parts/landmarks in the story and zooming out to the overall pattern.

You may not achieve all of these stages at first. It's an exercise that will stand repetition and development through different stories.

Curriculum connections

Beyond story learning: strange visions again

Exercises rather like these are useful beyond purely imaginative story work. Combine them with the suggestions in the last chapter for 'strange visions' of historical times and far-off places.

Future focus: exams, tests, performances *et al.*

The three exercises are also like those a person can do with test or examination material in advance. If one imagines one's way through material to be memorized, it becomes more sticky. If one imagines how one will handle an exam or a performance or an interview thoroughly and very positively, making sure one can deal with mistakes and upsets along the way, one is much more likely to do well on the day (see Chapter 10). Also in one-to-one coaching/counselling or in PSHE, the 'plot' to be imagined can be a new and more effective behaviour. Imagining well, telling oneself the story of what one is going to do and how, prepares a person for experiences, putting in place a template for action. It's the kind of technique sports coaches and therapists use with clients, but one doesn't need special training to utilize it at a simple level.

Simpler short tales for learning

The simplest kinds of stories to learn are short and quite simple, but interesting enough to be memorable. These might range from folk tales and legends to fables and other short teaching tales to jokes and anecdotes.

Probably the best way to introduce children with varying literacy skills to learning stories is simply to tell them stories, so that they enter into the story trance and the story 'sticks' almost by itself. A good CD or DVD may be a substitute here, though live telling is occasion and person sensitive.

A good way to encourage learning and then passing on stories is to have a whole set of tales on cards or sheets. These need to be quite simple, outline tellings of stories, though with a little extra effort you can grade stories to suit different reading abilities within a group. Fables work well because they are brief, but any short and interesting story will work. (Some sets are available commercially, whilst others are on websites.[1]) Cards or sheets are given out, ideally with a different tale for each member of the group. It's possible to use fewer tales, numbering them so that tellers won't be telling each other the same story. For example, suppose you have ten stories but 30 pupils, there will be three pupils learning each story. When those with story 1 have memorized it, they tell it to 2s, who then tell 1s their story. Meanwhile 3s and 4s are swapping stories, and so on. When the time comes to change partners and pass on the stories heard, 3s might tell to 1s and 4s to 2s until all of the group have heard all ten stories. (Incidentally, the permutations possible before stories are being repeated to people who have already heard them makes an interesting maths problem for pupils – or, as I've discovered for myself, a confusing conundrum if you are leading a session and haven't thought it through!)

Here are five short tales to learn. Each is told in flat, plain English with no attempt at more interesting storytelling. This gives the maximum scope to tellers in the way they will retell it. I will return to one of these in a later chapter to illustrate a little of what you can do with a simple plot.

The donkey and the lion

Donkeys were once not known in Uganda. A lion met the first one that came to visit, heard his deafening bray and believed the donkey when he said he was strong – until that donkey could only jump halfway across a stream the lion himself could leap over easily. But the donkey claimed he had been fishing for a large fish and the lion believed him again. Next the lion jumped over a ruined wall. The donkey knew he couldn't do that, so he kicked the wall over with his strong hind feet. Now the lion, awed by this amazing trick and a little afraid of this obviously powerful visitor, took the donkey to meet all the other lions. The donkey challenged them all to follow him into a valley full of thistles. They dared not, since thistles would hurt their paws, and were amazed to see this strange and obviously strong creature munching happily on the thistles. They were so impressed and indeed scared that they elected him as their king and so the donkey soon ruled over all the animals in Uganda – which might show that some power can be trickery, or it might mean that, just because it looks like a king, it doesn't mean it's not a donkey underneath.

(East African fable)

The blue jackal

A jackal once fell into a pot of blue dye, so that all of her fur was dyed a bright blue. The other animals no longer recognized her as a jackal, so she told them she was a queen. They believed her and she ruled over them for a time.

However, the other jackals were jealous, and one night they went up on to the hillside and howled at the moon, as jackals do. The blue jackal, hearing them and relying on her instinct without a moment's thought, joined in. It seemed a natural thing to do. When the animals heard that familiar sound, they were no longer deceived by the evidence of their eyes – their ears told them it was a jackal. They deserted her immediately. So, if you want to know who is the jackal, don't use your eyes but wait till they howl.

(Indian fable)

The mare's egg

A countryman was carrying a pumpkin across the lane – part of it had gone bad, so he was going to put it on the compost. Just then a city slicker, who had just stepped off the stagecoach, which had stopped to change the horses at the nearby inn, saw him. 'Whatever is that?' he asked, never having seen such a thing in his life.

'Oh,' the countryman replied, with a mischievous grin, not expecting to be taken seriously, 'this is a horse's egg. My mare just laid it.'

Now the city slicker knew little about vegetables and less about animals, but he did know you could get good money for a young horse in those days, so he asked the price. After a bit of haggling, he bought the 'horse egg' for a golden guinea and strutted off with it proudly – so proudly, in fact, that he tripped over a stone and the pumpkin flew out of his arms, the pulp of it splattering all over the track as it burst on landing. This would have shown him his mistake had not a startled hare in a nearby ditch started up and sprinted away across a field. Of course, he thought it was the foal from inside the egg escaping. He cursed his luck as he picked himself up and climbed back on to the coach. The country-man smiled and waved to him as the coach set off again.

(Sussex legend)

Three wishing cells

Three travellers arrive at an enchanted castle. A witch explains that, if they go down into the dungeons and brave the damp and the stench, they can enter what seem to be cells. But, if they say out loud what they wish to find there, they will find that very thing.

The first goes down into the dungeons, braves the dark and damp and foul smells and enters a cell, loudly saying 'Gold!' He finds the room full of gold and becomes rich.

The second follows him and finds a different cell and enters it, pushing aside all thoughts of the unpleasant sights and stinks and proclaiming 'Jewels!' He finds a room glistening with diamonds and rubies and pearls.

The third, a man who never really listens to anyone for long, still has a rough idea of what he has to do. He goes down into the dungeons, which are now even darker and damper and very much smellier. He opens a cell door, but suddenly, overcome with the horrid stench, he holds his nose and says 'Pooh!' Inside the cell he finds – a small stuffed toy bear wearing a red jumper.

(Children's joke)

The rich man's diamond

Once long ago, a rich man had his fortune told. Now next door to his mansion was a tiny hovel and in it lived a poor fisherman, his wife and 13 children. The rich man had always despised him. So he was horrified to hear the old fortune-teller say that one day that very fisherman would have all of his wealth. 'Not if I have anything to do with it!' he said to himself, and he made his plans.

The rich man sold everything he owned and used the cash to buy a fabulous diamond. This he kept hidden away in a secret pocket. Then he set out on a journey to a far and distant land, leaving the fisherman to his miserable little life. He gloated at the thought of how he had cheated fate.

But, sadly, the boat in which the rich man sailed was not a good one. Caught in a storm far out at sea, it sank and the rich man was drowned. The diamond was washed out of the secret pocket and a fish swallowed it. Time passed and then one day the fisherman caught that very fish . . .

(Arabian folk tale)

Advanced memorizing: two magical tales for learning

These traditional stories are told at greater length and with more elaboration (though there is still scope for more). Both are followed by some practical analysis of structures in the story and some tips on memorizing. Many other stories can be approached in ways similar to those suggested here. The stories have been chosen because they have some particular features that make them sticky and/or interesting as memorizing exercises.

Mohammed and the magician

The magician had tricked Mohammed, so Mohammed would trick the wizard. Hadn't that sly old fox promised to pass on the secrets of magic to the boy when he came to Mohammed's mother's house in Cairo and persuaded her to let Mohammed become his apprentice? Day and night Mohammed had worked for him at his desert lair, but not one little whiff of the magic had he been offered for three whole years, only chores and back-breaking tasks.

When his master had gone out, riding on the magic carpet on which he would cross vast tracts of desert to visit far-off palaces and steal away ancient secrets, Mohammed pulled aside the plain rug that covered the floor in his master's workshop. He had spied on his master through a crack in the door the previous evening and seen him do the same thing, uncovering a large flat stone in the floor, which he had raised using magic words Mohammed had memorized. He had disappeared down what must have been a staircase or a ladder beneath this for some time, returning with a strange smile on his wicked face. Mohammed was curious, naturally. He also knew by now that his master would tell him nothing of what was beneath the stone, so he would simply have to find out for himself. He recited the strange words and saw the stone rise to reveal a short staircase that led to an underground room. Lighting a candle and holding it before him, Mohammed went down into the shadowy chamber and found there a strange book, perched on a carved X-frame lectern of the kind he had seen reciters of the Qur'an use for the holy book. But there was nothing holy about this strange tome; the cover was jet black, decorated with stars and circles. The writing on it was odd too; it made no sense.

Puzzling over it, turning the pages and squinting at it from all angles by the flickering light of the candle, it suddenly came to him in a strange, unexpected surge of illumination – all of the magic that was in that book, swimming into his mind and being at once, so that he understood the power of transformation: how to change himself into this or that or whatever else. With it, too, came the knowledge that his master would kill him if he found out how he had stolen the power of the book.

Climbing back out of the room and looking out across the baking dunes, he saw a dove flying by. At once he knew how to become that dove and did so. It was strange to soar up into the air, to flap his wings and feel the hot sun, tempered by the desert wind that ruffled his feathers. But Mohammed could not enjoy it for long; even as he made his escape, the wizard was returning. He saw the open trap door and knew at once, by the second sight he had cultivated, that the bird disappearing over the horizon was his own apprentice, who must have peeped at the forbidden pages. In an instant, he transformed into an eagle and set off in pursuit.

Miles they both covered, but the eagle covered them much faster than the dove and would soon swoop down and tear it to shreds. At the very last moment, Mohammed spotted the danger. Looking down, he saw the waters of the Nile below him and dived into them to become a fish and swim away to hide in the weeds below the surface. But the magician became a crocodile to catch that fish and swallow it. Before he could do so, Mohammed looked up through the water and saw a date palm growing beside the water. At once he became one date upon that tree, but the wizard became a boy to climb that tree and pluck the date.

Just then the blare of a trumpet sounded, followed by the beating of a large drum. The sultan's daughter was passing in a palanquin, surrounded by fierce marching soldiers. Mohammed saw the flash of a diamond ring upon her finger and became the stone of that ring. The palanquin was carried on until it came to the palace, where the princess stepped into the safety of the women's quarters, with Mohammed as the ring upon her finger.

Now the wizard became a perfect replica of the chief eunuch of the harem, bearing a signed and sealed message from her father, demanding that she give up the ring upon her finger. The princess, who had just been served with a silver tray of refreshing sherbets and watermelon, obediently slipped the ring from her finger, but even as she did so the ring vanished as Mohammed became one of the water melon seeds. At once the wizard turned into a rat to guzzle up the watermelon seeds, but Mohammed became a stone to blunt the teeth of the rat. The rat became a huge hammer to shatter the stone, but Mohammed became the silk veil the princess had only recently removed. The wizard became a sheet of flame to burn the silk, but Mohammed became himself, quickly picking up a pitcher of water and putting out the fire. That was the end of the wizard.

The shocked princess had been shrieking in terror at this rapid series of strange transformations. Seeing the handsome youth appear and realizing that it was all now over, she greeted him as a hero who had rescued her from what must have been an evil genie. When her father heard her story (which quickly became a very exaggerated tale of spectacular heroics), he rewarded Mohammed richly and made him his court wizard. Mohammed made many secret visits to the magic lair of his old master and discovered many more treasures and secrets. These he used for the good of all, rescuing his old mother from poverty and eventually marrying the princess. But the adventures he had in winning her and his many other disasters and triumphs are different stories for different days.

General note

The stories of Mohammed Shattira (Mohammed the Clever) are traditional Egyptian tales. I first came across the model for the tale above in the notes to Burton's nineteenth-century *Alif Layla Wa Layla* (*The Arabian Nights*). However, I have simplified and altered it here, missing out an episode in which Mohammed escapes from the wizard with the ability to change himself into a camel, a horse and a dog, being caught again before escaping in something not unlike the magic chase sequence included here and pulling in some features of other magic chase tales – of which there are very many in folk literature. (See also the magic chase game in Chapter 8.)

Story map

1. The wizard takes Mohammed on as apprentice but teaches him no magic.
2. Mohammed reads the magic book secretly and decides to escape.
3. Mohammed becomes a dove but the wizard becomes an eagle.
4. Mohammed becomes a fish; the wizard becomes a crocodile.
5. Mohammed becomes a date on a tree; the wizard becomes a boy.
6. Mohammed becomes the ring on the princess's finger; the wizard becomes the chief eunuch with a message to give up the ring.
7. Mohammed becomes a watermelon seed; the wizard becomes a rat.
8. Mohammed becomes a stone; the wizard becomes a hammer.
9. Mohammed becomes a silk veil; the wizard becomes fire.
10. Mohammed becomes water and puts out the fire. End of the wizard.
11. Final stages – Mohammed made court wizard, etc.

Landmarks

Wizard's lair – secret cellar – magic book - magic chase (dove/eagle – fish/
crocodile – date/boy – ring of princess/chief eunuch – watermelon seed/rat
– veil/flame – water) – princess and court.

Chain

A chain or list of events is central in this story, in the famous motif of the
magic chase, which is explored further in Chapter 8 through a story game.

Simple three-stage frame

- *Beginning:* Mohammed works for the wizard and finds a way to read the
  magic book.
- *Middle:* The magic chase, with a series of eight paired changes until
  Mohammed wins.
- *End:* Things work out well for Mohammed.

The taming of Fenris

From his high silver throne in the heavens, Father Odin could spy on all that was
happening in the world. Something he saw one time as he looked down he did
not like at all. Something he saw made him shudder. In the darkness of a cave
somewhere in the centre of the world, three eggs were hatching. From the first
came a giantess, ugly and enormous and dangerous. From the second came
a serpent, again ugly, again dangerous, again large – very large and growing
longer by the minute. From the third came a wolf, and it too began to grow bigger and bigger. These were the children of Loki, god of mischief.

Odin called all the gods and they agreed on a plan. These three creatures,
left to themselves, would soon take over the world. Something had to be done,
and Odin set out to do it. To the giantess, whose name was Hel, he gave the
underworld to rule as goddess of death. To the snake, Jormungund, he gave
the oceans. That snake grew longer and longer still; to this day it lies stretched
right around the centre of the earth beneath the waves, biting its tail. The pulses
of its icy blood along its cold, smooth body make the waves and the tides.

As for the wolf, it was vicious and furiously fierce by nature, but Odin was
hopeful that the gods would be able to tame it by showing it kindness. He took
it to Asgard, the home of the gods. Gods they might have been, but not one of
them could tame Fenris. He growled and slavered and growled whenever anyone went near, snapping his huge sharp teeth and howling wildly.

So now Odin decreed that Fenris must be bound, since he could not be
trusted even in the heavens, which the evil that was in him might soon distort
and destroy. Yet, when they tried, Fenris, who by now was much bigger than
any wolf has been before or since, simply bit through the strongest chains they

could find in one bite. At length, Odin sent a messenger to the dwarves, who understood how to fashion the best of things. He set them the task of fashioning a chain to bind Fenris the wolf.

The dwarves pondered long and hard on this knotty problem; then they set to work. To make such a chain, they needed to capture six mythical things: the sound a cat's paw will make as it creeps up on a mouse, the spittle of a bird, the beard of a woman, the roots of a mountain, the dreams of a bear and the song the fishes sing beneath the ocean tides. It took time and patience and supreme cunning to gather together all of them in one place and superb craftsmanship to bind them in a magic chain that seemed less like a fetter than a strand from a spider's web.

The dwarves presented this to the gods, and in turn the gods took it to Fenris. 'Another game, Fenris!' they cooed encouragingly. 'See if you can bite through this one.'

Fenris looked at them suspiciously. The chains they had brought before had been massive. This one was very different. By now, he had learned language and he spoke in a rasping wolf growl. 'I do not trust the trickery of this chain. If you would put it on me, one of you must put their right hand into my mouth as it is done.'

The gods shrank back. None wished to lose a right hand, the hand with which they could fight and make and do. It looked as though Fenris had successfully bluffed them and would never be bound. But then Tyr, the god celebrated in the name of the second day of every week (Tuesday – Tyr's day), stepped boldly forward. He put his arm into the mouth of the wolf and put the chain the dwarves had made around his neck. Fenris pulled and struggled but could neither break nor bite through the chain – though he could bite easily enough through Tyr's arm and eat his hand.

So it was that that Fenris, spirit of evil, was bound by the gods. So it was that Tyr, god of war, lost his right hand, his sword hand. And, if there is a special meaning in that or if there is not, it's for you to decide and not for me to say.

General note

There are many variations on this vivid tale from Norse mythology. Fenris is also known as Fenrir and by other names too. At first sight, the story might seem to pose a larger memorizing challenge, if only because one seems to need to know something of Norse mythology (who Odin and Tyr are, what Asgard is, the nature of Loki, Odin's habit of scanning the world from a tower or high silver throne), whilst the names are unfamiliar and hence easy to forget and there is a bizarre list of ingredients for the magic chain in the middle. However, the structure of the tale is not difficult, whilst some details are extras (the names of the giantess and the snake, the silver throne, Asgard, etc.). It's a shame, though, not to have the central list, but that can be handled as a separate memorizing challenge (see below). Incidentally, for advanced memorizers, more details can be added by researching this story a little – the names of the chains the gods tried first, for example, or what happened to Fenris afterwards.

Story map

1. Father Odin scans world from high throne. (Optional extra mythical information.)
2. Sees three beings hatching: giantess (Hel), snake (Jormungund) and wolf (Fenris the evil).
3. Gives giantess the underworld, gives snake the oceans and takes Fenris to Asgard for gods to tame.
4. Gods can't tame Fenris, so he must be bound. Breaks chains.
5. Dwarves make rope from six special ingredients (see list below).
6. Fenris suspicious. Makes bargain with Tyr, the god of war – hand in mouth.
7. Fenris bound. Tyr loses hand. Question about meaning.

Possible landmarks

Silver throne – three beings hatching in cave (giantess, snake and wolf) – Fenris breaks chains – dwarves' chain (six ingredients) – hand in mouth – fine chain holding Fenris.

List memorizing

The list at the centre of the story is another kind of memorizing challenge. There are only six parts of the chain – some lists in traditional stories are much longer. However, although this is literally a chain, there is no link between the separate images. In order to memorize them, one has to go through the list and make a vivid image in the mind for each of them. It may help to link them, by for example imagining them spread out along a familiar path or road or in different places in a room one knows – or simply in the landscape of the story. This can all be handled as a memorizing challenge:

1. the sound of a cat's paw when creeping up on a bird;
2. the spittle of a bird;
3. the beard of a woman;
4. the roots of a mountain;
5. the dreams of a bear;
6. the song of the fishes beneath the ocean waves.

(See also Chapter 7, 'Listing'.)

Simplified frame

- Odin sees giantess, snake and wolf hatch from eggs in cave.
- Giantess gets underworld, snake gets oceans, wolf (Fenris) taken to Asgard.
- Gods can't tame him, try to bind him and fail.
- Dwarves make very fine, strange chain (see list).
- Fenris suspicious. Makes bargain with Tyr.
- Fenris bound. Tyr loses hand.

Memorizing longer stories

The two tales above are still quite brief. A skilled storyteller might elaborate them to fill between 10 and 15 minutes, possibly a little more. Yet there are stories that can take an hour and more to tell. How does a person learn long stories like that? The answer is that longer stories, especially if they are from oral traditions, break down into episodes that are essentially smaller stories. Hence memorizing a long story is not unlike recalling a chain of tales; in order to do that, one either formally or at least mentally breaks the story down into stages in exactly the same way as we have done above. (Performing storytellers may punctuate a long tale by playing music or putting in songs or riddles or tricks and so on at suitable points in the story, effectively breaking it up into episodes.) A good example of a longer wonder tale which breaks down into stages in this way is 'The water of life' from the Brothers Grimm,[2] which is structured around the classic three brothers/sisters style of plot (see Chapter 7).

The memory challenge

You can give memorizing some impetus and cachet by setting up a story memorizing challenge. It can be within a class or year group or, perhaps during a book week or other special focus event, across the whole school. Maybe you will set a list of possible stories to be memorized according to age and experience, with some stories described as simple, some of medium difficulty and some advanced.

- A simple story would be quite short and relatively simple – like the short fables and jokes included earlier in the chapter.

- A story of medium to easy difficulty might be one of those same stories with more elaboration cunningly applied (see Chapter 7) or might be an easier three wishes story (again see Chapter 7) or a tale with a chain of events that helps to fix it (as in the magic chase as the centre of 'Mohammed and the magician').
- A story of medium to hard level might have a more complicated structure or perhaps some mythology or a list to recall (as in 'The taming of Fenris' above).
- A more difficult tale might be a longer wonder or fairy tale with several episodes with subplots, etc.
- An advanced tale might involve tales within tales or a combination of lists and mythology and devious twists.

The memorizing challenge can be combined with stretching a tale in interesting ways, as in Chapter 7. One way to handle the logistics of hearing every pupil tell a story to the whole class or group is to get participants to test each other in pairs, trios or small groups. (They could play basic elaboration questioning games described in the next chapter whilst doing so.) Groups could nominate one or two members each to tell their stories to the whole class or larger workshop group. In a whole school challenge, classes can nominate perhaps two or three tellers (or groups of tellers) to present their memorized stories or sets of tales in an assembly or special event.

7

Stretching stories

The longer it gets, the shorter the road. What is it?

Framing ideas: stretching skill

Solomon Grundy,
Born on Monday,
Christened on Tuesday,
Married on Wednesday,
Took ill on Thursday,
Worse on Friday,
Died on Saturday,
Buried on Sunday.
This is the end
Of Solomon Grundy.

It's a strange little conundrum: a whole life in ten short lines. A whole life – but not a whole life story, not really. That is the humour of the thing; it leaves you guessing, even after you've worked out that the days don't have to be in the same week or even the same year. Who was this Solomon Grundy? Where did he live? What did he do? What was the illness that carried him off? Who was sad when he met his end? Was he really young when he died or did he confound the expectation created in the rhyme and actually live to a ripe old age? It's teasing and tantalizing.

A story sets up questions. Usually a storyteller anticipates and answers a lot of those questions before they are asked, as she or he shapes and tells the tale. It's what makes the story engaging. You can have a plot, you can have a synopsis of what happens, you can summarize and abbreviate as much as you like, but most of us know that that doesn't add up to a story. Most stories, to work as stories, have to be stretched. The more you stretch a story, the longer and more involved they could get. Answer all those questions at the end of the last paragraph fully, sparing no interesting and engaging detail, and you might just find that you have a Man Booker Prize-winning Solomon Grundy novel on your hands.

In Chapter 3, we found that asking questions about a big fib turns it into something of a story, which grows the more curious you get about it until you have a tall tale to tell. In Chapter 4, we saw how a tale shared between people and passed on through generations grows and develops even more and can even become a kind of truth. In Chapter 5, we went back inside the mind to find how the dreaming, metaphorical mind picks up on and develops the clues in a story almost automatically, whilst Chapter 6 laid down the basis for internalizing story structures. In this chapter, the starting point is elaboration itself, taken firstly as a natural talent, not unrelated to fibbing, dreaming and myth making, and then as a developed art and craft involving teachable skills.

There are, incidentally, some important differences between the way you elaborate a story on the page and the way you elaborate an oral story. There are vital overlaps too, but a told story is a direct interaction between teller and audience. So it has to be flexible – something that changes a little or a lot each time, because people are different and circumstances and times are different. With a written story, on the other hand, one attempts to shape an ideal expression of the story, cutting and polishing and refining. These don't have to be mutually exclusive; the one approach balances the other. If you think about it, both the improvisational, 'think-on-your feet' way and the carefully considered 'word sculpting' are of more or less equal value day to day in many work and life situations beyond the craft of creating and telling tales.

A tale for stretching

This magical tale, presented in brief, largely unornamented and neutral 'plain English', suggests a lot of possibilities for elaboration. It's possible to engage audiences of any age with it, suitably adapted. We'll find out some of the ways this can be done in ensuing sections to make a template for work with pupils on other stories.

The queen's palace

There was once a queen who had the finest palace in all the world. At least, that is what her loyal subjects told her, though somehow she doubted them. Perhaps somewhere there was a grander royal residence, a more magnificent ruler. She dearly wanted her palace to be truly the best.

An old woman came to her with a ring, claiming that it could give three wishes. The queen soon tried that ring, not expecting it to work, but being very certain of what she wanted for her first wish as she wished it. She doubted she would ever need the second and third wishes anyway, because she wished for her palace to become the greatest there had ever been or could be, containing all knowledge and every kind of delight.

In no time at all, the palace was growing magically, brick by brick, then wall by wall and mile by mile, until it stretched out as far as the eye could see. Excitedly the queen ran to explore this amazing edifice and found wonders beyond imagining, with fascinating knowledge of all kinds in room after room and courtyard after courtyard. For a whole year, she wandered through the stupendous building, finding ever new and more incredible things to see and do each day, served by magical servants who seemed to know exactly what she needed whenever she needed it. At length, though, she was weary with it all and desperate to return to familiar sights and sounds, but these she could not find. Everything was always different and new.

In desperation, the queen cried out 'This is far too big! I wish there were much less of it!' Since she still had the ring on her finger, most of the palace vanished instantly, including the distant quarter in which she had been standing. She found herself in the midst of a wilderness on the far borders of the realm. What is more, the sudden change had left her with no memory of the power of the ring on her finger, which could have saved her at once.

Staggering for miles along a dusty track, she came to a village and informed the people there that she was their queen. She commanded them to take her back to the city. Of course, they thought her only some mad woman and, though they treated her kindly, they did nothing to return her to her throne. She had no choice but to live with them and share their simple life for two whole years. One day in a rare moment when there were no chores to do, she found herself toying absent-mindedly with the magic ring. Suddenly it came to her that she was indeed a queen, not a mad woman, that she could use this ring to escape. Soon she found herself back in her own palace, with the old woman grinning toothlessly at her. Only three minutes had passed since she put the magic ring on her finger and made her first wish. She had never left the throne room, so the courtiers insisted, though the queen herself always believed otherwise. She certainly no longer wished for a finer palace than the one she had already.[1]

The three wishes

There are many versions of the three wishes plot – including a fair number of joke versions.[2] (Asking for three wishes tales usually brings out at least a couple of these from any group of pupils, and that can be a good way to start the ball rolling as well as encouraging plot comparison – there is an example in Chapter 6, 'Three wishing cells'. You may, however, want to establish some rules about acceptability for the school context in advance, since it's a popular theme in rude humour – though offering the odd tale of one's own that is just a little risqué gives the exercise 'street cred' with older pupils.) Wishes plots are simple to learn – the pattern of the three wishes is another 'sticky' one; it's also easy to use it creatively to make new tales, a theme we'll explore in the next chapter, where you will find a game for playing with this plot. The initial challenge, however, is to get this version to stretch out and grow in an interesting way.

Basic elaboration

Embroidery (key elaboration game)

Here's a questioning game not unlike 'Fantastic fibs', drawing on the liar and lawyer, this time to stretch an existing plot almost effortlessly. Again my version dates back 30-plus years to my early teaching experience.[3] It works very well with the above plot (or similar wishing tales) and with very many other (usually shortish) tales. The version here is adapted from my booklet *Yarn Spinning* (2007b), which includes a series of story games that complement work in this chapter.

Young children soon learn that, if they ask questions about the story they have been told or read, the story gets longer and more interesting – not to mention the fun of watching the mental squirming the adult does. 'Embroidery' formalizes that process in a game played in pairs or in groups large or small.

- One person will tell a story. It could be a story made up earlier through a 'Fantastic fibs' game or a legend or a tale based on guided imagining. It could be a traditional story or any other kind of suitable yarn. The story-teller has to know it well enough to repeat it without a script.

- A time limit is set for the story, usually between three and five minutes for a shorter tale (i.e. one that could be summarized in a minute or so). The storyteller aims to tell the story within the limit. The partner or the rest of the group try to stop him or her doing that.

- The storyteller must pause at the end of any sentence, at which point the partner or group will ask questions about the story so far. Lawyer questioning patterns are used to draw out as much detail as possible, so that the storyteller gets lost in it. In a first try at the game, one question only might be asked. In subsequent rounds this can increase to two or three at each pause. (More than this may make the game too long – though, as a fun party game, endless frustrating questions can be asked.)

- The storyteller must answer all reasonable questions. Clever storytellers may connect their answers immediately with the main narrative, smuggling in some more progress with the main plot before pausing for questioning.

- The game continues until either the story is finished or the time limit is up.

- (Optional) Go back over the story, noting as much of the extra detail as can be recalled. Write the elaborated story or tell it on in elaborated form in a 'Pass it on' round or two.

Three example questions for the opening of 'The queen's palace'

- When and where did all this happen?
- Can you describe the queen's palace before the wishes?
- Why did the queen want to have the best palace in the world?

Answers woven into a new opening narrative

(See also 'Beginning', page 117–118.)

So much time has gone by since that no one knows quite whose time it was. So many empires have come and gone that no one knows in which land it all happened. Wherever it was and whenever it was, it was someone's time, not yours, not mine, but certainly the queen's time. She was young, she was ambitious and she very much liked to have her own way. She also very much wanted to make her own mark on the kingdom her father had left her, especially on the grand palace in which she lived. It was built of the purest white stone, with gates of burnished gold. Fountains of silvery waters tinkled into crystal clear pools in the magnificent gardens; the heady scents of ten thousand flowers every colour of the rainbow filled the air. Inside the palace itself, there were rooms filled with wonders and treasures . . .

Using the dreaming mind with a story

Purposely imagining one's way through stories allows details to emerge almost effortlessly. This may have already come up through (for example) 'Seeing it through' (page 97) and other exercises in the last two chapters. These can be developed a little further.

Explorations (a mental routine)

'Embroidery' is played inside the mind, as a mental imaginative discipline:

- Map, landmark and frame an existing story.
- Think of three questions about each stage (using questioning skills developed in 'Embroidery').
- Answer these mentally, simultaneously 'seeing' the answers using different imagining modes.
- Zoom in and out on details.

'The queen's palace': seven-stage map

1. Palace, queen and her strong desire.
2. Getting the wishes: old woman brings them.
3. Using first wish and consequences: the amazing palace (details?).
4. Limits of the first wish.
5. Using the second wish.
6. Bad results of the second wish leading to use of the third wish.
7. Back to the palace as it was, but with a change in the queen's mind.

Memory landmarks

Queen – palace – old woman – ring – wish one: incredible palace – wish two: palace vanishes – wish three: back to throne – three years = three minutes.

Simpler frame

- Beginning: queen and palace.
- Middle: three wishes and extraordinary palace.
- End: back to the palace.

Watch it (imagining challenge)

Start from the 'Explorations' exercise above or from 'Seeing it through' in the last chapter. When a story has already been clearly imagined through, try watching the details of the story unfold whilst hearing and watching yourself as if you were someone else telling the story. This is best presented as a challenge ('You probably can't do this . . .' 'A few people find they can . . .') – it's not so much being able to do this 'trick' as trying that is interesting.

Discoveries (competitive task)

Group or class members are given a few minutes to mentally and imaginatively explore the same story outline (without writing anything). They then have several more minutes to list as many new discoveries about the story (extra detail, unexpected incidental events and characters, places that could be described and so on) as they can. This can be handled as a note-making task (in story clouds or anything effective) or, alternatively, as a more extended writing task involving brief descriptions. The competition element (if included) can be in seeing who can come up with the most extra discoveries. However, discoveries can be challenged by other group or class members if the discoveries do not seem to make sense when shared. They will then have to be explained by the 'teller' in order to be included in the final tally.

Discoveries about 'The queen's palace'

- *Younger:* In the magic palace, there is a room filled with games, toys and distractions. Next to this is a room filled with every kind of food and beyond that a room of costumes, fabulous clothes and strange disguises . . .
- *Older:* In one of the rooms, there is a map of every country there has ever been or will be on this earth, including some long since vanished under the ocean and some that have not yet come to be in places that would seem impossible even today . . .
- *Either with adjustment:* You can find magic potions and flying carpets in one of the rooms and study wizardry and witchcraft . . . There are rooms full of strange contraptions, horrors, thrills or adventures . . .

The role of role-play

Another way to develop detail and different perspectives in a story is to use role-play or empathy games like this one:

- Group or class members take it in turns to be a character in the story. In 'The queen's palace', they could be the queen herself, a courtier or servant at the palace, the old woman, a person from the village, etc. For a group, you can allocate roles to each person, perhaps by random choice (slips in hats or boxes), perhaps by volunteering.

- The group asks each character a series of 'lawyer' questions (probably between five and ten) about plot details he or she should know, things 'seen', etc., or about his or her motivations or feelings at different stages of the story and so on.

- Each character aims to convince listeners that he or she is the character (or, if you like, has a direct psychic line to that person's mind), answering the questions in character. (If confident with the idea, some might 'voice-act' the part, even adopt supposed physical style and mannerisms and so on, though this is not essential to the game.) As in 'Fantastic fibs' and other questioning games, what he or she says is true as long as it seems to match the story, though can lead to further questions.

Role-play perspectives on 'The queen's palace'

- You are the old woman (or, adjusting the plot, old man) with the ring. Tell us about the ring and its power, why you brought it to the queen, etc.

- (Group) You are people from the poor village. Tell us what you thought of the queen and what it was like having her to stay.

Rules and tricks of elaboration

Don't bore and confuse; do fascinate and engage: these would probably be reckoned the fundamental rules of any kind of storytelling. As with most arts, any rules in storytelling are there to be broken – when you understand them. In oral storytelling you get an immediate feedback, since you can see and sense when your audience is not with you, which is often a prompt for changing tack – hence the necessary 'bendiness' of the rules. But learning those bendy rules is well worth it: they reveal the tricks of the trade used to keep people listening or to re-engage them as necessary as well as to start and end elegantly. What's more, they are very creative places to work from with children, teaching them a lot about communication in general and feeding into improved written work.

Here is an outline of some basic rules and tricks, followed by some techniques for introducing them as ideas and practising them.

Beginning

Every teacher of literacy knows that you need to teach the art of making an interesting story start as pupils develop beyond basics. Every teacher of literacy also knows that it is not infrequently hard to wean pupils off the standard story formulae – 'One day . . .', 'Once there was . . .' and 'Long ago . . .' being some of the most obvious ones. Oral tradition has a lot to offer here because one can reassess the function of those standard formulae. That's where they started out, as spoken signals that story country is about to be visited.

An oral storyteller needs to draw an audience in, to announce the story. But, if too much vital plot information is put into the opening sentences, there is a chance that listeners won't take it in – they won't have switched in. The standard opener is part of the 'switching-in' process. You get them in very many cultures. Those from remote places may sound exotic, but they may firstly have similar functions to those of 'Once upon a time . . .'

Here are some common purposes for the standard opener:

1. an (approximately) agreed social signal that a story is starting;
2. (sometimes) something that requires a response from listeners – chorusing back words and phrases, etc., actively participating in the classic call and response, building up a feeling of involvement (see also Chapter 11);
3. (sometimes) an intriguing or baffling bit of language, a paradox, a riddle that gets people thinking and curious;
4. (sometimes) a mini-story that leads into the main story;
5. (quite often) a metaphor that encourages listeners to go into imagining, metaphorical mode.

Some traditional examples follow. As some fulfil more than one of these functions, I've put 'function numbers' corresponding to the list above after them. This is just my opinion; you are welcome to disagree. A good exercise with older pupils is to teach them the ideas above and then show them formulae like these and ask them to list what they think are their purposes at the head of a story. You can find plenty more examples from the hundreds collected by the remarkable American-French storyteller Sam Cannarozzi, a selection of which have been published by the Society for Storytelling in a booklet called *When Tigers Smoked Pipes* (Cannarozzi 2008), from which examples marked SC below have been taken. (This makes a very handy reference work for creative storytelling work on the pattern below, incidentally.)

- 'Once upon a time when the sun was just born and the moon was no bigger than a star . . .' Moldavia, SC (1, 3, 5, possibly 4).

- 'Stories come and stories go, and if this isn't a lie then the truth you will know . . .' Catalonia, SC (1, 3, 4).

- 'I'll tell you a story that's true – as true as I can make it on the day . . .' Anon. (1, 4).

- 'Beyond seven tall mountains and seven raging seas, beyond seven forests and thrice nine strange and empty lands . . .' Russian (1, 3, 4, 5).

- Teller: 'Siri!' (A story!) The listeners: 'Nam!' (Let it be!) Mali, SC (1, 2).

- Teller: 'How many ears do you have?' Listeners: 'Two.' Teller: 'Then find yourself a third one and listen to what I say . . .' Haiti, SC (1, 2, 3, 5).

- 'There was at the heart of the world a gigantic beech tree with its roots deep in the earth and its high branches scraping the sky. I saw it myself so I know that it's so. On the highest of those branches was sitting an old man whose beard almost touched the ground. He told me the ancient and wonderful and incredible tale that I'll tell to you . . .' Hungary, SC (3, 4, 5, possibly 1).

Formulae like these easily lend themselves to creative variation. Some activities around varying and developing standard openers follow. You can invent more around the formulae above or others.

Once upon a time . . . (variation on game from Yarn Spinning)

Threadbare and worn perhaps, but the old formula can be creatively restored to something like its original function in a fun oral game for beginning a session around stories:

- You come up with one or more examples of variations on the pattern, e.g. 'Once upon a strange time when seagulls squawked the truth and fish danced the tango . . .', 'Once upon a fantasy time when mountains could talk and forests could fly . . .'

- Next challenge the group to come up with more variations: 'Once upon a (. . .) time when (. . .) . . .' Class or group members can take it in turns or simply volunteer ideas, or you might make it into a team game:

  > Team 1 says 'Once upon a (. . .) time . . .', i.e. they specify what kind of time (funny, peculiar, future, ancient, puzzling, mathematical, etc.).
  > Team 2 answers 'when (. . .)', i.e. adding something to roughly match the kind of time it is supposed to be (e.g. mathematical: 'when triangles had no corners and wheels were square').
  > Team 2 starts a second 'Once up a (. . .) time . . .' and Team 1 responds.

There are very many creative possibilities in this game, so it's worth repeating on different occasions, with prompts to ensure variation and development. You can play quite similar games with formulae like 'Long and long and very long ago . . .', 'In a far and distant land and a far and distant time . . .', 'Beyond seven powers and seven seas . . .', etc. (See *Yarn Spinning* for some variations.)

Why is my story like a fish?

An oral riddling game like this one provides a great way to practise simile making and metaphorical thinking in general.

- First draw either on playing-card-size pieces of paper or on card pictures of things to compare a story to (fish, elephant, mountain, ocean, city, road, etc.) or simply write these words on slips of paper. Place in a hat or box.
- Players take it in turns to take cards or slips from the hat or box. A good way to do this initially in a class is for a group nominee to choose on behalf of a group, who will then work together to 'solve' the riddle.
- They must now compare a story they might tell to this object ('My story is like a fish because it is slippery and hard to catch . . .' 'My story is like a fish. If you want to see how fishes live, you must dive into the water. If you want to see how my story lives, you must dive into your imagination').
- Answers are only wrong if they are not really effective metaphors ('My story is like a fish because it stinks . . .').

On the basis of this game, you can then create new story openers, e.g. 'Listen to this story, everyone, because it's slippery and hard to catch like a fish. Like a fisherman, you need to concentrate now, so set the net of your mind . . .'

The tall tree

The last traditional opener above from Hungary, about the beech tree and the old man, has parallels in many other 'mini-story' openers from world traditions (see for example 'The bright yellow bird' in *Yarn Spinning*). Reducing it to an abstract framework, you get something like this:

1. I saw something impossibly large or otherwise miraculously different (the tall beech tree).
2. Somewhere on or in it was a person with an impossible feature (the long beard).
3. This person told the story . . .

Here's an example of a creative reinterpretation:

1. I went into a house as big as a city, casting a shadow a hundred miles long.
2. The cellars beneath it were ten miles deep, and in the darkest, deepest corners of those cellars I met a child two thousand years old.
3. She told me this story by the light of a glow-worm . . .

You can set the task of creatively reinterpreting this and patterns like it.

- First give and discuss the examples above (or other examples).
- Then get pupils to work in pairs.
- If doing this as a writing task, both write a first line giving the impossible thing seen. They then swap papers to do the second, in which the person who told the story appears.
- If doing this as an oral creative game, player one makes up the first line, player two continues, and player one recites the final line, suitably adapted (or embellished a little, as in my example reworking). Then player two begins another round, which player one continues, followed by player two's conclusion, and so on.

The rule or rhythm of three 1: stock descriptions

If you describe something or someone or somewhere, the description generally sounds complete when you have described three features. If you give three reasons why this or that was or is or should be, you will sound as though you know what you are talking about. If you mention three 'insider facts' about a country, people will think you've been there. Somehow or other, we look for that rhythm of three in speech – and indeed in writing. (Look back at the way I have structured this paragraph so far for an example.) You can hear the rhythm of three in the rhetoric of politicians and other public speakers, in the patter of comedians or the ranting of rappers, or in the way copywriters structure their ads, but you can also spot it in day-to-day talk.

In oral storytelling, the rule of three gives you a quick way of describing a person or a place. It also helps you to establish plot elements and character attributes quickly. A land is suffering from a series of disasters, so you describe three of them and, for the audience, it's enough to go on; their imaginations can fill in the rest. A person is lucky, so you describe three lucky things about her or three things she does that bring her unusual luck and we get the picture. More might tax our patience.

Some creative activities for teaching threes description are as follows.

Description challenges

- Explain the principle of a traditional description in three and give examples, e.g. an enchantress ('She was as cunning as a fox, quick to anger as fire kindled in a dry forest is to spread through the baked bushes, and strange and slippery as a silver serpent') or an old beggar ('He was so crooked and bent that his gnarled old nose seemed to knock on his knees, the coat on his back had more holes in it than fabric, and his fingers were thin as dead twigs and looked twice as brittle').

- Set three stock character types (or beings or locations, etc.) from traditional tales and ask the class or group to experiment with creating three-point descriptions of each of them (with a similar feel to the examples) through writing or group brainstorming or both. (Examples of stock characters, beings and locations could include wizards and witches, giants, monsters, kings and queens, poor men and women, merchants, knights, tricksters, fools, dragons, aliens, castles, palaces, forests and caves. You can also go to the stock characters in different styles of fiction – gangsters or geeks or ghosts, for example.) With refinement, these can make good short display pieces in themselves, similar to short poems, especially set out on three lines, with a line for each point in the description.

Chance likeness (oral game for improvising descriptions)

- Have a list of stock characters, locations, beings, etc. like that above displayed on the board or screen (or give them out on a prepared sheet).

- In advance, you will have prepared a series of slips of paper or cards on which are a random series of (say) 30 to 50 nouns (hammer, stone, sword, ring, tree, wood, elephant, banana, tap, water, fire, coin, table, box, cloak, shoe, etc.). Alternatively, you can get the class to contribute several suggested random nouns, each on folded slips. Slips or cards are placed in a suitably attractive story box or bag. Shuffle them in front of the group to add a little drama.

- Individuals or (in a larger group or whole class) teams pick or are allocated a stock character, being or location. They take it in turns to make a blind choice of three cards or slips from the bag or box.

- The stock character must now be compared to each of those things in turn to make a three-point description. For example, supposing I get 'giant' from the list and then draw 'hammer', 'elephant' and 'fire' from the bag or box, I might (after some work and refinement) come up with something like this:

> His heart was as hard as a hammer that has knocked in a thousand nails.
>
> He was as insensitive to the feelings of his victims as an elephant's hide is to ant bites.
>
> And his appetite for human flesh burned inside him like a furious furnace.

This is sometimes easy to do, sometimes hard – some random juxtapositions of ideas are easier than others to work with. Players unfamiliar with the idea will usually need time to think. Classes and smaller groups can talk it through and brainstorm; individuals could try some creative thinking strategies – jotting down lists of possibilities, trying them out each in turn, allowing for completely crazy contrasts, 'wrong notes', etc. With repetition, it will become more natural and quick. Meanwhile, it's best to be encouraging – problems are there to be solved. You might allow groups or individuals a second dip into the bag or box for alternatives – rules around this can evolve. The randomness stretches imagination and can encourage creativity and produce some unexpectedly dramatic or simply bizarre and funny descriptions.

Nice snouts and nasty noses (oral game)

This game is again similar to one in my *Yarn Spinning* booklet, originally invented by Ruth Herbert. It is for two people (or teams), though can work with more.

- First agree a (for school purposes respectable) part of human and animal bodies (noses, knees, feet, hands, paws, snouts, etc.) and a quality (nice/ nasty; beautiful/foul; intelligent/stupid, etc.). You might again make the choice using random choice cards or slips, or simply decree the choice to save argument.
- Players now take it in turns to swap lists of three qualities of the snout or nose or whatever. These can be 'real-world' or completely fantastical.

For example, a nice snout:

> Covered with delicate silky white fur
> and whiskers like fine gold thread,
> it is tipped with a soft, liquorice-black nose.

Or a nasty nose:

> A forest of green hair sprouts out of it at all angles.
> It is covered with purple and pink boils of varying sizes.
> And the nostrils are like enormous dark and dangerous caverns.

The principle in this game can be transferred to things other than body parts, for example character attributes and psychological characteristics, powers and abilities and so on, not to mention anything from sticks to stones, planets to palaces.

'The queen's palace' (pre-wishes): three-point description

1. 'This palace was built of stone that was the pure white of a new cloud in the summer sky or angels wings or a clean conscience.'
2. 'It had golden gates and jewel-trimmed windows that shimmered as the sun rose each morning.'
3. 'And it was surrounded by gardens filled with flowers every colour of the rainbow and tinkling fountains of silver water.'

The rule of three 2: plots and threes

Traditional plots often also follow the rule or rhythm of three, as of course happens with a three wishes variant like 'The queen's palace'. Or in a classic fairy tale there might be three brothers or three sisters. You might hear briefly about the failures of the first two before you get the tale of the third one who succeeds. Perhaps (not invariably) in doing so, she or he will have to perform three tasks or undergo three trials in order to find and bring back as many as three marvellous things – maybe an apple that heals all ills, the cap of happiness and the magic bird of truth. Or maybe it is one wonderful thing that has three special and extraordinary attributes, such as a ring that can give you strength, beauty and knowledge. You can easily find examples if you want to tell or read out a model story. One already mentioned is 'The water of life' from *Grimm's Fairy Tales*. The hundreds of other examples (from recommended collections) include beautiful wonder tales such as the

Russian 'The feather of Finist the Falcon' (Lines 1985: 31 or Wheeler 1995: 181), the Italian 'The fine green bird' (Calvino 1982: 315), 'The bulbul bird' from Latvia (Cole 1982: 395) and 'Farizad of the roses smile' from *The Arabian Nights* (Mardrus and Mathers 1986: 439).

Evolving a threes plot (plot structure and rhythm)

You can set a creative writing or storytelling task that involves following the rhythm of three in a plot. The set requirements might be:

- The story is about three characters.
- Each character has three particular qualities.
- Characters can (optionally) be described using the three-point description scheme as above.
- And/or each character will get three special (possibly magical) gifts.
- Each character goes on a journey to find three things (fairy tale example – fruit from the garden of life, the hat of happiness, the ring of truth).
- Each will face three dangers (enchantments, monsters, tasks, riddles, etc.).
- The first two will fail but the third will succeed.

Whilst this seems to imply a fantasy or fairy tale setting (as in my examples), this plot can be worked out in much more contemporary ways, at a level to suit the age, ability and interests of pupils. Requirements of the plot can be varied, of course – this is not a set formula.

Subverting the three

Experienced speakers often play with the expectation of three points, examples, features, etc., perhaps by stopping on only two, with the tantalizing suggestion of a third not mentioned. Traditional plots also cheat the expectation of three occasionally,[4] whilst modern children's writers have been known to play with this expectation and rhythm.

Activity

Once pupils have experience of creating threes, get them to experiment with two-point descriptions and see which sound complete and which seem to need a missing third.

The rhythm of three 3: dreaming awake

Five senses/three things (imaginative exercise)

As a back-up to descriptive work with any story, you can develop earlier imagining routines specifying the five (or six) 'sensory modes' in turn – sight, sound, smell, taste, touch plus the gestalt 'feel' of it.

- First map, landmark and frame the story or, if evolving a new plot, set out a rough common plan (as above).
- Discuss ways of imagining stressing use of the senses.
- Establish the imagining mood ('Imagination station', etc.).
- Choose the part of the story where there are (or will be) essential or incidental (but vivid) characters or places or things that can develop as landmarks or vital plot moments.
- Ask pupils to 'picture' some of these, invoking each of their five senses in turn, mentally noting three things their imaginations 'show' them about this part of the story.
- A good way to 'anchor' each noted thing, without interrupting imaginative flow, and also training memory, is to get them to go through each finger of a hand, one for each of the five senses and then the fist for the 'feel'.
- Note these (story clouds, etc.).
- Go on to dreamer and lawyer questioning and answering in pairs. Or go straight to writing about the things seen.
- Allow for the fact that quite a lot of what has been imagined may be difficult to recall initially. Repetition improves the skill.
- Also allow for differences in ease with imagining with different 'modes' – visual and 'feel' are easier for most than taste, touch and smell, whilst imagined hearing is variable.

To do a full story in this way requires a lot of mental focus and developed powers of concentration. Build up to the routine and the length of story sections, starting with particular incidents, characters and places. With younger children, you might precede this with some physical activity that disperses energy – simple stretches or maybe something more aerobic. Incidentally, working with this kind of quiet inner focus is a very important tool in the kit of the therapist or counsellor working with distractible young children – and, in the end, more effective than a lifetime course of Ritalin.

Listing

A list in a story usually has five or more features or qualities. Four features could feel as though you forgot to stop at three; as you go to five and beyond, people can sense that you are listing. A list in an oral story might be introduced when the audience is temporarily distracted and you want to freeze the action whilst you re-engage them. You might want to tease the audience at a moment of suspense or, if you can make a list bizarre and strange or very vivid and imaginative or perhaps simply funny, you might be seeking to engage them in a different way, perhaps making them lose sight of a plot element you don't want them to recall until you surprise them further on in the story.

Lists are again a creative and productive area to work on in teaching story elaboration both on and off the page.

Challenging lists (oral game)

This makes a good introduction to lists, is a fun workout for the imagination and can also be developed for further literacy/language teaching:

- Set an interesting list theme, for example fantasy clothes.
- Invite class or group members to take it in turn to see how many things they can list for (say) the fantasy clothes collection and count them as they list them (jackets made of steel, coats with working wings attached, hats that make you invisible, belts that give you strength, waistcoats that talk, etc.).
- Everything that is both an item of clothing and fantastical counts for a point. However, saying ten hopping socks or 1,000 flying pairs of pants only gives one point each, not ten or 1,000.
- As you repeat this game, you can make the challenge harder by asking for (say) as many different adjectives or adverbs (wow words) per item as possible. You might even given extra points for vivid description, use of threes in those descriptions or even including interesting wow words, metaphors, etc. ('A coat of so many clashing colours that positively insists the rainbow is dull, with enough concealed magic pockets in it to hide the entire population of a large city and the power to sidle around suggestively all by itself').
- You can also make the task easier for younger players or by way of introduction, with lists of trees or houses or cars that are simply (say) different.

- The game can also be played by two competing teams taking it in turns to add items to a list until one team can't go on so that the other wins the 'round'.

Tips for improvising lists

- Get inspiration by looking around the immediate environment. For example, what items of clothing are people wearing? Can you make them fantastic?

- Use memory. For example, think of the last time you saw lots of people outside school. What were they wearing? Make their clothes fantastical. Imagine a shop you know with lots of clothes. Imagine different departments and what is in them. Make the clothes fantastical.

Additional listing games and tips are in *Yarn Spinning*.

Lists beyond literacy

The listing principle can be applied beyond description of appearance and indeed literacy. As a 'change' exercise for some difficult, too critical or negative groups, for example, you can get them to list as many positive aspects about some (not too immediately controversial) aspect of school experience as possible in the 'Listing challenge', whilst the rest of the group pick up on and 'criticize' any stray negatives. No moral is drawn – moralizing is too easily rejected; one simply draws attention to what is good and doesn't comment on what is bad, subtly encouraging positive attitudes.

Creating and working with lists for 'The queen's palace'

- In telling or retelling this story (and other tales), you can informally ask for lists at different points. 'There was a room filled with foods of every kind, the very best in the world. But I don't know what those foods were. Maybe you do? . . .'

- Set the task of exploring at least three and up to seven rooms in the magical palace, listing three (or more) things that are in each room.

- Maybe set the task of memorizing the created lists of the different rooms that are in the palace or the different things that are in some of those rooms.

- Play 'List improvisation', as described above, with lists of rooms or things in rooms, seeing who can list the most.

More through listing

- *Alliteration through lists:* You can teach alliteration and its use through lists. For example, everything on an orally improvised or rapidly written random list must begin with the letter B – 'brown bread', 'beautiful butter', 'baked batter', 'broken bunks' and 'booted baboons'. Or perhaps a food room in the queen's palace might contain paired alliterative foods: crumpets and cakes, and tarts and tortillas, and pizzas and pies, and paninis and pretzels.

- *List songs and verse:* Many song lyrics are structured around lists. Old standards like *My Favourite Things*, classic pop like *Penny Lane* by the Beatles and many more are lists. Creating such lists follows the principles above, but adds the demands of disciplining the list into a verse structure.[5]

To make a list song or poem (very approximately):

- First, jot down random lists on the theme of the song you are writing.
- Then (unless you have already made up a tune) use the model of a known song to give a working rhythmic shape and form.
- Create an opening 'scene setter' or story introduction to frame the list.
- Fit your items and others that come to mind into the rhythmic scheme.
- Use the rhythm to invent a new tune.

Listing and imaginative focus

In similar ways to those described earlier, you can use the list as an inwardly focused meditative imagining challenge, including staying with the list, returning straying thoughts to it and reviewing things 'seen'. Afterwards, there can be discussion about this or debriefing through questioning and so on.

Motivations

Both three-point descriptions and listing can help you build a better impression of a character and his or her motivations in telling and writing stories. Generate lists (and threes) by asking 'lawyer' questions about the character. Note that sometimes the sense an established story plot makes is altered by the way you handle the answers in a list.

Motivation questions for 'The queen's palace'

- Why did the queen want a good palace?
- Why did she think she could cheat the three wishes?
- What really interested her amongst the wonderful rooms?
- Why didn't she like the magical palace in the end?
- What was it like living in the poor village?

Framing stories and tales within tales

Perhaps the best introduction to the idea of framing stories and tales within tales is the well-known tale that holds together *The Arabian Nights*, the tale of Shahrazad (Scheherazade), the clever daughter of the king's wazir (adviser). In case you don't know this one, in summary the king's first beloved wife had betrayed him (probably best to leave out the steamy details of exactly how and with whom for the school context). Because of this, he believed that all women were wicked. He hence developed the unpleasant habit of marrying one on a day, spending one night with her and having her beheaded in the morning. The last maidens suitable for marriage were Shahrazad and her little sister, Dunyazad. Shahrazad volunteered to marry the king. On the first evening, she began to tell him a story but (accidentally on purpose) left it unfinished when the hour for going to bed arrived, so that the king decided not to kill her until he had heard the rest at the time for telling stories the following evening, when she finished a tale and began another, which she again left unfinished, so that he again spared her until the following night, when she finished and began another . . . And so on and so on she went, finishing and beginning new stories each evening, sometimes weaving a whole series of stories together which took several nights to complete, always leaving the king in suspense so that he should not kill her. After one thousand and one nights of this (and 350-plus separate stories), the king told her that he had long since decided to spare her, no longer believed in the wickedness of all women and indeed loved her.

Another example of a framing story for short tall tales of wonder is to be found in 'The voyage of Mael Dun' (see Chapter 4). Amongst many other tales framed with tales, there is also *Kalila and Dimna* or *The Fables of Bidpai*, the Persian/Middle Eastern retelling of the ancient Indian *Panchatantra*, Boccaccio's *Decameron* and of course Chaucer's *Canterbury Tales*. Interrupting tales to begin others is not done in all of these – though of course the technique is familiar to many much closer to home as the technique of the soap, which runs several stories simultaneously, interrupting one to develop another and so on.

Framing stories: story challenge

- Develop a set of your own versions of traditional stories, perhaps with some original tall tales and likely legends.
- Invent a story about a storyteller or a series of storytellers who will tell these stories (framing story).
- Present the stories inside the framing story in a telling or in book form.

This is also a good way of doing a group presentation for an assembly, open evening or special event. Create a frame story and have a series of individual storytellers (or groups of storytellers) to tell the stories. This is most lively if the stories are told, but can be done with a mixture of storytelling and reading – especially if presented with some music (see Chapter 10).

Tales within tales: a scheme for advanced storytellers

To develop the tales-within-tales technique for live performance of stories or as a writing experiment, you can challenge pupils to work out an interlocking of stories (or work out a version with them, again for a presentation of some kind) using a pattern like this one:

- *Story 1:* Tell the first story to an interesting point; then find an excuse to start a second story. Perhaps a character within the first story starts to tell a story. Perhaps the first story is being told by someone who is reminded of another story by the part of that first story he or she has reached. Perhaps there is another reason altogether.
- *Story 2:* Tell the second story to another 'cliff hanger' moment; then find another excuse to start a third one. (Perhaps again a character in the second story starts to tell a story . . . Perhaps the character in the second story finds a book and reads the third story in it . . .)
- *Story 3, centrepiece:* You can tell all of the third story as the 'centrepiece'. Alternatively, introduce a fourth and then a fifth story and even more until you get to the centrepiece, though if you want to hold the attention of an audience with a series of unfinished tales there are limits. Three stories is an achievable number for the school context.
- *Story 2 again:* Once the central story is completed, find a reason to go back to the second story. (The reason may come naturally enough out of

the excuse for starting it – the storyteller in the second story has finished telling the tale, etc.)

- *Story 1 again:* Now find a reason to pick up and complete the first story. (Again the reason may have been established when the first story was 'abandoned'.)

Though not without complications, this gives a lot of creative possibilities for more advanced individual writers and storytellers or as a teacher-led group project. Where different classes are working on stories, it can be fun to present baffling tales within tales and framed sets of tales to each other.

'The queen's palace': a 'frame' story for the story

He looked thoughtful for a moment and then the smile lines around his mouth deepened. 'Endless wishes, you say? That's what you'd ask for from the genie? But that's against the rules – unless you're clever.'

I looked at him expectantly. I'd always reckoned it would be a crafty way to cheat the magic that always seemed to go wrong in those wishes stories – you know the ones: the sausage that ends up on the man's nose, the treasures that vanish and all that. But my grandfather wasn't having it. He shifted a little and then settled himself, looking me full in the eye as he began one of his stories. It's a tale I've always remembered, just as I've always recalled the look of my grandfather, the thick black bushy eyebrows and the strands of greying black hair on the end of his nose, the grey tufts of thinning hair still clinging to his balding head. It was a story of a queen and her wishes . . .

If I tell the story in this frame, I can go back to my grandfather at the end, or possibly remind you of the situation in the middle of the story, maybe even developing a story about something my grandfather did or said that interrupted the story. Or perhaps I will develop further stories inside the 'Queen's palace' plot.

'The queen's palace' tale as a framing story

- Perhaps when the queen meets the bringer of the ring, the old woman will tell her a story about the ring.
- Perhaps the queen herself will tell the old woman a story.
- Perhaps when she explores the magic palace she will meet magical storytellers who will tell tales of fantasy.

- Perhaps in the village she will hear different kinds of stories from the villagers . . . Perhaps the whole story will develop as a compendium of stories with a wishing and wanting theme . . .

- Perhaps it will conclude by returning to the grandfather and the remembered boy or girl (the writer's young self).

Ending

Just as there are formulaic 'openers' for stories, there are classic ways of ending stories in the oral tradition, used with many different stories. Again, the hackneyed fairy tale ending 'And they all lived happily ever after' has in common with such less well-known models at least one or two of these basic functions:

1. the agreed signal that the story is over;
2. something that might require a chorus of agreement that this is so;
3. a way of wrapping up the loose ends and lingering questions – what next? what did they do after that? etc.;
4. a bridge from the story world to everyday reality;
5. hence a presentation of something perhaps whimsical or paradoxical or metaphorical, perhaps only distantly related to the story, if at all;
6. a way of suggesting that there might be more another time;
7. a way of making you think a little about the story and its value.

Here are some examples. As with story 'openers', I've listed possible functions from the list above. Again you are welcome to disagree. Again identifying and discussing these functions (and identifying which match the 'happily ever after' one) are useful study for older pupils. And again I've drawn on Sam Cannarozzi's collection, in which you can find many more examples.

- 'And that's my story.' Scottish traveller tradition (1).

- 'Khattam shud' (The end – completely finished). Indian tradition (also the name of the evil character in *Haroun and the Sea of Stories* by Salman Rushdie (1990).[6]

- Teller: 'An animal's tail is long or short and so is a story tale. Long or short, everything must come to an end.' Listeners: 'Ahan!' (Agreed!) Buanda, Africa, SC (1, 2, 3, 4, 5).

- 'All went as well as it can for the rest of their days, and if they're not dead yet they're living to this day, if not in this world then in a world beyond this world or in a world beyond that . . .' Amalgam of formulae from different traditions – Middle East, Celtic, etc. (1, 3, 5).

- 'My story was just as true as you and I could make it, as true as me, as true as you, as true as this day and the night that will follow.' Anon. (1, 4, 5, 7).

- 'From the east and all the way to the west, may the wild ducks soon bring us the sweetness of dawn.' Mekkahiwak Indian, North America, SC (1, 3, 4, 5, possibly 2).

- 'I don't know if they lived happily, but the celebrations they had after all that lasted nine days and nine nights, and on the very last night I passed that way myself and told them one of my own tales. They liked it so well that they gave me three gold coins wrapped in a net, three snowballs in a red-hot cauldron and three amazing stories. Well, the gold fell through the net and the snow melted, but I kept the stories and one of them was the very one you just heard. As for the others, well those are for another day . . .' Adapted from various traditional formulae – Russian, European, Celtic, etc. (1, 3, 5, 6, 7).

Once again, playing with some of these and inventing more is a valuable creative exercise, teaching the 'feel' of ending, the sense of cadence, etc. as well as giving practical experience and resulting in alternatives that can be used in further oral storytelling. They can also form models for on-the-page endings. Games and ideas for varying openers and creating new ones work just as well with endings.

An ending for 'The queen's palace'

I went that way myself not long after all that happened and I told the queen a story and sang her a song. She liked them both so well that she told me her tale and introduced me to the old lady with the wishing ring. Well, first I wished for riches, but they were all soon spent, so then I wished for fame, but that was soon finished, and last I wished for someone to listen to me well, and that's how I came to be telling you that story today.

Shrinking stories

If the art of telling and writing stories is very much about adding fascinating and engaging detail appropriate to the story, it's also about being able to abridge and abbreviate too. The exercises in Chapter 6 for learning stories involved reducing stories to schematic outlines as part of memorizing them, through mapping, framing and landmarking. Once a story has been expanded, it's still good to stay in touch with the basic schemes. One way is to remap, landmark and frame and see what might have changed, but another is to try one or both of these activities.

Smaller and smaller/shorter and shorter (group and/or solo challenge)

Start with a long story known to the group.

The first stage can be done as a solo exercise or, to involve everyone in a class, in smaller groups (four to six):

- In either case, the first challenge is to summarize the story orally as quickly as possible in up to (say) four minutes. Allow some preparatory discussion or thought time.

- Group spokespersons or individuals take it in turn to summarize the story within the time. When the summary is complete, other people or groups may challenge the summary, bringing up essential points that seem to be missing.

- Judge whether the challenge is correct (using the opportunity to discuss what seems essential).

- Winners are those who summarized the story within the time limit and with no upheld challenges.

For stages 2, 3, 4, etc., issue further challenges to groups or individuals to summarize in three minutes, then two minutes, then one minute or less. Alternatively, set the task of writing the story within (say) 100 words.

How recognizable is the shortest possible version of the story as the original?

Guess the story?

Groups or individuals summarize a story (or, if more experienced, up to three tales) they will choose secretly from a longer list of stories everyone in the group knows. They will produce short summaries or descriptions of these stories, done in as vague a way as possible, without mention of identifying names, etc. This can be done as a writing task or through discussion and oral 'telling'. These short descriptions are relayed to the larger class, who attempt to guess which story it is. You might have a word or time limit for each description.

'The queen's palace': building an extended version – a checklist

1. Will you introduce a framing story – someone tells someone else the story of the queen?
2. Will you use the queen's story as a framing story, so that people within the story tell further stories? If so, will they be more wishing stories or other kinds of tale?
3. Will there be a formal 'opener' for the beginning of the queen's story or how will it begin? (Will there be variations on openers for other stories if included?)
4. How many questions about the queen's motivation can be answered as part of the telling? How will this change the story?
5. How far will motivations and detail of other characters such as the old woman or the people in the poor village change or add to the story?
6. What glories of the palace as it is at the outset will you have described?
7. What wonders inside the palace will be listed and how will others be left to the imagination of listeners or readers?
8. Are there other interesting detours the story might take at different stages?
9. What might the queen have learned (a) when she tired of the village, (b) from living with the poor people of the village, and (c) when she 'returned' to her throne?
10. Will the story conclude by returning to a frame story or with an imaginative variation on a traditional ending?
11. If you perform the story for a special event, will you use music and sound effects or other performance aids to set the atmosphere, to divide episodes of the tale, to suggest events or moods or to make a stylish ending? (See Chapter10.)
12. Will you weave in other kinds of interlude to vary attention in a longer version? (See Chapter 10.)

8

Stealing stories

I give you one; you get a hundred. What is it?

Framing ideas: why steal?

Perhaps it's a good job no one had invented intellectual copyright when Shakespeare wrote *King Lear*, since underlying all that word wizardry you can still spot the elements of a universal folk tale plot. Or maybe someone should have been standing before all the anonymous oral tellers of legends and myths, wagging a warning finger and telling them not to help themselves to what clearly was not theirs to take. Perhaps, but not many people would really think so. Stealing stories sounds wrong. After all, are we not supposed to try to be original, to come up with new ideas, new angles, new ways of interesting and engaging readers and listeners in story magic? Yet all story makers and tellers do it all the time – and indeed need to do it. And we all do it too, because it's another of those talents we have naturally, the marvellous ability to copy and then make free with what we've copied.

We inherit a vast culture of story ideas – plots, motifs, character types, myths and all sorts more. It is hard not to absorb at least some of this, even if only as audiences of mainstream popular film and TV, not to mention adverts and fantasy-based computer games, etc. Good, original story makers and tellers have necessarily absorbed a lot of it – through listening, through reading, through watching and then, very importantly, through imitating. 'Absorbed' is the right verb to use here: there is a process something like osmosis happening; it is not that there is always a conscious effort to study in intentional ways. It somehow 'goes in' and is there to use intuitively – rather as we absorb our own mother tongue. Contrary to popular notions of unique talent and extraordinary giftedness, the evidence seems to be that most good story makers and tellers have been exposed to all sorts of models and immersed in the whole milieu of fiction in exactly this way, through their own reading in a literate culture, but equally through family or local tradition and habit (in both oral and literary cultures) and through all sorts of other contexts and influences.

Learning consciously to steal stories – to adopt and adapt plots and plot elements in all sorts of ways – is a very effective way both of improving and refining the bank of story patterns those with a broad reading (etc.) background may already have and, crucially, of making up for the lack of those patterns in perhaps the majority of pupils who don't – or, maybe we should say, who need to connect with what they (kind of) know without (kind of) knowing that they know. It has a lot of benefits, some of them immediate and more measurable, some of them more long-term and 'invisible'. This is a preliminary list:

- *Sowing seeds* that will come up in different forms 'instinctively' in writing and telling. Pupils' stories often contain 'trace elements' of universal plots and widespread motifs they are usually unaware of. The more good seeds you plant, the richer the crop can be.

- *A repertoire:* When a pupil has purposely taken a plot and altered it, both that plot and the elements of it are available for further conscious 'stealing' in story work. He or she, like a professional teller of tales or a writer, has a repertoire of plots and can begin to appreciate that (as the storytellers' saying goes) 'learning one story is learning a hundred'.

- *Improved literacy levels:* Fluency and confidence in working flexibly with plot are literacy skills in themselves; they also provide a vehicle through which other oral and literacy skills can develop.

- *Good example:* Working with great plots that have stood the test of time gives young storytellers and writers a feel for how plots work and balance out. This 'feel' and example feed back into their own plot creation.

- *Respect:* Handled intelligently, it can develop respect for the depths in a good traditional (or other) model at the same time as developing the ability to be original.

- *Structured imagining:* The plot has to be reimagined, reclothed. Exercises around this are also exercises in controlled imagination.

- *Insight into diverse story elements:* This kind of work leads to many incidental learnings about stories and how they work, applicable both to creative story work and to literature study and analysis, for example insights into the importance or otherwise of character, gender, setting and social context, metaphorical depths, etc.

- *Insight into the underlying structure:* Instead of consuming stories as something always different because surfaces are different, seeing that there are similarities and common points. Young children will watch *Scooby-Doo* cartoons without noticing that the story repeats in different disguises. Older children can learn not only to spot the pattern but also to reinterpret it for themselves.

- *Oiling creative processes:* Changing stories requires the divergent thinking skills sometimes practised with much less context (and therefore relevance) in exercises like 'List ten different uses for a stick and a sponge'.

- *Creative challenge:* Dealing effectively with a circumscribed creative challenge inspires confidence in the ability to do so in more difficult circumstances.

- *Metaphorical meaning:* Seeing the underlying plot pattern can also lead to insight into how metaphors in a tale may work and to a deeper engagement with those metaphors.

- *General improvement in flexibility of thinking:* The more you understand how story patterns transfer and change, the more you may understand how other principles transfer. Velcro was developed when Swiss amateur mountaineer and inventor George de Mestral, noticing that both he and his faithful dog had returned home from a nature hike covered with burrs, decided to investigate how those burrs worked and discovered a principle he could apply to make a new kind of fastener. He transferred the pattern. Story transposition oils that kind of creative thinking transfer.

- *Life patterns:* Seeing the pattern also leads to the insight that is needed to spot other underlying patterns in life – a vital wisdom skill as well as a practical creative problem-solving one.

The idea of change

Underlying patterns: archetypes to memes to practical starting points

Were this a more theoretical book, there is a long debate I could detail here around apparently competing theories of the archetype and the meme as explanations of the underlying patterns in stories, not to mention postmodernist cultural theories. Very briefly, in case you are unaware of all this, archetypes are often associated with Carl Jung, though the concept had a long history before he introduced his take on it. It means literally 'ruling kind' and suggests an 'original model' for things like stories, which becomes the pattern for further 'copies'. In the transcendentalist philosophy popular prior to the dominance of Darwin's ideas, the 'original' exists in an ideal transcendent world. The term 'meme', on the other hand, only goes back to 1976, when Richard Dawkins introduced it in *The Selfish Gene*. It's now officially defined in the *OED* as 'an element of culture that may be passed on by non-genetic means, esp. imitation'.[1] It suggests an alternative conceptualization to that of an underlying and 'universal' archetypal pattern – something without such an essence beyond its survival value for the species, differing from a purely postmodernist perspective, in which the notion of underlying patterns would be denied with the insistence that everything is socially constructed.

Interestingly, Chris Nunn has recently brought together the notion of memes and archetypes, freed from what he describes as 'Jung's flummery', using the notion (from chaos theory) of attractors in the brain (Nunn 2007). Exploration of these ideas in more depth would take us way beyond the scope of this book. As a personal opinion, I suspect that Nunn's general drift may well be the way to go in the specific area of the story: recognizing that, on the one hand, there are robust, underlying and essentially meaningful patterns in many stories, which may however transmit automatically – and indeed transform automatically – in the process. I also suspect that there are optimal forms for any story pattern, ways in which they can become more focused, more meaningful and many layered, more relevant at any one time or place with any one person or group of people.

Anyway, practical work around changing stories (particularly traditional tales) needs a theoretical starting point. For this, I'm going to assume that most practitioners, in working with children, will want to retain the marvellous ability of many such stories to mean (for whatever reasons) at the same time as encouraging the maximum amount of flexibility in working with them. This leads to a basic set of further working assumptions:

- There are underlying patterns in many stories, though an original model may be hard to trace and define.
- Patterns can and should be changed and explored in different ways, perhaps especially by children, who are natural copycats and experimenters.
- This process has, anyway, happened repeatedly in the history of ancient

story patterns as they migrate from place to place, culture to culture and time to time.

- Part of the definition of a 'good' story pattern or plot is that it is flexible, a metaphor that *can* be adapted and changed without losing all of its identity: it traps some vital essences of an idea about life, human experience and all sorts more.

- There may hence be some essential elements in the pattern it may be sad to lose.

- Creative work with stories can be vitally informed by these notions.

Plot and motif

Put simply, a plot could be called the pattern of events that form a narrative, whilst a motif is a single event or occurrence or theme that crops up in that narrative, but which might equally turn up in another very different narrative with a quite different pattern of events. Supposing a traditional hero or heroine is going on a quest and has to go through an ordeal along the way, perhaps passing through an enchanted valley, ignoring distractions and threats. The plot is the overall pattern of the quest: there are many quest stories, often similar in structure. The ordeal is the motif: similar ordeals crop up in other stories, which are not necessarily versions of the quest. Sometimes the ordeal is an essential part of the plot; sometimes it seems almost a bolt-on extra. Or suppose, in some classic love tragedy, the lovers die, but then different plants grow from their two graves and twine around each other (as happens in various ballads and legends). The love story is the plot and the twining plants are the motif; the love story may gain in pathos and poetry from the image, but might not be changed beyond recognition by its absence. That seems simple enough – except that you could build a whole plot around an ordeal or even twining plants, so that each could be a plot in some circumstances and a motif in others. Similarly a quest might turn up as a brief motif in some stories. Hence the distinction can blur a little and, certainly for creative purposes, doesn't have to be thought of as rigid.

Ringing the changes: plot and motif transposition

What can change and what needs to remain the same underneath if one makes use of a traditional model? The principles above suggest caveats, but you don't learn about a subject by tiptoeing respectfully along its margins: there's nothing wrong with blundering around with stories and seeing what happens. It's part of the joy of learning an imaginative discipline. After all, these days you are much less likely to be the sole transmitter of a tale hallowed by long tradition than, say, the apprentice of some ancient bard. However, a plan for what and how one can change stories helps one to be more focused in doing so – and perhaps less blundering.

- *Plot:* How far can one change events, etc. on the surface whilst keeping the underlying pattern the same? At what point does the story simply become different, if similar? What might you be losing and what might you be gaining? These make interesting discussion points in story work (as do many of the points below). For example, pupils can be encouraged to comment on each other's stories, saying how much like an original plot the new version is, but also how it differs.

- *Motif:* A motif in a story can similarly change on the surface, whilst retaining some essential similarity. The mythical or fairy tale enchanted valley could turn into a shopping mall or gambling club. Similar questions can be asked about motif change as for plots, with the addition of the fundamental question of how important the motif is to this particular plot.

- *Small details:* A lot of minor incidentals in a story can change without affecting the main plot and setting very much at all. A magic sack in one version could become a miracle box in another very similar one; a mansion of marvels could change into a walled garden of wonders. A door might be blue in one tale and red in another.

- *Characters:* If it's essential that a character is, say, mean and grasping it makes no sense to make her generous, though you might choose to make her simply careful with what she has with only slight changes. If the character is beautiful, making him ugly may or may not work, but making him charismatic or hypnotically powerful might.

- *Gender:* Could the main character be a woman instead of a man or vice versa? What happens if you change the gender of any of the characters? Sometimes it obviously won't work. Sometimes such changes give the story a new relevance and strength. Changing the gender of characters in a suitable tale and then exploring and feeding back on the consequences makes a thought-provoking exercise for older pupils.

- *Social status:* How important is it that this character is a queen and that other one a pauper? Does the central character need to be rich or noble? If something of the sort is vital, you can still find an equivalence – which may be interesting in itself. If not, there may be more freedom, but how much? This is another stimulating exercise.

- *Time:* Can a story set in an ancient fantasy world become a twenty-first-century 'real-world' adventure? Can a folk tale morph into science fiction? Can a modern crime novel be disguised as a historical costume drama? Some plots will move to almost any time setting; others are more tricky, though this may only emerge as a person tries to make the changes.

- *Location:* A story set in the desert might work reset in the Arctic, but equally in a much more symbolic and psychological 'desert' in a European city. A town story could work in the country and vice versa. Some stories seem very much to belong to a place and a time; some local legends turn out to have universal elements. For example, the well-known Welsh legend of Gelert (the faithful hound killed by his master, Prince Llewelyn the Great, who misunderstood the dog's bravery in saving his infant son) has the same plot as the tale of 'The Brahmin and the mongoose', from the ancient Indian *Panchatantra*, a plot repeated in the folklore of a number of other countries too.

- *Culture:* Stories have moved freely from culture to culture for centuries, often because people naturally domesticate them (as with the story of Gelert), though sometimes through the more conscious efforts of authors importing tales. Changes of cultural setting that work the other way (from familiar to the more exotic) can be more challenging, if interesting; they may require research and sensitivity, which can in turn be a rewarding exercise for pupils in understanding another culture.

- *Story style (genre):* The style of the story is again something that may change. The same underlying plot could be in a folk tale or a sci-fi fantasy or indeed, as mentioned at the start of the chapter, a Shakespearian tragedy. Some modern urban legends are very similar to ancient 'true' Japanese tales (Schaefer 1990).

- *Metaphors:* If you change a story, how does this affect any metaphorical depths in the plot? Does the story lose them or does the change sharpen them? Are there any symbolic motifs in the original that could change to suit the new setting of the tale, whilst keeping the same or a similar meaning?

Practical exercises in story stealing

These 'plot stealing' exercises can be adapted to suit most pupils in the target age ranges, given adequate prior experience (from earlier exercises in this book or otherwise) and suitable build-up.

Guided transposition

This is a simple, straightforward formal scheme for introducing the idea of transposing a story, after discussing some of the above possibilities.

First map and landmark a shorter model story with the group or class, turning this into an abstract frame for reshaping.

For 'The queen's palace' in the last chapter, the abstract frame might be:

1. person with strong desire, need or ambition;
2. she or he getting three wishes (how?);
3. use of first wish to satisfy that blind desire;
4. result good at first but eventually leading to use of second wish to get rid of it;
5. result of second wish leading to use of third wish, which restores normality.

- Discuss what can change (e.g. the queen might be, instead, a mermaid with wonderful hair or a rock star with a mega backing band).

- Imagine: go through the stages of the story, encouraging pupils to imagine the changes they will (personally) make as vividly as possible (see below, 'Seeing it new').

- Tell the new story to each other in pairs or trios, playing the 'Embroidery' game.

- Then write the new story.

Share the new stories afterwards as far as possible, asking pupils to comment on how well the pattern underneath has been retained but disguised and developed. Perhaps also play elaboration games with the written stories if they are not sufficiently detailed.

Warps and whispers

This game makes a good alternative or complementary introduction to the idea of changing stories for groups that have already used some of the story games and procedures explained earlier in the book and who are able to do some basic but flexible storytelling. Many will know the game of 'Chinese whispers', and mention of it may help them to pick up the way this is supposed to work.

- The 'Pass it on' procedure is followed (see Appendix B) in a class or group story session, starting with several new story plots that will be passed on around the group. However, this time (after the first round) the tellers must change at least one aspect of the story they receive from other tellers on purpose when they pass the tale on (the number of changes can be stipulated – one to begin with, two and even three with repetition of the game). They must not tell anyone what they have changed. The changes they make can be left to their own free choice, but they should disguise them, making them match the story.

- Alternatively, you can list kinds of changes previously discussed and understood, using some of the categories from the list above (time, place, character, a small detail, etc.) and encourage 'players' to focus on one or several of these.

- After several moves, group members are chosen to retell the last story they heard in the form in which they received it. The original story is then compared and the changes are spotted. This can be done by getting the first teller of the tale (who received the original) to tell it, or by reading out the model (or playing the recording if it was learned in this way).

Seeing it new (imagination exercise)

Adapt this outline to suit the age and likely concentration of the imaginers.

- An already familiar story is mapped, landmarked and explored (as in 'Seeing it through', page 97).
- Lead pupils (or allow them to lead themselves) through each landmarked stage, thinking how they will change each surface 'landmark', substituting something different but equivalent. (In a group or class, this can be handled as a challenge or in a more coaxing style, perhaps with a veiled command – 'You can take your time, no need to rush, but you might be able to *do this now* . . .', 'Some people find that *it gradually starts to work* after a while . . .', etc.
- Track back through the new scheme at least three times.
- As you do so, allow any new details to emerge by 'imagination magic'.
- Zoom in on details of each stage to discover more detail, using as many sensory modes as possible.
- Zoom out to the overall summary feel of the plot.
- Tell it through to yourself, hearing your storytelling voice.

Play 'Embroidery' (described in Chapter 7) with a partner or group using your new version of the old plot.

Challenges

Group grilling (more advanced critical exercise for older groups, developing critical sense, close listening and a sharpened sense of plot)

- Tellers attempt to win through with their new tale, as a true new interpretation of the old plot. Individually (or in groups), they tell the new story to the rest of the group, all of whom know the original story and have (probably) also mapped and landmarked it.

- At each agreed stage, the teller pauses and the group ask questions about how the new plot works and how it compares to the original. New developments that stray too far from the agreed underlying model can be challenged.

- Challenges must be explained. The teller can 'win through' by creatively explaining the 'story logic' that led to the change or even by backtracking a little and adjusting details as necessary.

Allow a lot of encouraging scope initially, but develop more rigorous criteria as the idea becomes more familiar. This idea also works done in pairs or trios.

Change smuggling (game for more advanced players)

Developing the last exercise, this time tellers prepare two kinds of change to their plots. The first are straightforward 'transpositions' of the kind worked on above. The second are deliberate 'wrong' changes that don't correspond with the original pattern, but which the teller attempts to smuggle through by storytelling art and cunning pre-planning. The grilling group attempt to spot all of the 'wrong' changes. To make this competitive, storytellers can score points for any unnoticed changes and also for any incorrect challenges (i.e. challenges of changed details that do, however, match the original pattern). The ensuing discussion needs firm refereeing.

Games with specific plots

These two games are adapted from my *New Lamps from Old* booklet (Parkinson 2007a), in which there are more useful games for playing with specific traditional plots.

Wishes three

This of course follows on from 'The queen's palace' in Chapter 7 but can be introduced by and linked to any other versions of the plot. It can be played in pairs or with the whole group.

The storyteller gets three wishes and aims to use them to get and keep what he or she wants. The partner or group aim to stop this happening within the rules.

First the storyteller is chosen and has to say where and how he or she gets three wishes.

Then:

- Storytellers say what their first wish will be. (It is against the rules of the game to cheat by asking for endless wishes.)
- The partner or group now spoil this wish. They are not allowed to say that the wish doesn't work but must find a way in which it works, but in the wrong way (without killing the wisher).
- Storytellers must respond to this, getting themselves out of the mess and on track again. (Perhaps it's possible to dodge the results of wish 1 without using wish 2 yet.) Wish 2 is used (if not used already). Again other players try to spoil this wish by making it work in a way that the wisher didn't expect.
- The storyteller has to respond again, explaining how he or she copes with the consequences. This may or may not involve using the last wish.
- Wish 3 is used if not used already. If it has already been used to go back to safety (before the wishes), then the game ends here. If not, wish 3 can be followed by more spoiling, though the storyteller can again respond by turning those consequences to the good.

Finally, going back over ideas and answers given at each stage of the game can provide the outline of a new three wishes story in which the storyteller is the hero or heroine who was given three wishes with the consequences the game created. This can be told as a story and (perhaps) also later written.

The magic chase (story game)

This story game is based around the central motif or plot of the magic chase in 'Mohammed and the magician' (Chapter 6). The *New Lamps* version is based around a similar Scottish wonder tale about Jack and the magician.

Suitably adapted in the presentation, it has proved very popular with children and teenagers across a broad age range (including both younger and older than the target range for this book). It's for two players (or teams). One player takes the Mohammed role and tries to escape; the other is in the wizard role and tries to catch Mohammed. Both improvise their changes to match (and beat) the last change.

First:

- The group become thoroughly familiar with the story (or one like it) through reading or telling, maybe discovering through retelling the many ways to expand the outline telling in the book. Study and count the series of changes in the model story (see below).
- Decide on who is Mohammed and who is the wizard (or decide to be different figures – Delila and the witch, Zog and the alien, etc.).
- Also (optional) decide how the magic is obtained – is it from a book of spells or an internet site involving scientific formulae?
- Is the game set in a far-away culture (as in the Mohammed version), in the ancient past, the distant future or the present? (If played according to stricter rules, this will affect what it is possible to change into – cavemen might not know much about rockets, for example.)
- Is danger involved before the getting of the 'magic'?
- Will it be described as magic or is there some way to alter this?

Then comes the chase. ('Mohammed' and 'the wizard' are used for convenience here.)

- Mohammed makes his first change to escape the wizard.
- The wizard makes his first change to catch Mohammed.
- Mohammed makes another change to escape the wizard.
- The wizard changes again to catch Mohammed . . .
- . . . and so on through as many changes as it takes for Mohammed to beat the wizard – or for the wizard to catch Mohammed (unlike the story, in the game it can go either way).

In phase 3, retell the transformations in the game. Make a three-part story involving all of the changes (middle) plus the preliminary section (beginning), explaining how the Mohammed figure got involved with the wizard figure and read the spell book (or whatever) and bringing the story to a conclusion (end) – in the model story, Mohammed is greeted as a hero, becomes court magician, etc.

Pairs of changes in the Mohammed story (for convenience) are:

1. Mohammed becomes a dove, the wizard an eagle.
2. Fish – crocodile.
3. Date – boy.
4. Stone on ring – chief eunuch.
5. Watermelon seed – rat.
6. Stone – hammer.
7. Silk veil – fire.
8. Mohammed with a pitcher of water.

Note that there are seven pairs of changes and one single final change. If the Mohammed figure wins, there will always be a final single change, since the wizard hasn't been able to match it.

Tips for using this game

The game requires quick thinking. A basic rule has to be that no one can become a god or have god-like invincibility. You can evolve more necessary rules with repetition, to avoid too many disputes about possible changes. For example, players must be able to explain why their latest change makes them either more powerful than the other or able to escape him or her easily. As suggested above, it can be made more challenging by restricting the time or culture setting, but also by setting a time limit or a set number of moves in which to win, lose or draw.

Stealing motifs and mini-plots

Here are some examples of typical (and often imaginative and meaningful) motifs that migrate from story to story. For each there are ideas for playing with them creatively and creating new stories around them, in both telling and writing. Games introduced earlier in the book can be used to expand each idea in oral work.

The spring unblocked

A spring that used to gush clear, refreshing water with special healing and/or other powers has become blocked. No one knows why until the hero or heroine in the story comes by and discovers what has blocked the source. Maybe it is an enormous toad that has been sitting across it in an underground chamber or a snake coiled around the rocks at its mouth; maybe it is a hidden treasure hoard; maybe it is something else. He or she unblocks the spring (kills or tames the toad/snake or releases the treasure, etc.) and everyone is delighted. Maybe the hero or heroine gets to keep the treasure or gets a secret power from the snake or toad.

This is a powerful metaphor with many possible meanings, but pupils don't have to understand those to be inspired by it. Maybe one day it will yield some relevance, like a lot of metaphors. Meanwhile it's fun to play with. Analogous images from tradition include the dead tree that suddenly blossoms, the ruined or enchanted castle or palace that is suddenly restored, the stone statue that comes to life, the dark land that becomes light, and more.

Exercises

1. Find (or invent) more images like it. (Listed one after the other with a little artifice, these could suggest the beginning of an evocative list poem:

   Blossom at last on the long-dead trees,
   The stone statues stretch,
   The spell on the silent castle shatters
   As the silver spring surges . . .)

2. Work one or more of these into a story. These questions may help:

   • Will there be just one image of this kind or perhaps the classic three (three tasks for the hero or heroine)?
   • Where is the stream, tree, ruined castle or statue, etc.?
   • How did the stream get blocked? (Or how did the tree die, etc.?)
   • Who or what was responsible and why?
   • Who is the hero or heroine, where has he or she come from and where might he or she be going after unblocking the stream, etc.?
   • Why can the hero or heroine unblock the stream when people couldn't do so before?
   • How does this story end?

Begging disguise

The beggar seems thin as string and frail as an autumn leaf. The robe he wears has more holes than fabric. The girl in the story is, however, kind to him, sharing whatever she has to give. Later the beggar turns out to have been a king in disguise or a magician or another kind of powerful person who can change the girl's life.

Gender roles can easily change here. The beggar king could be a queen, the wizard a witch or a fairy or a millionaire; the girl could be a boy or a man. Similarly, implied age differences can be reversed or otherwise changed. The challenge is to create a new interpretation of the idea of a scruffy or poor exterior and an interior high quality in any disguise or setting.

Useful questions

- Who or what is the beggar?
- Who is 'the girl' and why does she need the change in life?
- How does 'the beggar' make the change for 'the girl'? (Perhaps he gives her a 'magic feather'; perhaps it is a task or a special journey, perhaps a treasure.)
- Will 'the girl' find out that the beggar is not just a beggar, and if so how?

Box in box

The box is beautifully decorated with marquetry in five different kinds of wood: pale sycamore, dark mahogany, creamy ash, rich brown walnut, a blush of cherry wood – all making interlocking star patterns. It is exquisitely made, very finely crafted. When you open it, there is another box, just a little bit smaller, with the same pale sycamore, the same dark mahogany, the same creamy ash, rich brown walnut and blush of cherry, all making the same star patterns, just a little bit smaller but just as finely done. When you open that, you find another box . . . and another . . . and another, until you come to the last box, so tiny you have to look at the patterns on it with a magnifying glass and open the lid with fine tweezers to find . . . another box.

Pupils will probably be familiar with Russian dolls and may also know the classic Dr Seuss story of *The Cat in the Hat*, both of which are expressions of the fascinating and perhaps quite profound idea of things within things, worlds within worlds.

Exercises

1. Set the task of coming up with a list of as many as possible 'things within things'. (Some preliminary examples that work well are: town within

town, bag within bag, ring within ring, sword within sword and house within house.)

2. When these are claimed at the end, pupils are challenged to explain in detail to the group (or, if set as an exercise for individuals, in pairs, trios or small groups) how the interlocking works (as in the example of the box above).

3. Write a story with this motif at its centre. (Perhaps the box is a wonder created by a master craftsperson who sets strange puzzles or hides mysteries. Perhaps the town within the town is visited by magic means.)

Alternatively, simply give the class or group a series of examples of things within things and challenge them to create the details for one or more in speaking and listening or writing exercises.

The custard pie

Slapstick humour appeals from a young age. The custard pie is a visual joke, but there are equivalents in told and written stories. Only the youngest children may laugh a lot just because someone has a pie splattered in his face. Clever clowns or pantomime actors set up the trick so that, for some reason, you want that custard pie to go in that face and are pleased when it does because it's rough justice. Maybe the owner of it is strutting around proudly; maybe she is unbearably bossy. Maybe it works differently. In a story, maybe someone trips over a stick or a stone; maybe someone falls into something unpleasant; maybe again it works differently.

After discussion of all that, set this challenge for telling and writing:

1. Find a 'custard pie' trick (i.e. something that works in a way you reckon is somehow like the custard pie).
2. Invent a character who will 'cop it'.
3. Find ways to make this character dislikeable enough to deserve it (character sketch).
4. Invent a likeable character who is put upon by the one who will get the custard pie.
5. Tell a story about the delivery of the 'custard pie', why it is well and truly deserved by the villain and how the likeable character gets away with it. Test it out through the telling and elaboration games given earlier in the book before writing it, or perhaps after doing a rough written draft.

Dashing devils and virtuous villains

Evil beings might officially be ugly and obvious, but stories are much more interesting and intriguing if the devil (or other villain) is handsome, even reckoned to be a fine example of true virtue by all and sundry, only gradually showing a wicked side. Equally, a story in which someone who seems to be vile turns out to be virtuous can intrigue and fascinate. Good–bad distinctions in younger children's stories tend to be very black and white, backed up by an 'Old Testament' version of morality. A character sketch around a 'dashing devil' or a 'virtuous villain' is one way to begin to challenge this simplistic style of plot development.

Useful questions

- What time and place does the character inhabit?
- In what ways does your character appear good or bad?
- How does he or she act to deceive people into thinking the wrong thing about him or her?
- How could you give a hint that the character is opposite to the way he or she seems?
- Is someone else (or are a series of people) involved in exposing the character's real nature?
- Does the dashing devil or virtuous villain choose to show his or her real nature in a dramatic way?
- What good or bad things come out of this and how does it all work out?
- Swap stories of dashing devils and ask each other lawyer questions about them.

More motifs

There are thousands more motifs, and many useful ones may come to mind with a little thought.[2] Here are just a few more many will recognize from traditional fairy and fantasy literature. Most crop up in several different forms. Similar approaches can be developed with any of these:

- healing potion;
- cloak (or hat) of invisibility;
- magic steed or carpet;

- genie in bottle/devil in bag, etc.;
- hidden treasure;
- good and bad luck;
- sword of sharpness (and other invincible weapons);
- crystal ball (seeing stone, etc.);
- transformation (from frog to prince and vice versa, etc.);
- enchanted castle/forest;
- ring, mirror, etc. of knowledge;
- trial of strength, bravery, power, etc.;
- magic musical instruments;
- special shields, suits of armour, protective ointment, etc.

Similarly there are classic character types or stereotypes in the many genres — tricksters, fools, ogres, giants, monsters, cheats, bullies, wizards, witches, bold and brave lads and lasses, cowards, mad scientists, wise women, sages, etc.

Card games: random choice

Using cards on which are elements of stories is a perennial workshop fun favourite, well worth redeveloping in this context. For example, it's quite easy to create and duplicate a set of cards (or slips of paper, etc.) on which are 20 to 30-plus different single motifs, perhaps supplementing the list above with some character types (or stereotypes), classic situations and locations, etc. for a particular story genre. These can be represented in words or in a picture or both. Sets can then be used in groups for oral storytelling games, where players take it in turns to draw (say) three cards without knowing what they are taking. (Cards can alternatively be dealt out.) Players must make up a story that uses all of the elements on the cards they have taken, suitably altered and transposed. (If stuck for a story ending, they might draw or be dealt extra cards.) Group members could use lawyer questioning methods to bring out the story. To begin with, they may prefer to have just one card each to explain and to use it just as it is on the card. When they are familiar with the idea, they might choose a more difficult challenge, drawing more cards (the practical limit is usually seven) around which to shape their tales, each of which has to be disguised as something else that is similar. The cards can also be used to create written stories in similar ways.

Disguise-a-story competitions

Story changing can be given a big boost by having one or both of these two kinds of story competition:

- *Hidden tales: storytelling competition:* People in a class or year group or whole school will secretly prepare a story, based on one of a number of models known in their original form by other pupils. They will not reveal what the model is. Models can range from the more obvious, very well-known 'nursery tales' ('Jack and the beanstalk', 'Cinderella', 'Sleeping Beauty', etc. – though note that it is quite difficult to disguise these very well) to much more adventurous and diverse tales, introduced to pupils during an extended focus on stories. An occasion is arranged (for example, a longer assembly, a special family evening or a book week get-together) at which the stories are told aloud by individual tellers or by a whole group or class. The audience guesses what the story is and then (perhaps) votes on which was the best disguised. To avoid bafflingly dissimilar tales with only the faintest likeness to the original scooping the prizes, points may also be given (by a judge or judges) for how well the story retains essentials of its original whilst disguising them. A party atmosphere can be encouraged around the event, with interludes of music and sound effects or other kinds of storytelling (see Chapter 10).

- *Disguise-a-story writing competition:* This works in a similar way to the telling competition (and can be run in parallel with it), but the task is to write a story, disguising and reshaping a traditional plot whilst retaining as many of its essential qualities as possible. A number of the most successful stories can be shortlisted for the prize and displayed, so that other pupils can read them and guess what the underlying plot is. To minimize the kind of copying that happens when one person correctly guesses the plot and passes on their idea or writes it on a list, guesses can be made (for example) on slips of paper (one only allowed per pupil) which will be placed in a box, and pupils can be asked to keep their guesses secret. (They probably won't keep them secret, but whispering and passing on guesses add to the excitement and generate more interest.)

Alternatively, a specific plot is set for reshaping either as a told story or as a written story – or possibly as both. Judging (either by staff members or by fellow pupils) is done not simply on the cleverness of the disguise but on how effectively and originally the story expresses the basic pattern – on how good a story it is.

9
Fooling with forms

To stay true, it must change. What is it?

Framing ideas: the nature of forms

If you hear a story, do you think first 'How can I categorize it?' Unless you are a folklorist or have an unusual obsession, probably not. The first thing you will do is respond to it, listen, accept, reject, be inspired by it, bored by it, whatever else. We don't pass on stories in order to record an interesting example of a form; neither do we necessarily keep the story 'shapes' we absorb in separate mental boxes. They move easily through our imaginations across conceptual boundaries.

It's very useful to teach and to learn that there are different forms of story. That is one kind of learning – learning *about* things and shapes and forms. Learning through and with stories starts to go beyond this first base as one stretches the limits of a form and plays with it creatively, discovering how one version might be a fable with an obvious moral, whilst another telling might bring out the fantasy elements or searing satire or poetic pathos with provocative mixed messages. Equally, a story might seem small and relatively insignificant in one presentation, yet be expanded to provide the bones of a major work.

This short chapter explores the process through some simpler examples. Hopefully they will suggest some ways of doing the same kind of thing with more complex material.

Two fable reshaping experiments

The jackdaw and the peacocks

This short fable is often attributed to Aesop. It is purposely chosen because, in its bare form, it probably looks less than promising, with some rather unfashionable and questionable notions. The ideas about how to develop it came out of practical work with the tale and again are not supposed to exhaust the possibilities.[1]

> A jackdaw was very impressed when it saw some peacocks. It loved the way they strutted around and showed off their magnificent tails and decided at once to join them. It gathered together as many different-coloured feathers from different birds as it could find, also taking some more and dipping them in wet paint human beings had left around. These it attached to its own tail and presented itself amongst the peacocks, pretending to be one of them. But they recognized it as an impostor at once and drove it away. The jackdaw returned to its own kind, but now they didn't want to know either and also drove it away.

Some relevant questions for reshaping (more can be generated in discussion)

The considerable scope for PSHE in reshaping work should be apparent here – PSHE and emotional literacy and so on, it should be clear by now, do not have to be divided from literacy work on developing stories.

- Some people might worry that the fact that the jackdaw is black gives this a racialist feel when told in the contemporary context. What do you think?

- How different does the story feel if it is about another bird not unlike a jackdaw, such as a magpie, which is black and white?

- Other people think that this fable is pessimistic about the possibility of changing your status and chances in life. Is this necessarily true?

- There may be things in the story that a person might want to emphasize. For example, it says something about what it is like to get an imaginative idea and make an effort to join another group or gang, something about being rejected by both one's own group and the new one. How could these things be brought out in more interesting ways?

- Maybe you can alter the story to make a happy ending for the jackdaw (or magpie). Maybe it goes and finds a new island where all the birds paint their own feathers. Maybe they like it and it gets on well there. Or maybe it finds the island and makes its own kingdom there, where birds have to paint their feathers. Maybe this is the origin of some exotic tropical parrots you might find in zoos today. There are quite a few possibilities, so how well can you make one work?

- Have you noticed that the jackdaw is called 'it' in the presentation, so that you don't know its gender. How different is the story if you make the bird female or male? Does this suggest a different emphasis?

The Elvis outfit

The more extended original 'modern legend' below is written simply, with reading aloud in mind, and is based on a short fable that appears earlier in the book, in the group of short tales for learning in Chapter 6. Quite young groups (down to Year 3) have related well to versions of this, presented through storytelling simply as an interesting modern legend. Work around it suggested afterwards shows how it combines use of a fable plot with extensive tall tale style elaboration.

Elvis Presley is famous; just about everyone knows that. Sadly, he died young, though there are a lot of people who worship him to this day. He's sometimes called 'the King of Rock 'n' Roll' – or just 'the King'. He was certainly a great singer. Especially in the later part of his career, he would wear very exaggerated costumes in his performances – tight white suits with gold and glitter and frills and all sorts. Those are the kinds of costumes people put on to do imitations of him – because there are many who like to pretend to be Elvis, some a lot better at doing so than others.

I want to tell you about one Elvis imitator who did something many who came after him probably wish they could have done. His name was Martin Stone and he was from Manchester, in England. Or maybe I should say *is* from Manchester, England, because Martin is still alive and living in that part of the world. He told me this story himself, which is how I know that it is true.

Now Martin had been crazy about Elvis since he was 12. At the age of 22, he scraped enough money to pay for a cheap flight across the Atlantic and to take a series of Greyhound buses down to Las Vegas, where Elvis was going to do some live shows at the Hilton Hotel to relaunch his performing career after many years of films, hit singles and albums. It turned out, though, that Martin just couldn't afford a ticket – it was a sell-out, and the only tickets left were in the hands of greedy touts who wanted a fortune. Martin hoped he might just get a glimpse of his idol. He had styled himself on Elvis, wore his hair just the way Elvis was wearing it, had practised doing all the Elvis moves, watched Elvis in all his films, could curl his lip and snarl like Elvis, could smile cutely and show his perfectly white teeth like Elvis, had mimed to Elvis's records over and over again and probably knew more about Elvis than the singer did himself. The only thing he couldn't do was the most important thing of all. He could walk like Elvis, even talk like Elvis, but he could never sing like Elvis.

Martin spent days just hanging around in the right places. Sometimes he thought he saw Elvis; sometimes he even thought Elvis had seen him. There were other fans, amongst them guys dressed up like the star the same way he was. It was all very strange, as if there were mirrors all around reflecting that one incredible person. He talked to some of these lookalikes, shared Elvis stories and facts. Some were friendly; some were definitely odd, weird even. But anyway, the word went round one day that Elvis was doing a photocall to publicize the new show. He found out about the location, dressed himself up in a dark, sober suit instead of his usual Elvis jeans and check shirt and managed to get there. Frustration again. He soon found there was no way he was going to get inside with the photographers. He was lingering in the street nearby when he suddenly saw a figure walking along the street towards him. He was wearing dark glasses and was hunched down sulkily into a big long coat despite the sunshine and hazy heat, with a hat crammed on to his head. Maybe it was supposed to be a disguise, but that wasn't going to put off a dedicated fan. This was no second-rate copycat; this was Elvis himself, in the flesh. You just knew that straight away if you knew Elvis the way he did. Martin just stood there gaping, too shocked even to hold out the autograph book. He was even more shocked when Presley stopped, looked at him for several seconds and then said: 'Hey, fella! I've seen you before. You're good; you're just right, in fact. You wanna job? Come with me.'

Martin says he walked beside Elvis in a kind of a dream, wondering if he'd died and gone to paradise, whilst Elvis steered him into a hamburger joint several blocks away and ordered coffees and a burger with fries each, paid for them and then told him what he wanted him to do. 'You see, fella, you look so darn like me that I reckon it might work.'

It seems that it had all been too much. Someone had designed these costumes for Elvis to wear and they'd really gone over the top. Gold and glitter and frills and . . . well, he showed Martin some of it under his coat. Elvis had worn some gear in his time, but this was too much. Trouble was, his manager, Colonel Tom Parker, wanted him to wear the crazy things: part of the new image, he reckoned. Presley had stormed out, hence the hasty disguise. Seeing Martin had given him an idea. He wanted Martin to change clothes with him in the toilets, go back and take his place for a while, strut his stuff in front of the cameras. 'Sometimes it gets kind of lonely being Elvis, you know,' the star told him. 'Sometimes I just want to be an ordinary guy in a black suit, walking the streets for a while. If everyone knows I'm in there, they're not gonna notice me out here.'

What could Martin do? Of course, he said yes, anything to help Elvis. Actually, he says, he suddenly felt sorry for the singer, suddenly saw him as just a human being like himself, with human feelings and problems. But there wasn't much time for those kinds of thoughts. He and Elvis changed clothes and Elvis gave him his security pass and a few other things, telling him exactly how he was to get back into the venue, what he was to say, how he was to act. 'Just don't say much, fella,' he insisted. 'Pretend you're still in a bit of a sulk, OK? They're used to that from guys like me.'

The long and the short of it is that, surprising though it seems now in the days of high-tech security, it actually worked. What seemed only a few minutes later, Martin had turned up at the rear door and was inside being hastily hustled through final preparations with a make-up artist who had fortunately never met Elvis and was much in awe of this person she thought was the mega-star. They were all in a hurry, because there were a lot of people waiting and getting restless, people the Colonel wanted to stay impressed. Everyone behind the scenes had been frantically searching for Elvis, and there had even been rumours he'd been kidnapped. They were all so relieved that the hunt was over that no one looked too closely. Martin was bustled along and soon found himself walking out on to a platform, whilst flash bulbs went off all around him and the strains of 'Teddy bear', one of his old fifties hits, blared out over the sound system.

There was a kind of mass gasp as he appeared. The sight of all that stagy glitter and the King of Rock 'n' Roll himself in the midst of it . . . well, it sort of hit people, even the seasoned press guys who had seen all kinds of things – including by then the hippies and the flower people, of course. They were as shocked as Martin had been in a different way half an hour or so before. Martin reckons that, to begin with, somehow or other he just seemed to know exactly what to do. He felt high on all the attention, even believed for a while that he was Elvis. So he strutted his stuff just like Elvis had said, just like Elvis in fact. Or maybe even better, because Martin was younger and probably fitter – he used to work out regularly.

It all went fantastically. The cameras clicked; the bulbs flashed; everyone was calling out and cheering. He was doing brilliantly when suddenly he looked and he saw them there, amongst the crowd but somehow separate – two, three, four . . . maybe even seven or eight of them. Elvis lookalikes, Elvis fans, Elvis imitators just like him – except that, unlike him, they had managed to get press passes to the event. There was something about them, something that told him that they were not quite taken in, that they suspected something, all of them in their different ways. It was one of them who started the chant: 'Elvis sing! Elvis sing! Elvis sing!' They did it with such power and conviction that soon the pressmen and everyone there joined in. Somewhere near the stage, he could hear an intro being strummed out on a piano. The Colonel had guessed something like this would happen, even if Elvis had not. He and the pianist had decided that Elvis would prove that he was as great as ever by singing one of his biggest hits, 'It's now or never', a number based on 'O sole mio', an old Italian song that was nearer to popular opera than rock 'n' roll, a number that took some singing in fact, a song in which he was supposed to hit an incredible high G sharp.

Martin says his blood really did seem to run cold at that moment, as the hush fell and the piano meandered through a suggestion or two of the melody and a bit of improvisation, then the intro all over again to give him time to settle. Now the pianist began to stab repetitively at the same chord, waiting for 'Elvis' to come in. Martin knew he had to go for it, really sing it out, and he managed the first line, hearing his own voice coming back at him, thin, hoarse, not rich and full like Elvis at all but breathed into the microphone in a way that suggested that the King might be teasing his audience. Then he faltered, stopped, coughed a lot, several times over . . . 'Hey, wait a minute, fellas!' he wheezed between the coughs. 'Let me get a drink someplace. I'll be back.'

He rushed off stage and out to his dressing room. Maybe he could buy a bit of time, not long, just enough to think of a better excuse. That's when he saw Elvis, grinning broadly. 'Nice one, boy! You did a good job. But, listen to me, don't give up the day job! You ain't no singer.'

It was Martin's turn to be relieved then. It turned out that Elvis had been in the audience watching – he had a spare pass so he could get back in and couldn't resist joining the audience, watching what was supposed to be himself. He reckoned Martin had given him some great ideas about how he could use that costume in his act and he pressed a generous bundle of dollar bills into his hand, despite Martin's protests. Martin took the fancy costume off in the dressing room, Elvis put it on and the King himself went back in front of the press, sang his song and knocked 'em all flat, as they say – he had something to prove after Martin's false start on 'It's now or never', which now he sang fantastically.

Presley went on to do a series of performances in Las Vegas that has become legendary. He was brilliant. The first night, as is now well known, he appeared unexpectedly in a simple black suit – no glitz and glamour, just raw talent, so they say. What people don't realize is that he got that same suit from Martin that day. As the season progressed and was followed by further seasons, though, Elvis took to those over-fancy costumes, and they became his trademark. Martin got to stay in the penthouse suite with his hero, to ride in the limo with him too, and he was given a whole lot of things he'll still show you if you ever go and visit him – pictures and shirts and boots and even a guitar complete with a fur-lined crocodile skin case, all of which had belonged to Elvis, the kinds of things collectors pay a fortune for. But, you know, even though he still thinks Elvis is the greatest, he has never ever dressed like him again, never even mimed to a record in private. In fact, if you looked at him now, you'd find it hard to imagine that anyone ever took him for Elvis at all. 'I don't know', he told me, 'somehow you grow out of those things. I'm just happy to be me these days.'

The strange thing is that, if you see some of the pictures of Elvis that fans still put up on their walls, it is actually Martin Stone from Manchester underneath, photographed on that day before he tried to sing. Have a very close look if you ever see one and you might realize just how true this story is.

To work with this story, ideally first seed the use of it by presenting the original from Chapter 6 amongst several others in an earlier session, so that pupils will know it well enough but will not automatically know which story is being used and can be persuaded to take the tale above (or an oral telling of it) for a true-life tale. (To give some feel to adult readers for this kind of exercise, I am purposely not identifying which fable it is, though it should be fairly obvious.) You might, indeed, leave work showing how it has been made up for a later session, so that it has time to 'sit' unchallenged.

Some example questions for exploring this telling

- Which short story or fable does it resemble?
- How closely does it follow the pattern of that story?
- In what ways is it the same plot with a different surface?
- What changes have been made to the structure and why? (For example, in the original the 'fraud' is exposed and the other creatures no longer believe in their 'king'. In this version, Martin is never found out.)
- What bits of elaboration in the story help to make it more convincing?
- How have bits of research and reported facts about Elvis been woven into the telling?
- Is this still a fable?
- Is it equally other kinds of story?
- Does it have different kinds of meaning now?
- Can you use the pattern of the original fable to make a different story with a different setting and different characters?

Using dilemma tales

Dilemma stories leave some aspect of a story unfinished, usually asking you to make a judgement. They are traditionally related to the fable, suggesting an exploration of some moral or practical issue, and are a very useful tool both for considering alternatives there may be in developing plots and for raising life questions. You can turn many traditional stories into dilemma tales, asking a question about what should or could happen to resolve the tale instead of providing the denouement yourself. For example, the story of the jackdaw (or magpie) can be left at the point when it has prepared its false colourful tail and is about to meet the peacocks, and you can ask what will happen. This can be a group discussion or a writing task. You can also tell the story of historical or contemporary characters and the dilemmas they faced, again pausing to consider the possibilities before exploring actual events.

Mary and the Devil in the nut

It wasn't in my time nor was it in yours, but whenever and wherever it was doesn't matter. Mary was walking from one town to another – and whichever towns those two were is not important either. She had a bag of nuts with her and she'd crack one open as she came to each milestone, discarding the shell and eating the kernel to mark each mile she'd walked. With only one nut left, she'd still three miles to go, so she saved it, steeling herself to walk on past two milestones and only pausing at the last with just one mile to go. But wasn't she in for a disappointment! There was a tiny hole in that last nut, and some creature must have wormed its way in there, gobbled up the insides and slept for long enough to thin down and find its way out again. There was nothing at all inside it; you could tell that straight away.

'Devil take me!' Mary exclaims angrily – the very words a person should never say when out on the open road, for Old Nick himself was hiding nearby and out he pops at once. 'Dear lady,' he says, very smooth and suave, 'here I am. Let's be off at once.'

Now this was not at all what Mary wanted. She had only meant to curse her luck, but now she had the Devil himself ready to whisk her off to hell, so she had to think quickly. 'Wherever did you spring from?' she says.

'Behind that stone,' leers the Devil. 'I can make myself very small when I need to.'

She shook her head, disbelievingly. 'You could never fit behind that!'

'I could so!' cries the Devil. And he shrinks down to fit behind the large stone.

'But', says Mary, 'that's really just a trick of the light I'm sure. If you can make yourself really small, can you fit into this nut?'

The Devil wanted to show off, so he turned himself into the finest little wisp of a thing and he squeezed himself through the tiny hole into the very nut Mary held in her hand. So she of course blocked it up at once with a piece of straw and now she had the Devil trapped in a nut. From within that nut, he called out and begged and promised treasures beyond imagining, to make her famous and rich, queen of the world and all sorts more. What should she do?

(Based on a traditional tale)

With each dilemma, one has to pause over answers to the final question for some time, avoiding the tendency of pupils to be glib and to dismiss the options rapidly. The implications of any one decision have to be thought through. So if Mary just throws the Devil in the nut away, what is she losing? Is it a good idea to leave the Devil inside the nut, not just for Mary, but for the world? How do you interpret what the Devil (or in other versions of this plot, the genie or the sprite or the ghost, etc.) is? Can you use its power in some way or is that too risky? What real-life dilemma is this like? Could you write a story exploring one of her options, perhaps creating an adventure or a mystery around it?

Way beyond literacy?

It is very hard to keep story work that has any depth to it within a narrowly skills-focused box, since stories are part of how we create and relate to meaning in our lives in general. Good English teaching is bound to consider this anyway – you make better stories with better word skill if they mean something to you, understand literature better if you pick up on some of its less literal content. There is, however, much further one can go in using stories not only to explore meanings, but to create practical positive change in individuals and groups. Many stories create new perspectives, put dilemmas and situations into new frames, suggesting new possibilities – which can be very powerful. Whilst this is largely beyond the scope of this book, being aware of such dimensions in story work keeps a teacher alert to pupils as, let's say, a little more than numbers on a list. There will always be occasions, too, when story work will make a huge difference to some of those engaged in it.

10 Performing stories

If I show it to you, you may see something else. What is it?

Framing ideas: storytelling as performance

Storytelling may be something we all do naturally, but it can also be a sophisticated performance art. Even when you tell stories one to one, there is truth in that statement; when you tell stories to a lot of people, there may seem to be a lot more truth in it, because of course there is clearly quite an art in holding the attention of large numbers of people. Yet there is a consistent common factor.

When you tell stories to one person, you are most successful if your story takes that person into that absorbed state where you could say that the storyteller almost disappears and the story becomes the real thing. It's the same if you tell stories to a hundred people or even a thousand. The purpose of any art and indeed any artifice involved is to achieve and sustain that inwardly focused attention – but also to vary it suitably.

There are long traditions involving the combination of storytelling with other performing arts. In schools, performing stories to audiences, whether within a class or year group, for assemblies or for special events, gives pupils a chance to explore performance connections. It also gives them a focus for developing some more advanced communication skills, not to mention personal confidence, as well as giving them something to aim for in story work. Then there are some fascinating discoveries about the way people interact that one can spotlight, particularly through learning to tell stories in changing circumstances, not to mention the other side of the bargain: the improved listening capacities of pupils as audience.

Through the rest of this chapter, we'll explore some of the directions you could take in moving stories and storytelling beyond basic literacy in this direction, from public performance to more effective and direct personal communication.

First principles

Attention

In our default state, attention is multiply directed and needs to be. It's not wise walking through a jungle, whether it's an ancient tropical rainforest or the modern urban kind, with your attention fixed in one place on one theme. Our ancestors would have been gobbled up by unnoticed lions and bears had they done that; for us it's being flattened by a tram or a tanker, but the principle is the same. We need to be alert in several directions. Attending to a story is different; we need to be comfortable enough in circumstances that are conducive enough to focus attention narrowly on the telling, and we need to have that attention drawn inwards towards that 'dreaming awake' state by the story itself and the manner of its telling. A storytelling performance works around those two simple parameters. Hence ways of telling and things one does around the telling are intended to do one or more of several things:

- switch listeners from default multiply directed attention towards an imaginative state;
- focus the storyteller in his or her story better;
- develop a rapport between storyteller and audience;
- make use of the natural, non-verbal language of the body;
- underline verbal language devices used in other ways;
- make use of the natural dynamics of group interaction;
- maintain attention and interest, manipulating curiosity, suspense, fascination, etc.;
- provide a second, complementary 'narrative' (as may happen when music or other arts are integrated with the telling);
- adjust and readjust conditions to improve the attention focus;
- make the storyteller appear more interesting;
- distract the audience and alter the mood.

In a picturesque old metaphor, an untrained mind is a marketplace filled with noisy hawkers, all shouting their wares. Story listening and telling are a training of attention and focus, a training in effective communication and concentration. Since getting attention from others is also a natural human need, it's also a training in both receiving attention and not craving too much: you have to learn to attract attention and then to get out of the way of your story, to 'disappear' and let the story world live. Show-offs spoil their stories by giving you too much of themselves; excessively shy people do the opposite.

Doing what you can do

No one should be made to try to do what they can't do. One-to-one telling is something almost all who can talk should be able to manage *at their own level*. Performing in front of a larger group is a leap some can make instantly; many others need a careful build-up, talking to two, then three then four or five and learning the skill of confidence as they do so. It's well known that many adults shirk public speaking; one shouldn't expect children to differ – though one should expect to be able to teach them to improve. Equally, if individuals work around their own strengths and find new ways to use and develop them, they are more likely to flourish than if one imposes a style and a series of skills that all must master. If someone can juggle or dance, why insist that they sing? If someone can fix your attention with a steady voice and a poised stillness, why make them shout and jump around?

Essential communication

Ways in this book have been a lot about mind and imagination: how we get story thinking working alongside imagining skill. But, to tell a story well, one has to use two basic physical instruments.

Voice

Storytellers pay attention to the way the voice 'sings' a story. Though both drama and musical coaching techniques can work to improve this, the main 'test' is whether they make a story come over clearly, imaginatively and in an unselfconscious way. A hint of over-selfconscious 'thespian' tends to get in the way, however resonant and powerful the voice becomes. This is something professional actors who turn to storytelling often fail to grasp, so maybe you can excuse school pupils if they are a bit 'off' sometimes. The main thing, though, is to encourage them to speak clearly and confidently and to trust and develop their natural voice rather than trying to sound like someone else (unless you're doing a form of role-play or they are 'voice-acting' characters in the tale).

Simple exercises useful in warm-ups for storytelling performance and to improve voice sound in general would include humming more loudly and softly, imitating open- and closed-mouth sounds at different pitches, learning to spot (and release) the tense feel of talking too much on the throat, getting the feel of talking from different parts of the mouth with lips in different positions, drama-type role-playing (pretending to be this or that character) and simply listening to and imitating different voices with different accents and sounds. (You can present some on audio if you don't do voices yourself.)

Voice-acting a story is natural for many, though not for all. You will hear people putting on this or that voice to convey what this or that person said and how all the time in everyday gossip and banter. Doing the same thing in a story helps to make it come to life, firstly (and fairly obviously) drawing attention to (say) how a bully or a gangster or a dragon or a witch could sound, but also, secondly, perhaps suggesting quite a lot of other 'messages' if you give such characters particular accents or vocal mannerisms with particular cultural or other associations. You can get a certain amount of humour and even satire out of making (for example) an ogre or a gangster talk with the same accent and mannerisms as a prime minister – or indeed a headteacher. Discussing this with pupils and finding out who likes to do voices and how is usually fruitful.

Telling it odd (exercise/game)

Participants are challenged to tell all or bits of a story already known, switching into these modes in turn on a signal:

- as if you were someone else;
- with a different part of your voice;
- slowly and dragging;
- lightly with lots of energy;
- with mouth almost closed;
- with mouth wide open;
- shouted like a series of insults;
- whispered like a secret;
- (any other ways that occur).

Finally just focus on the listener(s) and tell it.

Body

Rapport skills

Watch pupils involved unselfconsciously in a one-to-one story game or simply swapping tales they know and you'll see the absolutely natural language of rapport that we inherit from our pre-verbal ancestors. When two people are getting on well in any kind of conversation, they automatically adopt similar postures and do similar things. When they're not, there's a mismatch. You can get pupils to be more aware of this as they speak by getting them to match on purpose some of the time as they listen to and/or tell a tale and then to experiment with mismatching – folding arms and looking away as they listen, for example, or telling as if to the floor or ceiling. They can then report back and discuss how this made them feel. This kind of awareness can improve both one-to-one telling and social skills in general. It works between three or four people too, but as groups get bigger a different dynamic takes over.

Rapport with a group

In telling a story to a larger group, there is less chance to be in direct and close rapport with individual group members. But good storytelling to a group still involves sensitivity to people present – adapting to them and learning how to monitor their attention and respond to it. Some pupils unselfconsciously do this anyway. Being aware of some factors involved helps you to teach those who don't 'get it' as well as to improve the skills of those who do.

- *Leadership:* When you step up in front of a group (as most teachers will appreciate) you are stepping into the shoes (or maybe the paw prints) of the pack leader. This is emphasized if you are standing and they are sitting on chairs or (especially) on the floor. For the purposes of storytelling (and other kinds of group communication), it's important to occupy them properly. Listeners unconsciously want their leader to be definite; otherwise he or she seems to be an impostor. They want him or her to have what is called 'presence'.

  Presence (exercise): After discussing the idea, get pupils to take it in turns simply to occupy the space in front of a group and act *as if* they had 'presence' (probably starting with small groups). Get them to sit at different levels as well as to stand, generally inhabiting the space and acting the leader *without saying anything*. Combine this with the exercises below.

Discuss the 'feeling' of it. Get listeners to feed back what they see and sense.

- *Space and form:* If you stand in front of a group sitting on chairs (or, particularly, on the floor), you are automatically larger and, on a non-verbal level, dominant. Moving towards the audience makes you larger still and potentially threatening, whilst moving away makes you the opposite. Sitting on a chair could make you seem 'less', also taking you more to eye level, though maybe still a little 'up'; sitting on the floor can make you either equal or, for a moment, 'down', which can be useful. Even lying down (a rare strategy for most speakers) can occasionally have a useful non-verbal meaning in telling stories.

  Shape shifting (exercise): Following on from or combining with the 'Presence' exercise, get pupils to experiment with position in front of groups, moving towards and away from watchers, making themselves smaller or larger, etc. Ask watchers or listeners to stay quiet and notice the automatic feeling such alterations create. Discuss effects.

- *Eye contact:* In easy one-to-one talk, people shift their gaze constantly. If you look away and down a lot and fail to ever meet the eye you may look shifty, but equally if you stare people out you could make them uncomfortable; staring can be aggressive. Speaking to a group might involve catching a listener's eye every now and them, even sometimes returning a gaze, but generally scanning around the group, checking and responding to attention levels and then, perhaps, looking steadily off into a 'distance' where the story is 'happening' to allow listeners freedom to imagine. This is a sophisticated skill, and pupils in front of a group will mostly be concerned about their own performance. As in everything, however, they can begin to learn.

  Eye-balling (exercise): Add to the previous exercises the requirement to look some people in the group in the eye without speaking for (say) ten seconds without giggling (or perhaps conveying a particular mood like anger or sympathy).

More body language

You might draw attention to and discuss how the body tells the story or works against it in a variety of different ways. How poised and confident does a person seem to be *before he or she says anything*? Do people look as though they are shrinking into themselves or projecting outwards? What happens if they make more gestures? Or fewer? Can they use their faces to express part of the story better? Are they too expressive? How does posture affect the voice? How do you move fluently between, say, sitting and standing? How much do you need to act the movements of characters? How much can you minimize a tendency to overact, implying movement and action with gestures, head tilts and all sorts more? Can you tell without these 'extras'? All of these and many more features of the way in which a body expresses a story can provide themes for practical warm–up exercises in a workshop session. People are different; the storytelling style that suits them may be different. But it's useful to think about all these things, accepting that no one gets it right all the time; being self-consciously 'correct' in the way you do all things is one way to get it very wrong. You don't choreograph storytelling performance; you simply make it almost possible to obey the famous impossible instruction 'Be spontaneous'.

- *Stealing styles (exercise):* Pupils pick their own favourite performer in any style of performance – anything from acting, dancing, singing, to sport or even teaching or preaching, essentially someone admired they have watched or listened to or otherwise studied. Ask them to focus on the style and energy of that person, not to literally copy it but to pretend that the person is advising them, showing them how to walk their own talk. Perhaps get them to try the 'Presence' and 'Shape shifting' exercises above as well as to tell stories using these 'stolen' styles. Using imagination in this way certainly helps some (not all) students a lot and is an interesting illustration of holistic learning. You can work on a series of skills as described in the last paragraph individually and self-consciously, but then get them instantly at an unconscious level simply through imitation.

Event parameters

Audience shape in performance for larger audiences

Many are used to experimenting with audience shapes – horseshoes, semicircles, in-the-round, etc. The simplest and most obvious of these work best for telling stories – gentle arcs where listeners are all looking in towards the storyteller without leaving too much space in front of him or her being probably the best. Old-fashioned rows can be fine if lines are not too long. In-the-round, often excellent for involving watchers in an acted drama, is generally out – storytellers are always talking to some with their backs, and audience members may become observers witnessing someone acting the part of storyteller, not listeners in rapport with a speaker. Similarly, deep horseshoe shapes tend to distance the audience from the speaker too much.

Sitting in a circle in smallish audiences all at the same level, as favoured by many workshop leaders, robs speakers of some non-verbal possibilities already mentioned, condemning them to constant scanning, not to mention rather imperfect contact with immediate neighbours. This is not to say that none of these alternatives can ever work; if pupils are very familiar with storytelling, you can experiment. But it is easier and generally more effective to use what works most naturally as first base, rather than to impose ideas about audience position appropriate to other styles of communication.

Groups of storytellers

In assemblies especially, you may want to involve a large group of storytellers in presenting stories, and some ways of working out stories for the purpose have been suggested elsewhere in the book. At the simplest level, you can have stories told in relays, with storytellers taking over to tell episodes of longer tales, with others providing music and other supporting effects and arts. It's useful if you can still make a central space where the story is told and into which individual storytellers will move, without rows of waiting tellers in the immediate background to distract the audience with their separate moods, occasional inattention – or indeed overacted attention.

Audience size: large or small?

It takes a lot of energy, presence and skill to draw in large audiences. A large audience is also potentially more stupid – what you say has to be telegraphed more thoroughly and it's less possible to amplify the responses of the few with whom you can establish a more direct eye-to-eye rapport. You are dealing with a big beast called an audience. Hence you have to know what you are doing well and the storytelling becomes more of an act – you talk to the audience *as if* you were relating to each of them individually, rehearse your story (mentally and perhaps literally too) and then deliver it *as if* presenting to a few people, at the same time as using larger voice, gestures and so on.

If you are training pupils to perform their stories and are planning an assembly or a special event where audience numbers are larger (say a hundred or more), you need to be aware of this transition, of how the audience size can change the nature of the communication. If you want them to continue to value and use storytelling that is less formal and more improvisational and personal at the smaller scale, you also need to avoid implying that a stagy performance version is the apogee of the storytelling art with natural extraverts as the best tellers of tales. With all those caveats, however, you can still make it work extremely well. When a lot of people are thoroughly involved in a story, there can be an extraordinary and powerful atmosphere that makes a strong impression on the people involved.

One to a hundred (preparatory exercise for coping with audiences)

Develop each of the points below (in an age-appropriate way) to allow storytellers to imagine their way thoroughly around an effective performance in front of an audience:

- First imagine telling your story to one person you know. Hear your own voice confidently speaking, feel yourself telling the tale, etc.

- Next imagine telling your story to two friends. See them smiling and laughing (or otherwise responding, depending on the story). Hear them congratulating you on telling it well.

- (You might build this one friend at a time to five or six or go directly to the next stage.) Now imagine someone you don't know joining your friends and catching the mood, joining in and smiling or going silent and alert and fascinated. Add more, one or two at a time to begin with and then by fives or tens.

- As the audience swells towards a hundred (or more), you can make the audience members seem quite small for some of the time, as if they had shrunk and the teller had expanded.

- You can also try imagining the audience as a large but secretly friendly creature you have successfully tamed and are persuading to have its tummy tickled or its chin stroked.

- Practise coping with interruptions or picking up the thread after you have made an occasional mistake, using these 'invisible blips' to strengthen your focus, hearing the story developing and growing as you tell it, drawing everyone in.

- Imagine the energy with which you will draw the story to a conclusion and accept the applause.

This kind of imaginative rehearsal can be very powerful, suitably adapted for age and experience. It's a useful counter to the automatic negative imagining too many people do when approaching an event; you imagine practical success.

Technical aids

If available, technical staging devices can enhance storytelling performance in larger spaces with a larger audience – though sometimes at a price. So microphones, for example, may be very useful, though using them unobtrusively is certainly a skill to master, whilst boomy amplification risks distancing listeners. Acoustics in many school halls will make them essential for many quieter pupils speaking to audiences of any size, however (see below). Lighting can be used to good effect for special events, but bright spotlights may dazzle storytellers and limit them in relating to audience members through eye contact and picking up clues about general audience attention and mood. The best lighting allows speakers to see audience members enough to relate, yet enhances the look and feel of an event. Again it's essential not to make lighting assumptions based on theatrical performance style.

Acoustics

Few school halls are blessed with good acoustics. Some are dreadful and require a very powerful voice to penetrate the mushy wash of echoes, whilst any restlessness in the audience is unreasonably amplified. (Evidently the fact that school halls are primarily intended for communication escapes the average school architect.) If you have such an unfavourable acoustic, you may be used to it, of course, but pupils' voices are still too easily lost. Microphones (as mentioned above) are one solution, voice projection lessons another. You might also consider ways of deadening the acoustic for an event – borrowed carpets, hangings and curtains, etc. Alternatively you can consider the possibility of using a different space if that is possible. The effect of an acoustic has to be given very serious consideration; an acoustic that enhances communication is a huge invisible advantage.

Costume

You don't have to go in for elaborate costume for special storytelling events. Ordinary clothes may well be fine, perhaps (in the school context) even staying with uniform. But sometimes, if you have an event and a theme that suits the idea, you might alternatively work around (for example) medieval or ancient Greek or Indian outfits. There is scope for imagination in designing special costumes too – according to legend, the king's storyteller in some cultures wore special robes of office such as multicoloured coats or cloaks or patchwork robes, the kinds of garment very much open to imaginative reinterpretation. Since the objective is to promote a theatre of the imagination, the question will always be: does costume help or hinder that?

Background visuals

Some styles of storytelling might benefit from a not-too-elaborate set to suggest a background atmosphere or indeed some kind of projection. For most school events, though, you can be relatively minimalist – perhaps a colourful backdrop using a rug or a hanging or an ethnic bedspread thrown artistically over a free-standing display screen, gym equipment or the back of a piano, perhaps a simple, large, painted design, poster or picture to make a central focus behind tellers. This is not essential; you might use nothing at all if the space already has good colour and atmosphere, and you certainly don't want to set up a distraction. However, making the performing space just a little bit special and different helps to draw listeners into imaginary worlds and forget the mundane, so it's worth giving it some thought and indeed imagination.

Programming

It seems logical that you programme a storytelling event, perhaps even print a list of who is doing what and when. However, as you become more used to the distinctive, improvised nature of storytelling performance, you could build in more flexibility. If Alicia has an upbeat tale with a lot of humour, you might decide during the event to slot it in earlier if Ben has made them go a little bit more quiet than expected with a solemn story. An experienced professional teller of tales does this kind of thing constantly, wheeling in tales from his or her repertoire unexpectedly to develop and vary audience mood; pupils usually need more predictability, but you can encourage flexibility. After all, adapting the plan is a life as well as a performance skill.

Following on (exercise)

Get pupils who have learned a series of stories to 'follow on' from each other as they think (or agree) fit. Ask them sometimes to pick up on the subject matter, theme or meaning in the last story ('That reminds me of one'), sometimes to pick up on the mood ('This has a similar feel') and sometimes to provide a complete or partial contrast ('Forget all that; listen to this'). Discuss why you might amplify mood sometimes and change mood at others.

Extra material (jokers, riddlers, tricksters, jugglers and so on)

Some pupils could offer 'optional extras' at different times in a performance, accepting that they won't necessarily use all of what they have prepared – though it's a good idea not to disappoint them by allowing them no time at all. So you might have one or two people who can come on with a couple of riddles or jokes or tricks between longer tales. If you have young performers who can juggle or do card tricks or conjuring, this may also suitably vary performance, as can short pieces of music or dance (see below).

Performing nous

Working with group mood

Performers learn to sense group mood, noticing variations in concentration, levels of excitement and so on and responding accordingly. This is one reason why experienced storytellers change tack, switching their material or perhaps moving to jokes, riddles, songs or whatever else they can do to guide attention. It's an advanced skill, depending on quite a bit of experience, but you can sensitize pupils to developing it, rather than implying that they must always plough on regardless. You might discuss different audience moods, what is useful about them and what is not, how to recognize them and what you might do to change them. For example:

- *Hysteria:* The symptoms are that everyone gets carried away and overexcited or they begin to overreact in other ways. A joke or two may seem to be pouring petrol on the fire, but releases some of the energy and puts tellers onside with listeners, whilst a serious tale told strongly with conviction to follow brings them down.

- *Focus:* Most audience members are clearly drawn in and imagining more deeply (see the list of markers in Chapter 2). Amplify this by intensifying 'imaginative input' – building up multi-sensory imagery, becoming more static and focused yourself, perhaps sitting down if you are standing.

- *Boredom:* Few audiences will forgive much boredom these days, and inattention in young audiences especially spreads easily; restless fidgeting and shifting are more obvious signs but, long before that, the look often described as 'going glazed' could be spotted. The important thing then is to arrest attention. There is no set way to do this. A loud bang on a drum is a good example of a shock tactic: it's swift and quick and wakes listeners up. Unusual instruments with an unexpected sound are also good, but there are very many alternatives you can draw out through discussion.

Also discuss other possibilities for group mood. There are quite a few.

Call and response

There's a famous UK promoter of 'performance storytelling' called the Crick Crack Club, which draws its name partly from the kind of traditional call-and-response formula storytellers (particularly, though not exclusively, African and African influenced) use to begin storytelling.[1] The storyteller says 'Cric' and the audience, to show that it wants a story, calls back 'Crac'. The storyteller does this several times, insisting that the audience gives back enough enthusiasm. Quite a few storytellers with more European roots and ethnicity favour this formula, though it is only one among many such. A lot more are listed in Sam Cannarozzi's short manual *When Tigers Smoked Pipes* (2008),[2] such as:

Teller: 'Siri!' (A story!)
Listeners: 'Nam!' (Let it be!)
                    (Mali)

Teller: 'Gatan gatankou!' (A story!)
Listeners: 'Tazo ta komo.' (That it come and we listen to it.)
                    (Hauser, Niger)

Using some of these formulae in school is justifiable for developing cross-cultural understanding alone. To achieve that whilst also reaping the benefits for understanding performance, it is useful to point out that more or less the same thing is happening when a British pantomime dame calls out 'Are you enjoying yourselves, boys and girls?' and the audience choruses back 'Yes', so he/she says 'I can't hear you!' and they all shout 'YEEES!' It's all about getting a response, getting the audience to do something, to say yes to paying attention to you, even if the spoken word is actually no. There are many ways of doing the same thing, some more natural than others. Even a song where people have to join in the chorus or clap along is having the same function in terms of audience dynamic. It doesn't have to have an exotic feel to it at all, unless you want to add that element, in which case it's best to normalize its function, avoiding the suggestion that it's something weird.

Creating calls (exercise) (pupils create a call-and-response pattern)

Here's an ironically insulting example version to appeal to older pupils:

> I say 'Listen up!' and you say 'Shut up!'
> So I say 'Shut up!' and you say 'Listen up!'
> (Repeat getting faster and louder over several repetitions of these two
> lines till some of the audience are muddled; then conclude)
> And now we're even so I'll start my story.

Chorusing

This technique you can adapt to almost any age, though it is easiest to learn with younger listeners. Training your storytellers through presenting to (say) Key Stage 1 pupils is both a good way to learn the skill and very relevant, because it keeps young listeners involved in the same way the call and response draws them in.

Many traditional stories contain repetition or are otherwise predictable. Once the pattern is established, you hold back as you come to the bit that is pure repetition and give a (usually non-verbal) cue that they can join in. For example, in 'The Emperor's truth' (Chapter 3), the Emperor always says 'Yes, I believe you' when the first tall tales are told to him and, by the third example, audiences will be ready to join in saying exactly that along with you. Even adult audiences can be persuaded to chorus back in this way with the right approach. When an audience is doing that, it is agreeing with the teller and endorsing the story.

Exercise

Go through a story (or several) finding where it works to cue chorusing and where you might build it up more.

Riddles and puzzles, short jokes, etc.

As already mentioned, these help to break up a session. Riddles and verbal story puzzles also get listeners into (or keep them in) story mode. For example, there is the well-known one about the two brothers who live at the fork in the road. One always tells lies and the other always tells the truth and you need to know which of two roads to take to get to your destination, since the wrong one leads to a forest infested with dangerous fierce beasts whilst the right one leads through a forest of good fortune. You can ask only one question.[3] Some riddles are very poetic and metaphorical, keeping listeners very much in imagination country, also exercising memorizing skills for the teller/reciter of them.

> White bird featherless
> flew from the heavens,
> perched on a castle wall.
> Along came Lord Landless,
> picked it up handless
> and flew away horseless
> to the King's high hall.[4]

Blending

Our perception of any event is a blend of what is presented with the circumstance in which it is presented. Many of our art forms are intended to be, as it were, relatively circumstance insensitive. We put them in halls and arenas and expect to minimize the influence of, for example, weather conditions or the political situation. We want to escape from all that and focus down into the art form. Maybe we insulate them entirely in DVD or CD or online.

Storytelling is, however, potentially circumstance sensitive. You can blend in many things that are happening around, as long as they are not too distracting and obtrusive. For example, if the wind were blowing, perhaps you could compare it to a convenient gale in the story or to the contrastingly still, hot mood you want to conjure up. This could be as simple as saying 'It's hard to imagine sometimes when the wind is blowing the way it is today how still and hot and dusty and silent the desert can be sometimes, even if the wind howls across it on other days and whips all that sand up into a storm . . .' You are turning a potential distraction into an aid to imagining.

Blend it (exercise)

- First prime pupils by getting them to listen to sounds and notice smells and all other kinds of sensory information around them.

- Now ask them to begin to tell their stories in pairs. At a given point, call out 'Blend it!' They must all stop, listen, watch and otherwise pay attention to what it going on around. When you say 'Go' after around 15 seconds (or more) they must blend as many things as possible that they have noticed (sounds, sights, happenings) into their stories.

- You can repeat the 'Blend it!' instruction several times in a longer story.
- Change partners so that the listener tells, and repeat.
- Finally discuss how easy it is to blend and who was able to do most blending. Hear some examples.

Embarrassment

Embarrassing audience members might be at the cutting edge in comedy and some drama or installation art, but it's unlikely to be very effective in storytelling. It's generally best avoided, even when it involves practices natural in association with storytelling in other cultures. You generally want to be effective in this one.

Sound spells and stories: using music

The use of music with stories goes back a long way and has taken many forms in different cultures and in different ages. From Celtic or Homeric bards with harp and lyre to medieval minstrels strumming gitterns and plucking psalteries, from the Nordic skops and skalds with crwth and bagpipe to saz-toting Turkish ashiks, vina-plucking Indian kathakars or West African griots with the silvery cascading notes of their koras, there have been many traditional figures who both played instruments and told tales, to say nothing of other traditional tale tellers who have worked alongside musicians. It's a large subject, worthy of a much more extensive treatment than there's space for here – there is a lot to be discovered. But even a little is fascinating – and remarkably accessible too. You don't need to be a virtuoso musician or a bardic initiate to make a convincing start on the spellbinding art of sound and story.

First we need a somewhat extended concept of what music in association with stories can do. Many will think first of what in Western classical music is called programme music or simply of sound effects, i.e. the music will describe what is happening in the story in some way. That is fine, and good ideas for doing that come up easily enough, but here are some alternative uses, some more obvious, some less so:

- setting up or amplifying atmosphere and mood (as happens with modern theme tunes, introductory music, background music, etc.);
- creating excitement and involvement, breaking down barriers and reserve (e.g. songs, chants, answering choruses, clapping along, etc.);
- lulling and calming, even mildly hypnotizing, developing a meditative

mood conducive to imagination (e.g. the music of gongs and bells, the sound of rainsticks, harps, etc.);

- attracting attention, shocking listeners into waking up to the story;
- expressing or releasing or suggesting emotion;
- reflecting a mood in a story and/or foreshadowing a new mood in a new tale or part of the same tale;
- hence, changing temperature between stories or between episodes of longer tales;
- suggesting images and ideas to prepare the way for a narrative to come (especially in a song through both words and music);
- puzzling and intriguing;
- providing a constant or variable accompaniment – a background tapestry of sound (usually featuring repetitive motifs or drones, etc.);
- making a separate narrative – the music speaks in one way not necessarily directly related to what is happening in a story but somehow underlining it;
- dialoguing with the speaker (this is comparable to the way the old blues guitarists sang a line and then answered it with a blues 'fill' before singing the next line; bardic performers from different cultures use this technique between 'lines' of the story);[5]
- filling the space between words and allowing the ideas in the words to 'breathe' – as well as giving the performer space to focus and adjust;
- contrasting with the voice, giving listeners a rest from it, and also allowing the performer to rest his or her voice;
- singing all or part of the story (as in ballads and narrative songs or indeed in modern stage musicals);
- topping and tailing – intros, endings and interludes can also be signals that mark stages of the telling and pace the whole event.

Some, though not all, of those uses you will find in the sophisticated modern art of film music, as well as in musical storytelling forms like stage musicals and opera. Using music with stories is a good introduction to these, but has some unique qualities. And, whilst it's tempting to use computer music technology to prepare music for stories, that could be a wasted opportunity for another kind of learning. A sensitivity can develop between players and the teller(s), so that music can be varied in intensity and improvised in different ways to respond to audience mood – as indeed happens in the Javanese *wayang golek* puppetry performances, where a gamelan ensemble has to respond to the audience mood as well as to the performance on the direction of the *dalang* (puppeteer).

You can interpret any of the above ideas in your own way, of course: the main guide is what is effective. Incidentally and to reiterate, the simple descriptive, sound-effect version of music with stories is entirely valid, used intelligently. You may have to work against pupils' tendency to be literal and obvious, for example 'There was a knock on the door . . . (BANG BANG) and then the door creaked open . . . (CREEEEEAK!)' This simply interrupts the narrative; much better if the BANG BANG of the drum or whatever comes before you tell about the knock, and again the CREAK anticipates the description. That's how it's done in films and on radio anyway.

Here are some simpler musical ideas presented mostly for non-musicians to use practically with pupils:

- *Rhythm:* A very simple way to generate accompanying rhythms for an introduction, background 'tapestry' or interlude is to use titles, names or short phrases from the story. For a short example, just the title of the story from Chapter 6 could be recited over and over with emphasis on the underlined syllables:

	1		2			3		4
Mo -	_hammed_		and the		Ma -	_gi_ -		cian

The rhythm can be tapped on a drum and/or other percussion. (You can generate much longer rhythms, perhaps even using whole sentences.)

- *Ostinato:* This is a short musical idea repeated over and over again. To make a pitched ostinato, you could take a simpler pitched percussion instrument with labelled notes such as a xylophone and play the syllables of your title, phrase or sentence to a set pattern. For example:

	1		2			3		4
Mo -	_ham_-	med	and	the	Ma -	_gi_ -		cian
A	B	C	D♯	E	F	G♯		A

Repeated over and again to a regular beat, varying volume and, later, speed, sometimes switching to just the drum playing the rhythm, sometimes having several instruments all playing with the drum, sometimes just one, perhaps also including chanting of the words from a vocal group sporadically, you already have a piece of introductory or background music for the tale.

- *Drone:* You simply accompany your ostinato or tune or whatever on one note, repeated over and over – usually using longer, sustained notes

A				A				etc.	or	A		A			etc.
1	2	3	4	1	2	3	4			1	2	3	4		

- *Riff:* Your pitched ostinato could be turned into something more like a riff for more variation. There are some confusing alternative meanings of the word 'riff'. Briefly, in its original use in jazz and related music, it meant a melodic/rhythmic figure repeated at different pitches to match a chord sequence (see below), a set piece. In the pop world, it's now used more loosely – often simply to mean something like 'the catchy instrumental bit', whilst in comedy 'riffing' has come to mean something opposite to its original sense, a kind of improvisation. Anyway, to convert the ostinato into an eight-bar riff (original sense) based around two 'pitch centres', you would simply play the same tune on different notes, something like this:

	1		2			3	4
Mo -	<u>ham</u> - med	and	the	Ma -	<u>gi</u> -	cian	
A	B	C	D♯	E	F	G♯	A

Repeat four times on these notes; then change:

	1		2			3	4
Mo -	<u>ham</u>- med	and	the	Ma -	<u>gi</u> -	cian	
D	E	F	G♯	A	B	C♯	D

Repeat four times on these notes; then begin the cycle again. If using a drone, you can stay on A throughout or use A for the first version, D for the second (i.e. the starting and ending notes of each pattern).

- *Motifs:* A motif is again a short musical idea, probably repeated at different pitches. For illustration of how you can use it practically to build atmosphere and complement a story, we can use some of the same notes. Supposing you have set a rhythm/ostinato/riff idea at the start of the story, you come now come to the part of the tale where Mohammed is learning the secrets and will soon be escaping the wizard. To build tension, you use just a bit of the above 'tune' sporadically, just once each time to hint about the danger of the magician:

	1	2	
The	Ma -	<u>gi</u> -	cian
E	F	G♯	A

You might play with variations on this throughout the story at strategic points, with the motif and the longer 'tune' appearing at different pitches on different instruments. You could even play it backwards (A G♯ F E, etc.).

- *Chords:* A chord is a combination of notes, usually at least three (though what is called a 'power chord' in rock music has only two). Young players of instruments like guitars or pianos/keyboards may well be able to play chords and even to combine them in 'chord sequences'. If you have those available to join your ensemble, the two–pitch centre riff sequence above gives this chord progression in 4/4 time:

    Am (four bars)   Dm (four bars)

    (Or use power chords A5 and D5.) Chords can also be used as one-off colouring effects without putting them into sequence, especially slightly more exotic ones. For example, if on pitched percussion you use the notes C E G♯ (technically a C augmented triad) one after the other and/ or together, this sounds a little scary and could again be added at strategic points in our tale, maybe contrasted with the more restful sound of a C E G B (C major 7th) at other points.

- *Scale/mode:* Most people know the sound of the major scale (or Ionian mode), often represented as *do re me fa so la te do*. There are hundreds of other scales or modes (an alternative name), some using unfamiliar systems of tuning, but many accessible on contemporary instruments. The one I've used for 'Mohammed and the magician' above is, to most from this culture, an exotic-sounding scale, sometimes called the Hungarian minor – A B C D♯ E F G♯ at first. (For the riff this has been transposed to a different pitch starting on D, keeping the same distances between notes.) Here are two more scales with a distinctive feel. Again you can play them at different pitches:

    A Japanese pentatonic: E F A B C
    Blues scale: E G A Bb B D

Any of the above ideas for use in music with stories can develop in all sorts of ways. Anyone prepared to experiment whilst remaining sensitive to the main aims of supporting the storytelling and drawing in listeners' attention can find excellent ways into them. It's not what is correct here, but what works.

Musical odds and ends (story making idea using music)

Many people know the story making technique in which a series of objects are presented and you have to turn them into a story. This is a musical variation. Various sounds, ranging from instrumental effects to noises, are introduced one after the other. Perhaps a range of happenings or actions they might suggest could first be discussed and recorded. These now have to be linked to make a story. You can do this orally with the group, using the instruments as you go along (not always with the preliminary stage of discussion and recording). If they want to be chosen to play an instrument, pupils must make up part of the story to go with it; you can hear more than one idea and choose what works best, perhaps on a vote from the group. When the story is complete, it can be replayed with each chosen storyteller contributing their effect and the part of the story they invented. With repetition and work on the narrative, you can develop a performance piece.

Using other arts with storytelling

Some arts can be combined directly with storytelling, enhancing narratives without changing their nature. Music is probably the prime example; you can develop it to a high level with older pupils. Conjuring (not a skill you can readily adapt for school use but not impossible) also works remarkably well in limited doses. The same is true of some juggling skills, card tricks, acrobatics and various other 'jongleur' skills used in castle hall and marketplace in the past. Returning to skills more conventionally available in schools, adding dance and mime can work, whilst as already suggested you can involve designers and artists in creating supporting visuals in all sorts of way. Puppetry is a more obvious possibility – stories told using puppets in a simple way make a good contrast with the 'theatre of the imagination'. There is clearly a point at which storytelling crosses over to become drama; there is no harm in blurring the distinction a little, if not a lot, with memorized 'performed' or recited items as well as more spontaneous ones. Similarly, you can have interludes of almost any art form – from poetry to paper folding to spontaneous painting. I've stressed in this book that storytelling has some unique qualities that it is a pity to miss through preconception based on more familiar art forms or simply muddled thinking; it's also a pity to miss the many opportunities there are to combine with as many of those art forms as possible, creating fascinating hybrids.

Performance perspective

A storytelling performance makes an excellent focal point in a term or year. Given a strong and positive profile in a school, it can encourage an interest in telling stories immensely, especially if it becomes a regular special event towards which pupils can work. It's not the only way to encourage storytelling and will naturally favour pupils with a performing bent, so it's as well to value other kinds of less formal, day-to-day storytelling as much and maybe more. Making performance storytelling for formal audiences the only model on offer is likely to produce a distortion. Storytelling connects on all sorts of levels, across the curriculum and also at a deeply personal level. It's important not to lose sight of that.

Itinerant telling teams

Telling teams can give storytelling an enviable profile in a school, also bypassing the need for special performance events, dedicated performance space and so on.

- *Class team:* Three to six tellers are picked at any one time. The class collaborates in coaching them in telling their stories and framing their tales using any complementary arts (e.g. music, paper folding, puppetry) or short jokes, riddles, etc. The team visit other classes to perform their tales at set times, swapping teams with similar-age classes or simply visiting younger groups. Membership of the team is varied to give different people a chance, but is a badge of honour, not a right – in the same way that a sports team is chosen on skill, team playing and so on.

- *School team:* This is similar, but the tellers visit any suitable community events to tell their tales as well as arranging exchange visits with other storytelling schools (if available). The school team is given a strong status within the school, performing as part of assemblies and on special occasions.

11

A storyteller's vision

Answer (in all cases): a story.

According to a little tale, a think tank composed of distinguished education specialists decided that they should investigate an onion and define what it was, by way of setting up an example of the kind of practices to be promoted in schools. They took it apart layer by layer and then found nothing at all – except tears.

'Joined-up thinking' is one of those clichéd terms people chuck into political arguments, usually to berate thinking that certainly isn't. Yet, in this world at this current time, we really do need thinking that brings disparate things together so that we can understand them and use them with a better sense of what might be their organic integrity. Our education, however, continues primarily to stress analytical skills, the ability to criticize and take things apart, the ability to reduce things to their component parts, to understand the bits and pieces and nuts and bolts. Whilst this is a very important skill, it needs to be balanced by a thinking style that is more holistic. That kind of creative, integrative thinking is nurtured, reflected and fed by story work. Stories are a way of joining-up thinking imaginatively.

This book has been written with the underlying conviction that stories and the telling of them, both oral and written, with the ability to 'think in story', need to be given a role much less on the margins of educational effort. Perhaps one day we will be automatically weaving all our educational plans around story. Perhaps we'll be teaching many and most subjects as much through memorable narrative and imagination as through logical, sequential exposition. Perhaps we will regard school leavers unable to tell or to make up at least a tale or two in their own style and language as being as disadvantaged as those who remain illiterate and unable to calculate. Perhaps, too, we will understand that anyone unable to listen and imagine long enough to take in a yarn or two is dangerously undeveloped, however clever they may seem. Perhaps we will be directing the attention of pupils as much to the work of great oral storytellers who communicate directly with their imaginations as we now direct them towards great novelists, painters, musicians or film makers. Perhaps, but that is all a long way off.

Meanwhile we can start to find out what stories and storytelling have to offer and expect to find a lot more than tears.

Appendix A

A plan for a storytelling activity session

This is an outline plan based around a typical storytelling questioning/activity such as 'Fantastic fibs' (Chapter 3) or 'Embroidery' (Chapter 7). The general objective is to speak clearly using imagination in developing the story and to listen and question intelligently. Specific learning objectives depend on the specific game or other technique:

1. Ideally start with a short story example told or read, listened to on CD or watched on DVD. Alternatively, refer to a story familiar from a previous session, drawing out a few relevant details.
2. Introduce and explain the story game you are working around.
3. Choose a person (or group) to take the lead as storyteller (or liar) and respond to the questions (or other procedures) that will develop the story. (You can allow the storyteller to choose his or her questioners initially, but you make need to take over choosing to avoid involving only cronies.)
4. You can coach the group on the kinds of questions likely to yield more information as you go along (see Chapter 3).
5. After this stage, get the storyteller to go back through the story including the answers to questions, with promptings from the group, to show how this has developed the tale.
6. Pupils work in pairs and play the game. With odd numbers, you can allow one trio or, if available, a 'spare' adult can make up the numbers.

7. When both partners have played the game, they put up their hands and look for others also with hands up and swap partners to try the same idea again. They can swap partners again if there is time.

8. You can then progress to the 'Pass it on' method (described in Appendix B). If you have a longer session, this can be allowed to run for a longer time: it generally gathers positive momentum for 5 to 15 minutes at least, often much longer.

9. Bring the group back together and hear some stories (a) invented or elaborated in the first rounds and (b) passed on. Pick up on teaching points as appropriate.

10. To develop this further orally, you can allow pairs and small groups to prepare further stories to be told together to the group and subjected to questions (or other procedures as suggested).

11. Alternatively, you can progress to writing/planning stories (see Chapter 2).

Appendix B

Simulating oral traditions 1: 'Pass it on'

Stories told orally change and develop with retelling and then as they are passed from one person to another. You can simulate this process with groups:

1. First find a way that pupils can get to know a story. It can be made up or developed in a story game (as in the pattern above) or it might have been written on a previous occasion or it might be a story from a book or CD or indeed from newspaper reports or the TV. (Chapter 6 explores ways that stories can be learned most effectively.)

2. Follow a procedure something like that in stages 1 to 7 in the outline in Appendix A so that pupils have had some practice in telling and passing on the story they have invented or developed.

3. Now make a surprise announcement. When they next change partners, they will tell not the story they have been developing but the story they have just heard from their partner. Before they leave that partner, they must get him or her to teach them the story thoroughly.

4. They must tell the story in their own way. If the story learned was a first person story, they must tell it as a third person story about the person from whom they heard it. If they can't remember it, they have to make up whatever is missing. They must also listen to and respond to and then learn the passed-on story the other person is passing on so that, when they change partners again, they can pass that one on.

5. This can go on through several exchanges, so that players are learning and passing on more stories. Eventually return to the group for a stage similar to stage 9 in the outline in Appendix A.

This basic version of 'Pass it on' can be varied in all sorts of ways. Pupils could, for example, pass on the same story heard from someone else two or three times before picking up the other person's story. Various ideas for developing and even slightly warping the basic passing-on procedure are suggested in Appendix C.

Apart from the story content, this way of getting group members to talk to each other is a good way of breaking the ice where pupils don't know each other or where you want a better mixing. You can, for example, insist that they choose partners to talk to that they don't know or who are members of the opposite sex. You could draw attention to the fact that you can get to know people in a different way through the stories they tell you.

Appendix C

Simulating oral traditions 2: three more ways of spreading stories

Over time, you need more ways to vary and indeed to stretch the 'Pass it on' ideas. These more advanced suggestions work on from a familiarity with those.

Story shopping

This is designed to build memory as well as creative retelling skills. The shopping 'frame' can make it seem more contemporary, but it's possible to use different terms – collecting or storing, for example. It develops from a basic 'Pass it on' procedure, either continuing straight on from it or building on a previous session. In either case, stories will have been created/developed in a story game or learned from a source (perhaps a short traditional tale on a card or sheet) or written on a theme and then memorized for telling and (probably) passed on in the ordinary way at least once.

1. First explain what this title means. They will be 'shopping' for a set number of tales other than the one they 'bring' themselves (start with two; build up the number with repetition) to meet some agreed criteria you establish at the outset. For example, they will find the tales particularly fantastical or funny, or the tales are fables that mean something to them or whatever (depending on what you are working on). They will listen to and pass on more, but they have to hold on to the set number of new stories for retelling.

2. Announce (for example) 'Shop now – two stories!' either in the midst of 'Pass it on' rounds or to begin the session. Participants continue from where they are in 'Pass it on' or find partners to tell stories to if you are using it to start a new session.

3. In telling, they aim to 'sell' the story they have received – get their listeners to take it on as one of their two stories by making it as interesting as possible.

4. Watch partner changes, allowing these to happen a suitable average number of times (usually at least twice your target number), calculated approximately, since they will change at different rates.

5. Call 'Show purchases now!' With a new partner (or in a group) pupils swap their two (or more) stories. They can add to the stories' funny or fantastic or fabulous qualities as they tell them.

6. Find out which stories were 'bought' most often and also who 'sold' those stories. Have the favourite stories told by one or more 'seller' to the rest of the group.

(You can progress from this to writing a set of interlinked stories as recommended in Chapter 7.)

New angles

This time the aim is to receive a story from another participant through 'Pass it on' (or in any other way). When it is passed on, however, the aim is to tell it not as received but from a new angle. The simplest example would be telling a first person story as a third person story (as is required in developing first person games such as 'Fantastic fibs' in Chapter 3) or vice versa (i.e. a received third person story has to be told in the first person as if you were one of the characters in it). More complicated 'new angles' (for more advanced groups who need a challenge) might include telling a story about (say) a knight in battle from the point of view of his horse, a queen's story from the point of view of her maid, the story of events in a pub from the point of view of the doorstep, etc.

You can call 'New angle for the next change, please!' in the midst of a 'Pass it on' round (if the idea has already been explained or is familiar), leaving decisions about what will be the new angle up to tellers, giving them a little time to think through the new angle before they take the story to a new partner for telling. Alternatively, you can set the kind of new angle you want. ('Tell it in the first/third person now . . .' 'Non–human angle:

living thing . . .' 'Non-human angle: inanimate object . . .' 'Tell it in the present/future tense next time . . .', etc.)

Twisting tales

Participants must change the stories a little on purpose as they tell them. They keep the plot, but alter some detail. Perhaps they change the gender of characters or (for example in an animal fable) make it a different creature. This idea is explored in 'Change smuggling' (Chapter 8) but is relevant elsewhere too. Each time the story is passed on a new change is added. At the end, stories are compared to their original models.

Appendix D

Using professional storytellers

Bringing in someone who has developed storytelling skill to a high level has very many values, the full spectrum of possibilities probably only fully realized in a tiny minority of schools, despite the much more widespread awareness that storytellers are available. Storytellers can inspire by performing with spontaneity and brilliance or by enabling pupils to practise their art in workshops, showing the way towards excellence. A couple of points need to be made, however.

Thirty years ago there were almost no professional storytellers available to schools. Now, partly because of the renewed interest and partly because of the highly successful work of storytellers who blazed a trail in the 1980s and 1990s, there are hundreds, with the number steadily increasing. It has to be said that the standard is variable; there is nothing to prevent anyone saying they are a storyteller and sending out publicity, with the result that some teachers book people who have little real idea of the art and find themselves a little underwhelmed. On the other hand, despite the claims of some groups to represent 'the best', there is currently no organization that has researched the work of all experienced storytellers in any systematic way. Any exclusive claims have hence no real factual basis and are more likely to mean simply 'These people do it our way' – which may of course represent a certain vision of excellence, but certainly should not be treated as a universal gold standard.

The best way to choose a professional for your context is direct experience of their work. Recommendation is good too. It helps to be clear about what you want, the kind of questions to ask and indeed what you should reasonably expect. This will lessen the chances of disappointment.

What you should expect

- An extensive repertoire of stories rather than a couple of fixed menus.
- Ability to adapt to the target age groups in your school.
- Clear speaking (not necessarily, however, in standard received English).
- Imagination and a distinctive but effective style.
- Ability to engage pupils for the full length of time agreed (different storytellers are comfortable with different-length sessions).
- Ability to adapt to circumstance within reason.
- A professional attitude.
- A clear idea of what reasonable requirements they may have in respect of preparation time, timetabling, audience numbers (for performance-type sessions) and effective workshop group size (on a project, etc.).
- Lack of pretentiousness.
- Formal or informal references or recommendations from comparable schools if required – though not necessarily from schools within your authority or area.
- Formal requirements in place (in the UK, this would currently include any necessary creative arts insurance, CRB checks, etc.).

Depending on the circumstances and the kind of storyteller you are working with, you might also find them offering additional specialisms such as:

- intelligent and worthwhile INSET sessions;
- helpful background notes and resource materials;
- a range of themes relevant to school groups of different ages;
- workshops and themes on special subject areas relating to personal and social development (themes such as bullying, developing confidence, etc.) and other uses of storytelling approaches;
- creative and original ideas for developing story work in general;
- particular cross-cultural insights.

What you should not expect your storyteller to do (one-off/occasional visits)

- Work all day with no breaks between sessions.

- Produce exactly the repertoire you require without any extensive direct discussion.

- Work with unfamiliar themes or authored material unless specifically agreed in advance.

- Cope with endless distractions (as, for example, when a hall used for a session is also a thoroughfare and no restrictions are agreed).

- Give their best whilst being treated without due politeness, ordinary respect and basic courtesy.

- Fulfil conflicting briefs given by different members of staff.

- Be pleased that you obviously have more important work to do on your laptop or in marking books and are not listening to what they are saying.

- Work in exactly the same way as another storyteller or author.

The better you treat your visiting professional, the better the work you will get from him or her. This may seem like common sense, but the above widespread difficulties are based on extensive comments from experienced professionals.

An ongoing relationship

There is a lot to be said for developing an ongoing relationship between school and a storyteller where funding and time allow and where the 'match' between what you want and what he or she offers is good. The model most schools work with is consumerist – tried that one, let's buy in another. This is often necessity as much as anything: storyteller visits are not usually cheap – though many storytellers will reduce their rates for repeat visits to schools where their work is particularly appreciated, especially in their own locality or if already visiting the area. Sometimes also rare funding allows for a project where the storyteller can work in partnership with the school, developing pupils' skills, cooperating with staff, acting as consultant and inspirer. This can help to stretch possibilities in ways that have been explored in this book and in many more ways too. There is still a lot to be discovered about the possibilities of the art of storytelling.

Notes

Introduction

1. Parkinson (2004, 2005, 2007a, 2007b). Titles in this series referred to in various places in this book provide much useful complementary material. Full information from www.imaginaryjourneys.co.uk.
2. Parkinson (2009).

1 Thinking about story

1. The popular psychology notion of 'left brain' (critical/logical/sequential) as opposed to 'right brain' (dreaming/imaginative/holistic) is a simplification based on the apparent dominant function of left and right cortical hemispheres. It's useful, however, to invoke it here, because imaginative work appears to involve brain functioning that differs from that of logical/sequential processing.
2. For an interesting, useful and accessible read here, see Rossi (1991).
3. See for example Claxton (2001, 2002) for an introduction to building learning power (BLP).
4. Books by the four authors mentioned have stood the test of time remarkably well and, allowing for some archaisms, are well worth investigating. Some are listed in the bibliography.
5. Books by these authors recommended to complement work in this book are listed in the bibliography.
6. See Idries Shah's *World Tales* (Shah 1979) for an enduringly fascinating and astonishing collection illustrating this phenomenon. Cole (1982) and Yolen (1986) are also both excellent collections to add to a reference library of such tales, yielding plenty of patterns useful for use in creative story work.
7. Richard Pollak's devastatingly convincing exposure of Bettelheim as a cruel charlatan, liar and plagiarist (Pollak 1997) should be enough to make anyone dubious about *The Uses of Enchantment*, but very few of the specious, self-consciously Freudian 'interpretations' of the images in fairy tales he advances stand up to closer inspection anyway.
8. The noted folklorist and academic Jack Zipes described some excellent ideas based on his occasional work with school pupils and gave a useful 1990s critique of the pretensions of 'cult' storytellers that still resonates in his *Creative Storytelling*. The ideas with which he framed them, however, seem to suggest that violent (and other) abuse is an integral part of 'normal' parenting, an idea that hinders actual abuse survivors and echoes another cult

that swept the therapy culture in America during the same decade, the fashion for identifying dubious 'abuse memories' (see for example Tavris and Aronson 2007).

2 Practical protocols

1. Explored thoroughly in my *Transforming Tales* (Parkinson 2009). Storytelling can positively influence people's personal development in unexpected ways, school pupils much included.
2. See for example Rossi (1991).
3. 'Unexpected influences' mentioned in note 1 above are achieved partly through using the metaphorical 'dreaming' mind. This is relevant to general teaching too. For example, it's more effective to obliquely show pupils how they can change behaviour in an imaginatively engaging story than to nag and harangue them.
4. See Claxton (1997) for a fascinating and elegantly written review of the science of the 'cognitive unconscious', showing how we learn in all sorts of ways that are unlike the intentional mode education has conventionally stressed.
5. These are further examples of positive influence. See notes 1 and 2 above.

3 Telling tall tales

1. Versions of this game appeared in my notes for storytelling courses for teachers from 1986 and subsequently in *Storylines*, the magazine/newsletter of the Society for Storytelling, in 1994. Others seem to have discovered similar ideas in recent years.
2. A relevant example, suitable for school use, is a delightful recent collection of the 'fine Welsh fibbing' of Pembrokeshire legend, *Shemi's Tall Tales* by Mary Medlicott (2008).
3. An example of family themes (and also of no. 8, improbable accidents) is the title story of my CD *Will's Clogs* (Parkinson 2003a), which follows the pattern of 'Abdul Kasim's slippers' from *The Arabian Nights*.
4. For this and other principles of influence, see for example Cialdini (1984).

4 Likely legends and marvellous myths

1. Recorded by George Aitchison, a contributor to *Sussex Notes and Queries* (Simpson 2009: 68).
2. Heard on a hotel's radio over breakfast (probably BBC Radio 1), 22 January 2010.
3. For example, Healey and Glanvill (1992). A more serious study of the genre is Brunvand (1983).
4. As listed on a popular science website, http://www.livescience.com/bestimg/result.php?back=myths_greatwall_china_03.jpg&cat=myths (accessed 8 February 2010).
5. I heard this story a long time ago from a Nigerian student who told me it was from the Bini peoples.
6. You can find the original with the full list of islands in a reissue of an old study (Rolleston 1985: 309), also online at www.imaginaryjourneys.co.uk as a free download (accessed 23 April 2010).

5 Dreaming awake

1. This simplification is admittedly controversial. For differing perspectives on the origins of imagination and the connection with dreaming, see Griffin and Tyrrell (2004) and Lewis-Williams (2002). For a different view of the evolution of mind, see Mithen (1996).

2. Flow states (effortless absorption in peak performance) have been studied at length by Mihalyi Csikszentmihalyi (1990). Sportspeople talk about being 'in the zone', which is a similar conception. Both are vital ideas for anyone involved in practical creativity (in story or elsewhere): you want pupils to go into flow at least some of the time in their work – and, because the 'in the zone' framing has had some media exposure, you can usefully invoke this alternative 'cool' metaphor with pupils.

3. Sports coaches routinely use forms of guided imagining to train sportspeople in the mental side of their performance. See for example the classic 'Inner Game' books, e.g. Gallwey (1997).

4. See for example 'The Spanish game' (Parkinson 2009: 71–2).

5. Again a theme thoroughly explained in my *Transforming Tales* (2009).

6 Learning stories

1. A handy fable card set I've used a lot is from Fax Pax and is simply called 'Fables'. An extended set of varied short tales will, at the time of writing, soon be available as a free download from www.imaginaryjourneys.co.uk.

2. There are many editions of the classic collection. In mine (Hunt and Wenhert 1984), it is on page 455.

7 Stretching stories

1. This version of the plot is original and developed out of varying the version mentioned in note 2 below.

2. The first reworking of this plot I ever created was 'The king's beard', which was recorded on my first published cassette of stories, *Will's Clogs* (1991), reissued on CD (Parkinson 2003a). It's useful for comparison. Tony Collingwood wrote and directed a film in 2002 using the same idea of a king who wished for a magnificent beard.

3. I first published versions of 'Embroidery' informally in notes on school workshops and teachers' courses in the 1980s, and then later more formally in the Society for Storytelling's Storylines newsletter/magazine in the 1990s. As with 'Fantastic fibs', others have discovered a similar idea more recently.

4. For example 'The luck of the cards', recorded on my *Will's Clogs* (Parkinson 2003a).

5. As a songwriter myself, I've used the technique often. My two popular CDs of songs for children (Parkinson 2003b, 2003c) include many examples.

6. This is a wonderful book with which to back up storytelling themes, incidentally.

8 Stealing stories

1. Folklorist Jack Zipes has explored the meme in relation to the passing on of traditional fairy tales (Zipes 2006).

2. For those seriously interested in following this up, the scholarly reference work to find in a library is Aarne (1961).

9 Fooling with forms

1. More examples of old fables updated and brought to life in a similar way and giving good examples for this kind of work are in my *Fabulous Fables* CD collection (Parkinson 2008).

10 Performing stories

1. The other part of the punning meaning of the name is relevant too: the *craic* or crack is originally an Irish term describing another aspect of group mood – fun, entertaining, enjoyable conversation, easy social 'flow', etc.
2. See also notes on beginning and ending formulae in Chapter 7 for other aspects of this very useful publication.
3. Answer: 'If I asked your brother, what would he say?'
4. I think this is originally medieval. The answer I know is snow, but there may be others.
5. Youtube.com is currently a good source of online video footage of bards. For example, search under 'gusle' or 'guslar' (names for a bowed one-string fiddle still played by Serbian bards) and you may find some dialoguing examples.

Bibliography

Aarne, A. (1961) *The Types of the Folktale* (translated and enlarged by Stith Thompson). Helsinki: F.F. Communications.

Bearne, Eve and Mottram, Marilyn (2009) *The Story Spinner Project: Final Report and Evaluation Online*, August, online, http://www.thestoryspinner.co.uk/wp-content/.../Final-Evaluation-of-Story-Spinner.doc (accessed 19 February 2010).

Bettelheim, B. (1976) *The Uses of Enchantment*. London: Thames & Hudson.

Bruner, J. (1986) *Actual Minds, Possible Worlds*. Boston, MA: Harvard University Press.

Brunvand, J.H. (1983) *The Vanishing Hitchhiker: Urban Legends and Their Meanings*. London: Pan Books.

Calvino, I. (1982) *Italian Folktales*. London: Penguin Books.

Campbell, J. (1976) *The Masks of God*, Vol. 1: *Primitive Mythology*. London: Penguin Books.

—— (1993) *The Hero with a Thousand Faces*. London: HarperCollins.

Cannarozzi, S. (2008) *When Tigers Smoked Pipes*. Reading: Society for Storytelling Press.

Charlton, B. (2007) Review of *The Feeling of What Happens: Body, Emotion and the Making of Consciousness, Medical Hypotheses*, September, online, htttp://www.hedweb.com/bgcharlton/damasioreview.html (accessed 6 January 2010).

Cialdini, R.B. (1984) *Influence: The Psychology of Persuasion*. New York: William Morrow.

Clark, E. (1927) *Stories to Tell and How to Tell Them*. London: Hazell Watson & Viney.

Claxton, G. (1997) *Hare Brain, Tortoise Mind*. London: Fourth Estate.

—— (2001) *Wise Up: Learning to Live the Learning Life*. Stafford: Network Educational Press.

—— (2002) *Building Learning Power: Helping Young People Become Better Learners*. Bristol: TLO.

Cole, J. (1982) *Best Loved Folktales of the World*. New York: Doubleday.

Colwell, E. (1980) *Storytelling*. Oxford: Thimble Press.

Cone Bryant, S. (1910) *How to Tell Stories to Children*. London: George C. Harrap.

Csikszentmihalyi, M. (1990) *Flow: The Psychology of Optimal Experience*. New York: Harper Perennial.

Damasio, A. (1994) *Descartes' Error: Emotion, Reason, and the Human Brain*. New York: Avon Books.

—— (2000) *The Feeling of What Happens: Body, Emotion and the Making of Consciousness*. London: Vintage.

Gallwey, W.T. (1997) *The Inner Game of Tennis: The Classic Guide to the Mental Side of Peak Performance*. London: Random House.

Gladwell, M. (2008) *Outliers*. New York: Little, Brown.

Grainger, T. (1997) *Traditional Storytelling in the Primary Classroom*. Leamington Spa: Scholastic.

Green, M.C., Aldao, A., Pollack, B., Rozin, P. and Small, A. (2004) 'Effect of story details on transportation into narrative worlds and identification with characters', University of Pennsylvania Department of Psychology, presented at IGEL, Edmonton, August.

Griffin, J. (1997) *The Origin of Dreams*. Worthing: Therapist.

Griffin, J. and Tyrrell, I. (2004) *Dreaming Reality*. Chalvington: HG Publishing.

Hamilton, M. and Weiss, M. (1990) *Children Tell Stories: A Teaching Guide*. New York: Richard C. Owen Publishers.

Haven, Kendall F. (2007) *Story Proof: The Science behind the Startling Power of Story*. Westport, CT: Libraries Unlimited.

Healey, P. and Glanvill, R. (1992) *Urban Myths*. London: Virgin Books.

Herbert, R. (2009) 'Range of consciousness within everyday music listening experiences: Absorption, dissociation and the trancing process', unpublished Ph.D. dissertation, University of Sheffield.

—— (forthcoming a) 'Consciousness and everyday music listening: Trancing, dissociation and absorption. In D. Clarke and E. Clarke (eds), *Music and Consciousness*. Oxford: Oxford University Press.

Herbert, R. (forthcoming b) *Everyday Music Listening: Absorption, Dissociation and Trancing*. Farnham, Surrey: Ashgate.

Hernandez-Serrano, J. and Stefanou, S.E. (2009) 'Knowledge at work: Learning and transferring expert reasoning through storytelling in education', *Knowledge and Economy: A Journal for Education and Social Enterprise*, 3 (1), pp. 55–80.

Hilgard, J.R. (1979) *Personality and Hypnosis: A Study of Imaginative Involvement*. Chicago: University of Chicago.

Hunt, M. (trans.) and Wenhert, E.H. (illus.) (1984) *The Complete Illustrated Stories of the Brothers Grimm*. London: Octopus Books.

Kariuki, P.N.K. and Bush, E.D. (2008) 'The effects of total physical response by storytelling and the traditional teaching styles of a foreign language in a selected high school', paper presented at the Annual Conference of the Mid-South Educational Research Association, Knoxville, TN, November.

Lewis-Williams, D. (2002) *The Mind in the Cave*. London: Thames & Hudson.

Lines, K. (ed.) (1985) *The Faber Book of Magical Tales*. London: Faber & Faber.

McDonald, J.K. (2009) 'Imaginative instruction: What master storytellers can teach instructional designers', *Education Media International*, 46 (2), pp. 111–22.

Mardrus, J.C. and Mathers, P. (1986) *The Book of the Thousand Nights and One Night*, Vol. 3. London: Routledge & Kegan Paul.

Medlicott, M. (2008) *Shemi's Tall Tales*. Ceredigion: Pont.

Miley, F. (2009) 'Storytelling project: Innovating to engage students in their learning', *Higher Education Research and Development*, 28 (4), pp. 357–69.

Mithen, S. (1996) *The Prehistory of the Mind*. London: Thames & Hudson.

Nell, Victor (1988) *Lost in a Book: The Psychology of Reading for Pleasure*. Newhaven, CT: Yale University Press.

Nunn, C. (2007) *Neurons to Notions: Brains, Mind and Meaning*. Edinburgh: Floris Books.

Parkinson, R. (2003a) *Will's Clogs: Unlikely and Fantastical Tales*. Tonbridge: Imaginary Journeys Publishing.

—— (2003b) *The Wonderful Store: Strange, Fantastical and Ridiculous Songs*. Tonbridge: Imaginary Journeys Publishing.

—— (2003c) *Wild Imaginings: Weird, Wacky and Wonderful Songs*. Tonbridge: Imaginary Journeys Publishing.

—— (2004) *Tall Tale Telling: 24 Fun Games for Making and Telling Incredible Stories*. Tonbridge: Imaginary Journeys Publishing.

—— (2005) *Imagine On: 24 Fun Ways to Picture and Tell Marvellous Stories*. Tonbridge: Imaginary Journeys Publishing.

—— (2007a) *New Lamps from Old: 24 Games for Making New Tales from Old Plots*. Tonbridge: Imaginary Journeys Publishing.

—— (2007b) *Yarn Spinning: 24 Fun Ways to Stretch a Tale in the Telling*. Tonbridge: Imaginary Journeys Publishing.

—— (2008) *Fabulous Fables: Witty and Wise Tales from World Traditions* (CD). Tonbridge: Imaginary Journeys Publishing.

—— (2009) *Transforming Tales: How Stories Can Change People*. London: Jessica Kingsley Publishing.

Peissel, Michel (1984) *The Ants' Gold: The Discovery of the Greek El Dorado in the Himalayas*. London: Collins-Harvill.

Pollak, R. (1997) *The Creation of Dr B: A Biography of Bruno Bettelheim*. New York: Simon & Schuster.

Rolleston, T.W. (1985) *Myths and Legends of the Celtic Race*. London: Constable.

Rosen, B. (1988) *And None of It Was Nonsense: The Power of Storytelling in School*. London: Mary Glasgow Publications.

Rosen, S. (ed.) (1982) *My Voice Will Go with You: The Teaching Tales of Milton H. Erickson*. New York: Norton.

Rossi, E. (1991) *The Twenty Minute Break*. Los Angeles: Jeremy P. Tarcher.

Rushdie, S. (1990) *Haroun and the Sea of Stories*. London: Granta.

Sawyer, R. (1977) *The Way of the Storyteller*. New York: Penguin.

Schaefer, D. (1990) *Urban Legends and the Japanese Tale*. London: Institute for Cultural Research, online, http:www.i-c-r.org.uk/publications/monographarchive/Monograph29.pdf (accessed 28 April 2010).

Shah, I. (1979) *World Tales: The Extraordinary Coincidence of Stories Told in All Times, in All Places*. London: Allen Lane/Kestrel.

Simpson, J. (2009) *Folklore of Sussex*. Stroud: History Press.

Stallings, Fran (1988) 'The web of silence: Storytelling's power to hypnotise', *National Storytelling Journal*, Spring/Summer, online, http://www.healingstory.org/articles/web_of_silence/fran_stallings.html (accessed 31 January 2010).

Sturm, Brian (1999). *The Enchanted Imagination: Storytelling's Power to Entrance Listeners*. Urbana-Champaign, IL: ALA Archives, online, htttp://www.ala.org/ala/aasl/aaslpub-sandjournals/slmrb/slmrcontents/volume219vvol2sturm.cfm (accessed 31 July 2008).

Tavris, C. and Aronson, E. (2007) *Mistakes Were Made (but Not by Me): Why We Justify Foolish Beliefs, Bad Decisions and Hurtful Acts*. London: Pinter & Martin.

Tooby, J. and Cosmides, L. (2001) 'Does beauty build adapted minds? Towards an evolutionary theory of aesthetics, fiction and the arts', *SubStance*, 94/95.

Wheeler, P. (1995) *Russian Fairy Tales*. London: Senate.

Yolen, J. (ed.) (1986) *Favorite Folktales from around the World*. New York: Pantheon Books.

Zipes, J. (1995) *Creative Storytelling: Building Community, Changing Lives*. New York: Routledge.

—— (2006) *Why Fairy Tales Stick: The Evolution and Relevance of a Genre*. New York: Routledge.

Index

Note: Where more than one page number is listed against a heading, page numbers in **bold** indicate significant treatment of a subject